# CODE

OF

# FLOTILLA AND BOAT SQUADRON SIGNALS

FOR THE

## UNITED STATES NAVY,

PREPARED BY

COMMANDER THORNTON A. JENKINS, U. S. N.

---

BY AUTHORITY OF THE

HON. GIDEON WELLES,

SECRETARY OF THE NAVY.

---

SECOND EDITION, REVISED AND CORRECTED.

---

BUREAU OF NAVIGATION, NAVY DEPARTMENT,

1868.

---

WASHINGTON:
GOVERNMENT PRINTING OFFICE.
1869.

# INTRODUCTION.

---

THE *Signal Flags* for use in signaling with this Code in daylight, and the *Coston Lights* for service at night, are the same as those used with the NAVAL SIGNAL CODE and the TELEGRAPHIC DICTIONARY.

The rules for general signaling and for using the Secret Signal Keys, will be found in the INTRODUCTION to the Naval Signal Code, and are applicable to this Code.

When the Boat Code is used elsewhere than on detached boat service, the Boat Code Pendant must be exhibited to indicate that it is to be used in reading signals.

When a GEOGRAPHICAL SIGNAL is to be made by this Code, the Geographical Pendant will be exhibited, and if not on detached service the Boat Code Pendant also, at the same time.

For Boat Squadron signaling the army mode will be found to be well suited both for day and night service. At night two white light lanterns may be used; one placed at or between the feet of the operator, and the other for making the numbers by waving to the right and the left in place of the flag for day use, and the torch ordinarily used at night.

As flags cannot be used without masts of considerable length, the making of signals with flags, although of a small size, must ordinarily be limited to the launch or senior officer's boat; the others merely answering the signals. Each boat and vessel of a Boat and Flotilla Squadron should be provided with a Boat Code and answering pendant, and each Division or Squadron Commander with a set of signal flags and the necessary number of Coston lights for making signals.

If the army mode of signaling is used, each boat should be supplied with a small *red* or *blue flag* for day use, and *two globe lanterns for night* signaling. In that case the senior officer's boat, or the senior of each Division should have the necessary flags and lights for making signals by this Code.

Boat Squadrons under sail should be manœuvred according to the different orders of *Fleet Sailing*, and those propelled by steam or oars according to the orders for *Steam Fleet Manœuvres.*

HOMOGRAPHIC SYMBOLS may be usefully employed on occasions when other means are not available.

The DISTRESS and ASSISTANCE signals, if taught to boat's crews, would enable them to give information and ask for assistance at times when it might be of great importance to them.

For the prescribed equipments, armaments, &c., of boats going on expeditions or other service in squadron, see the Ordnance Instructions of the United States Navy, Part II, from page 1 to 27, inclusive, 1866.

# FOG SIGNAL SYMBOLS.

## STEAM WHISTLE OR FOG HORN.

### NUMERALS.

**1.** One short, sharp blast.
**2.** One long blast.
**3.** Two short, sharp blasts in succession.
**4.** Two long blasts in succession.
**5.** Three short, sharp blasts in succession.
**6.** Three long blasts in succession.
**7.** One short, sharp blast, followed by one long blast.
**8.** One long blast, followed by one short, sharp blast.
**9.** Two short, sharp blasts, followed by one long blast.
**0.** Two long blasts, followed by one short, sharp blast.

### DURATION OF THE SOUNDS.

**1.** A *short blast* should be about three seconds of time duration, and should be made to sound *sharp*, as though by a mere jerk. A little longer time, however, may be required in practice.

**2.** A *long blast* should be of between thirty and forty-five seconds duration, or of not less than thirty nor more than sixty seconds duration; and should be made to sound as though modulated at the beginning and end of the blast.

**3.** The interval of time between the blasts of the same numeral should be as nearly as possible three (3) seconds. A little longer time may be necessary in practice, but the intervals should at least be uniform, or as nearly so as possible.

**4.** The interval of time between the completion of the blast or blasts representing a numeral and the commencement of the first blast of the succeeding numeral should be not less than five (5) nor more than ten (10) seconds.

**5.** It may happen, through the carelessness or want of skill of the operator, that a false blast or blasts may be made, entirely changing the interpretation of the signal, or, in any event, confusing the listener. When this happens, sound six or eight short, sharp blasts in rapid succession, as an indication that an error has been made, rendering it necessary to commence again. This "*error signal,*" as it may be called, should be answered before repeating the signal to be made.

### THE PREPARATORY SIGNAL

**6.** Consists of *one long blast,* of about twice the duration of time occupied by the ordinary long blast representing a numeral, say from sixty (60) to eighty (80) seconds, and it should in all cases be *answered* before making the signal it precedes.

### THE ANSWERING SIGNAL

**7.** Consists of *one short, sharp blast,* made as though by a jerk, of about three (3) seconds duration. No signal should be answered until all the numerals constituting the numbers representing the signal sentence shall have been made. It may be assumed that the signal is complete at the expiration of fifteen (15) or twenty (20) seconds after the sound of the last blast ceases.

**8.** When two or more numerals of the same value follow each other, or occur in the same number, they must be repeated by a repetition of themselves in the same manner as with (Coston) night signals, as there are no "*repeaters*" among the symbols for fog signals.

---

## UNITED STATES ARMY SIGNALS.

**By Albert J. Myer, Colonel and Signal Officer of the Army.**

The following Code of Signals, and instructions for working the same, are published for the information and use of all concerned.

The "General Service Code" is intended to be used for general communication between different vessels or between vessels and parties on land. It is for the purpose of transmitting such messages only as may constantly occur in service and concerning which it does not matter whether they are interpreted by the enemy or not.

*Ciphers, either to be agreed upon by particular commanders or published generally through the command, must always be used in the transmission of messages of importance, or for any communication which might give information to an enemy.*

Every signal officer ought to be able in a few minutes to devise a cipher for this purpose.

### GENERAL SERVICE CODE.

| | | | |
|---|---|---|---|
| A | 22 | P | 1212 |
| B | 2112 | Q | 1211 |
| C | 121 | R | 211 |
| D | 222 | S | 212 |
| E | 12 | T | 2 |
| F | 2221 | U | 112 |
| G | 2211 | V | 1222 |
| H | 122 | W | 1121 |
| I | 1 | X | 2122 |
| J | 1122 | Y | 111 |
| K | 2121 | Z | 2222 |
| L | 221 | & | 1111 |
| M | 1221 | ing | 2212 |
| N | 11 | tion | 1112 |
| O | 21 | | |

3—End of word.
33—End of sentence.
333—End of message.
22.22.22.3—"I understand," or "message is received and understood," or "I see your signals," or "affirmative generally."
22.22.22.333—Cease signaling.
121.121.121—Repeat.

212121—Error.
211.211.211—Move a little to the right.
221.221.221—Move a little to the left.
Flag waved successively from side to side until attention is attracted—"Attention; look for signals from this point."

1. 21112—Wait a moment.
2. 12221—Are you ready?
3. 22122—I am ready.
4. 22212—Use short pole and small flag.
5. 22221—Use long pole and large flag.
6. 12222—Work faster.
7. 11222—Did you understand?
8. 11112—Use white flag.
9. 11211—Use black flag.
10. 22222—Use red flag.

| | | | |
|---|---|---|---|
| a—after. | b—before. | c—can. | h—have. |
| n—not. | r—are. | t—the. | u—you. |
| ur—your. | w—word. | wi—with. | |

The signal for, "The address of the message is now complete," is made thus: the flag being in the first position is dropped to the front, and then waved in full circles twice to the right, then resumes the first position. The signal for, "The message is signed as follows," is made thus: the flag being in the first position is dropped to the front, and then waved in full circles twice to the left, then resumes the first position.

## INSTRUCTIONS FOR USING THE CODE.

The whole number opposite each letter, stands for that letter.

The numbers are made by motions of the flag or signal, to the right or left or in front of a vertical position.

## POSITIONS AND MOTIONS.*

There are one position and three motions. The FIRST POSITION is with the flag held directly above the head, the flag staff vertical. To make the FIRST MOTION or "one," or "1," the flag is waved to the ground to the right, and instantly brought to the first position. To make the SECOND MOTION or "two," or "2," the flag is waved to the ground to the left, and instantly brought to the first position. To make the THIRD MOTION or "three," or "3," the flag is waved to the ground in front, and instantly brought to the first position.

When the latter number consists of more than one figure, the motions of the flag for each figure follow each other without any pause between them.

Thus to make "A" or "two, two," or "twenty-two" or "22," the flag is waved without pause twice to the left, and then brought to the first position. To make "B" or "two, one, one, two," or "twenty-one twelve" or "2112," the flag is waved without pause once to the left, twice to the right, then to the left, and then brought to the first position. That is, one "first motion" followed by two "second motions" followed by one "first motion," the flag not stopping between the motions. To make three "fronts," or "three, three, three," or "three thirty-three" or "333," the flag is waved directly to the front to the ground three times, and then returned to the first position.

* See plates.

At the end of each letter the flag is held in the first position about two seconds, to show that the letter is finished.

## TO SEND A MESSAGE.

First call "Attention" by waving the flag successively from side to side until it is seen and answered by the opposite station. The station called will "answer" by making 22.22.22.3, the general signal for assent or affirmation, to signify that it is ready to receive the message. The communicating station then makes 22.22.22.3, signifying "I see you are ready to receive the message," then proceeds to transmit the message, letter by letter. A pause is made at the end of each letter to show that the signal for that letter is finished. At the end of each word the flag is waved to the ground directly in front, "3," to show that the word is finished. At the end of each sentence there is a pause, and the flag is waved to the ground twice directly in front, "33," to show that the sentence is finished. At the end of a message the flag is waved to the ground three times, directly in front, "333," showing that the message is finished.

When the signal "333," "end of message," is made, it indicates "my communication is complete; I await your answer." The station receiving the message will, upon noticing the signal "Message complete," if the message has been correctly received, immediately answer with the signal of assent, 22.22.22.3, and will then signal in turn such messages as it may have to communicate. If, however, the message or any part of it has not been correctly received, or is not understood, the receiving station will make the signal for "Repeat," 121.121.121.3, followed by the part of the message to be repeated; as, 121.121.121.3, after or before the word—(here signal the word after or before which the repeat is required.) If the message is not understood at all, the signal "121.121.121.3," "all," is made. In commencing a repetition, the sending station will always commence by making the signal of assent, to show that the call for repeat is understood. This signal of assent, meaning "I understand," will be used habitually at the commencement of all communications.

## RECORDING SIGNALS.

When circumstances render it necessary, a pause will be made at the end of each sentence to permit that sentence to be accurately written down. With skilled signalists such pauses are not necessary. Each signal number may be taken down with a pencil as soon as it is seen, and afterwards transmitted by reference to the code. When the signalist is accustomed to the code, this may be dispensed with, and only the words and sentences are written down during the pauses. When two men are together at a station, one man looks through the glass and calls the numbers as fast as they are seen to the other, who writes them down. Messages are thus recorded in the signal numbers composing them. This is done by writing for each letter the signal number which stands for it, thus the word "W A S," written in signal numbers is, "1121 22 212," each letter in signal numbers being separated from the next by a small space. Each complete word is separated from the next by a dash, as "W A S—N O T," is in signal numbers, 1121 22 212—11 21 2.

When secret or cipher codes, codes devised for the occasion, or codes not before used, or when the commander wishes a message signaled of which he and his correspondent alone shall know the meaning, the message may be thus reduced to signal numbers before being placed in the hands of the signalist, who then becomes simply a medium for the transmission of the message, without knowledge of its contents. By this plan of reducing a message to its signal numbers written upon paper before it is sent, and of recording upon paper the signal numbers made by others as they are received, translating them afterwards by the code, it will be found that messages may be almost immediately exchanged by those having knowledge of the principles of the codes without the study or practice of any particular code.

In calling off from the glass, signal numbers to be recorded in writing, each signal number should be given distinct and complete by itself, as for instance, "one twenty-one," "twenty-two," "one twelve," and so on.

When signals are made by a flagman detailed and practiced for the purpose, the flagman properly placed and equipped, and standing with the flag and staff in the "first position," each signal is ordered by calling off briskly, as an order, the numbers for that signal; the flagman making promptly, on hearing each order, those motions with the flag indicated by the signal numbers ordered. Each letter number must be called plainly, distinct, and clear by itself, that the flagman may know before commencing the signal what numbers are to be made together without pause, so that the motions may be made rapidly and well timed.

Thus in orders A "22," would be ordered "twenty-two," B "2112," "twenty-one twelve," C "121," "one twenty-one." Following the same general plan, it is evident that persons practiced as signalists need not be limited to the use of the signal equipments or of any apparatus. A handkerchief or hat held in the hand above the head and waved to the right for "one" "1," to the left for "two" "2," and lowered to the waist for "three" "3," can be readily used for any short distance. With a handkerchief attached to a walking-stick or a boat flag on any staff, messages may be sent a mile or two, or even to greater distances. A man standing with his coat off, with his hands touching upon his breast for the first position, making a wave of his right arm for "one" "1," a wave of his left for "two" "2," dropping both hands to his side for "three" "3," returning always to the first position after each motion, can thus transmit any message.

The simple methods of application are numberless. Enough are here given to be suggestive to those whose duty it may be to study the subject.

To make clear the mode of signaling, let us suppose the word "Able" is to be signaled. There are made first the signal numbers of the letter "A" "22;" there is then a pause of two seconds, the flag being in the first position. The signal numbers of the letter "B" "2112," are then made, followed by another pause. Then the signal numbers of the letter "L" "221," succeeded by another pause; the signal numbers of the letter "E" "12," are then made, and the flag is then dropped to the front, "three" "3," returning to the first position, to indicate that the word is ended; and thus word by word until the message is completed.

## NIGHT SIGNALS.*

To be made with signal equipments; staff 12 feet long; flying torch 1½ inch in diameter; wicked, filled with turpentine, lighted and attached to upper extremity of signal staff by clamp screws. Copper foot torch two inches diameter, wicked, filled with turpentine, lighted and placed at the feet and in front of the flagman. The positions, orders, and motions for signaling at night are identical with those used in the day; the lighted foot

* See plate.

torch being the "point of reference," in relation to which all motions are made. Each torch is fitted with an extinguisher. At the conclusion of each message the flying torch is extinguished. The foot light, or some other light in place of it, is left burning as long as signaling is continued, to the end that the communicating station may see to what point to direct their signals.

When, during the transmission of a message, the flying torch is lowered to the left and is there extinguished, it indicates that it is extinguished to be refilled, and so soon as filled and relighted, the message will be resumed without any further intimation.

In night signaling, great care must be taken that the reference or foot light is always and certainly within view of the communicating station. To ascertain this, placing the eye on the level and in the place of the foot light, it must be noted whether the foot light at the communicating station can be thence seen; if not, the foot light must be raised or moved to a position certainly visible. This precaution should always be taken. The foot light must be always in front of the flagman and directly beneath the flying torch, when that is in the first position.

The torch should be refilled every fifteen minutes and carefully trimmed after each message. When not in use the wick should be covered with the extinguisher.

Lanterns are sometimes substituted for the foot torch, especially on board of vessels where there is danger of fire. In this case, lanterns giving the most powerful light should be selected. Lanterns with reflectors can be used, taking care that the lantern is so placed as to throw the light upon the communicating station. A lantern may be substituted for the flying torch, and attached to the extremity of the staff in its stead. This will be found difficult, however. The light is not nearly so brilliant or so distinct as that given by the torch.

In signaling at short distances, lanterns may be used instead of torches; one lantern being placed stationary as the foot light, the other may be held directly above the head in the hand as the first position. The lantern is then waved to the right for "one" "1," to the left for "two" "2," and lowered to the waist for "three" "3," or pause signal.

Signals can be made in this way very conveniently for ship use, by placing one lantern upon the rail, and waving the other to its right or left to make any required signals, the general principles of the signals remaining the same. Signals made in this way are of convenient use in boats.

A convenient foot light is often made on shore by lighting a small fire near the feet of the signalist. With a single lantern then held in the hand or attached to a small staff, any message can be sent. Or, if for any cause lanterns are not attainable, and fires can be kindled, a small fire may be used as a foot light while the signal motions are made with a brand from the fire, or a lighted pine knot, or a piece of tarred rope, or with almost any combustible substance capable of showing a flame and a light, held in the hand or attached to a staff, and properly waved to either side or to the front to make the required signal motions.

[From Colonel Myer's Manual of Signals.]

## SIGNALING IN CIPHER.

If signals are to be displayed in the presence of an enemy, they must be guarded by ciphers. The ciphers must be capable of frequent changes. The rules by which these changes are made must be simple. Ciphers are undiscoverable in proportion as these changes are frequent, and as the messages in each change are brief. When alphabet ciphers are used, the aim should be to never allow any letter to appear twice alike. The number of letters under each key is to be as small as possible. The terminations of words are to be concealed. The letters in each word ought to be made in unusual sequence. For this purpose a message to be enciphered may be wholly reversed; that is, written with the last word appearing first. Each word may also be reversed. It does not do away with the utility of ciphers that they may be sometimes deciphered, for we must often use them, conscious that, with sufficient time and the appliances they can be interpreted; but knowing, also, that the time interpretation will require, will render the message useless to an enemy. Simple devices, unused for such purposes, it is believed, before the war, have rendered it practicable to so exhibit signals that their interpretation becomes almost impossible. The entire code may change with every day, with every message, or with every word of every message.

The signal disk of the signal corps is as follows:

## DESCRIPTION OF SIGNAL DISK.*

On a small disk of card-board, or any other material, are written or printed the letters of the alphabet in irregular sequence, and arranged around the circumference of the disk. The letters are so placed that when the disk is properly held all the letters are upright. On this small disk are also printed those combinations of letters which frequently occur in words, as "tion," "ing," "ous," &c., &c., and a sign to mark "the end of a word." On a larger disk are written or printed, arranged around its circumference in the same manner, either the letters of the alphabet or the symbolic numbers of signals which are to be used. The disks are fastened concentrically together in such manner that one may revolve upon the other, and that they may be clamped in any position. They are of such size that when so fastened, the letters, &c., upon the inner disk will each appear close to, and directly opposite one of the signal combinations upon the outer disk. (See plate d, Fig. 1.)

The figures "1" and "8" are sometimes used instead of the figures "1" and "2" to symbolize the elements "one" and "two," because the figure "8" is upright in most positions of the disks. Having a disk arranged and clamped, as at Fig. 1, in plate d. it will be clearly understood by any signalist that so provided, he has before him an alphabetic code with every letter opposite its signal symbols; and he will comprehend that by referring to the disk he can transmit a message without the study of any particular code, and can transmit it in secret signals or cipher, by moving the disks upon each other, and so making changes in the code.

Thus, to make "A," the combination "112," "one, one, two," is signaled; to make "C," the combination "1221," "one, two, two, one," is signaled; to make "T," the combination "211," "two, one, one," is signaled; to make "ing," the combination "2112," "two, one, one, two," is signaled; and there is so signaled the word "acting." To denote the end of the word, the common "pause signal," "3," "three," may be used, or whatever combination may be in the compartment opposite the character for "end of the word." This is arranged by preconcert, and so for any words. Clauses, &c., are made by repetitions of the pause signal. Now, it is evident that with any change of the relative positions of the disks made, as by rotating one upon the other, the whole code of alphabetic signals is changed. Thus, suppose the inner disk rotated until the letter "A" is opposite the combination "1112,"

*See plate.

"one, one, one, two." Then referring to the same figure in the plate to signal the word "acting:" "A" is "1112," "C" is "2121," "T" is "22," "ing" is "2212." The signals do not in any way resemble those before exhibited for the same word. The signal for the "end of word" may also be different. These changes can be indefinitely varied. It is for making them that the disks are movable. Where different parties, as the officers of a corps or of an army are to be in communication, rules for the changing of the disks issued to all, enable each to use them whenever they are in view of each other, each finding that his cipher will then correspond with that of the officer with whom he is signaling. And this may be, though the signalists have never met, and may be serving with detachments which have these communications with each other for the first time.

The following is a general rule for the use of signal disks. The signal disk is supposed to be arranged for a code of two elements. The communicating parties have disks similar.*

## RULES AND EXPLANATIONS FOR THE USE OF SIGNAL DISKS.

### I.—*Explanation of the signal disk.*

The numerals on the outer rim of the disk represent the combinations to be made with a flag or torch. Each combination represents, when made, that letter on the inner disk which coincides with it.

### II.—*To make signals.*

The signals for whatever code signals may be represented by the symbols upon the outer disks are made according to the rules heretofore given while treating of the different codes.

### III.—*The adjustment letter.*

The adjustment letter is any letter selected on the inner disks which, together with a given combination on the outer disk, forms the cipher, and is the key to any communication sent in that particular cipher. The letter R is understood to be the adjustment letter, if no other letter is given.

The combination to be used with the adjustment letter is called the key number.

The adjustment letter and the signal combination being given, the inner disk will be turned so that the letter R will coincide with the combination. Example: The combination is "1212," adjustment letter R—the inner disk will be turned so that R will coincide with "1212." Any letter may be the adjustment letter. Any signal combination may be chosen for the key number. Example: the signal "1221—3—1122—333," would indicate that "W" was the adjustment letter; and "1122" the cipher combination. The disk would, in that case, be arranged as follows: "W" would be brought to coincide with "1122."

### IV.—*To send a Message in Cipher.*

Station "A" calls station "B" and gets "B's" acknowledgment. "A" gives "B" the cipher combination in which he intends to send the message.

* See the plate.

Example: "A" gives "B" "2122, (right, left, right, right,) 333;" "B" answers by repeating "22.22.22.3,—2122 333;" which indicates to "A" that "B" has got the correct cipher. "A" and "B" adjust their disks as follows: each turns the inner disk so that the letter R will coincide with the combination "2122" in the outer disk. (See plate Fig. I.) The disks of both parties are now alike, and the message commences.

To signal the word "pickets" in the foregoing cipher, station "A" would make "221-11-1221-2211-1212-211-122, 3"=Pickets. If "W" was the adjustment letter and "1122" the cipher combination, then "W" would coincide with "1122," and the word "Pickets" would be represented by "122-1211-212-2-2222-112-2111"="Pickets."

* * * * * * * * *

## VI.—*Record.*

The officer receiving the message will have another officer or an enlisted man to write down the combinations as they are received, each being called off in its turn by the person at the glass. At the close of the message the officer will take the disk and decipher or translate the combinations thus written, acknowledging the receipt of the message in the usual manner.

---

## To use the Naval Telegraphic Dictionary with the Army Symbols.

To do this, in daylight, exhibit the CORNET anywhere, except at one of the mastheads, to indicate that the Telegraphic Dictionary will be used, and call attention at the same time with the army signal flag.

The first nine letters of the alphabet will represent the nine digits, and the tenth letter the cipher. Thus:

| No. | Symbol. | Value. |
|---|---|---|
| 1 | A | 22 |
| 2 | B | 2112 |
| 3 | C | 121 |
| 4 | D | 222 |
| 5 | E | 12 |
| 6 | F | 2221 |
| 7 | G | 2211 |
| 8 | H | 122 |
| 9 | I | 1 |
| 0 | J | 1122 |

At night the call with the torches or lanterns and the prescribed night indications for telegraphing with Coston lights will apprise the lookout that the Telegraphic Dictionary will be used.

By using the Naval Telegraphic Dictionary* with the army symbols, words and short sentences may be communicated instead of letters, and may be found in practice to be useful, especially at night and at short distances, when two lanterns may be used in place of torches or Coston lights.

* Boat Signal Code pendant, or a Green light, when it is to be used.

Example: It is desired to communicate the word or sentence in the Telegraphic Dictionary answering to 159. Having called and been answered and the CORNET exhibited, proceed to make two, two,—one, two—one; or 22-12-1. The Naval General Signal Book may be used with the army symbols by calling in the usual manner, and when the call is answered make the letters S, B, U, and wait for an answer. The answering officer should reply by repeating the numbers answering to the letters S, B, U, which will indicate that he understands that the signals which will follow immediately thereafter will be from the Naval Signal Book. Or instructions may be issued to the different vessels, and to signal officers on shore if there be any to communicate with, that when a particular army signal flag is used it will indicate—

1st. Regular army signals.

2d. Telegraph Dictionary.*

3d. Naval Signal Book.

The first might be a square Red flag with a white square in the centre;

The second a square Blue flag with a white square in the centre*; and

The third a square Red flag.

The flags for army signaling should be as nearly of the same size as possible, and when used for calling should be waved or held so that the colors may be readily distinguished by the observer.

At night the colors of the position lantern lights would serve to indicate whether the signals were to be the regular army signals, from the Telegraphic Dictionary,* or the Naval Signal Book:—

First, a White Lantern light.

Second, a Green Lantern light.

Third, a Red Lantern light.

The disk may be used for secret combinations of numerals as well as for the letters of the alphabet.

---

* Boat Signal Code pendant, or a Green light, when it is to be used.

Plate 1.

First Position - or "Ready"

Bureau of Navigation 1868.

Plate 2.

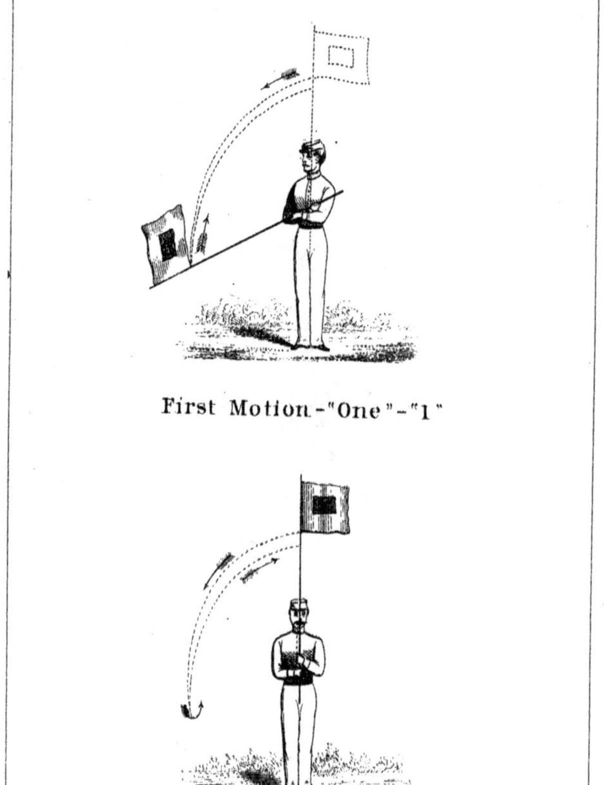

First Motion-"One"-"1"

First Motion-" One"- "1"

Bureau of Navigation 1868.

Plate 3.

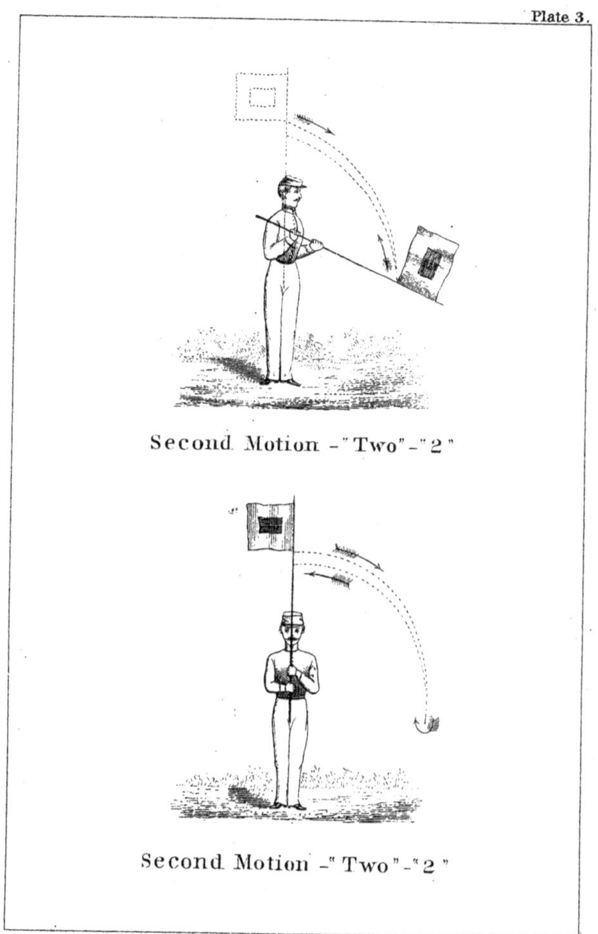

Second Motion - "Two" - "2"

Second Motion - "Two" - "2"

Bureau of Navigation 1868.

Plate 4.

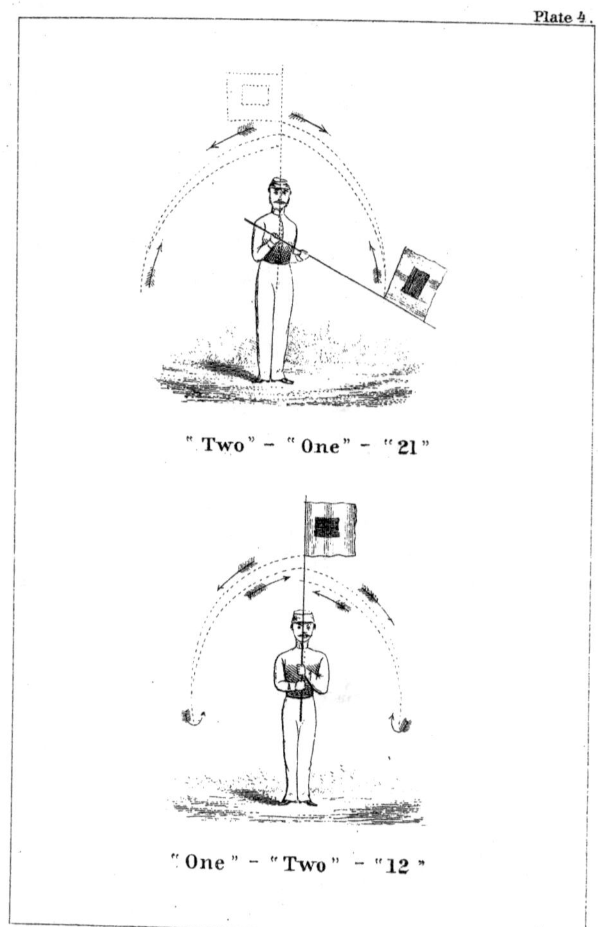

" Two " – " One " – " 21 "

" One " – " Two " – " 12 "

Bureau of Navigation 1868.

Plate 5.

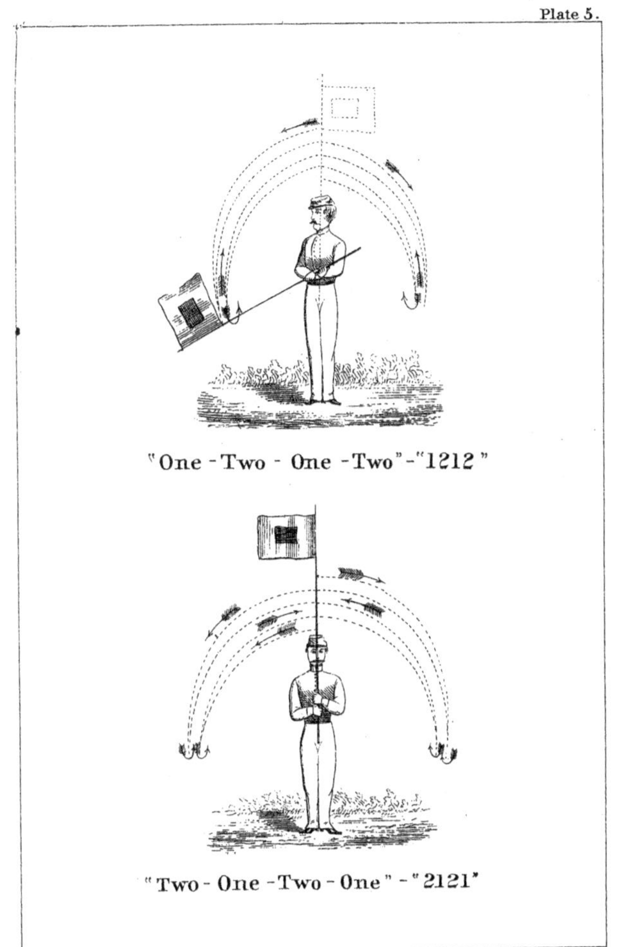

"One - Two - One - Two" - "1212"

"Two - One - Two - One" - "2121"

Bureau of Navigation 1868.

Plate 6.

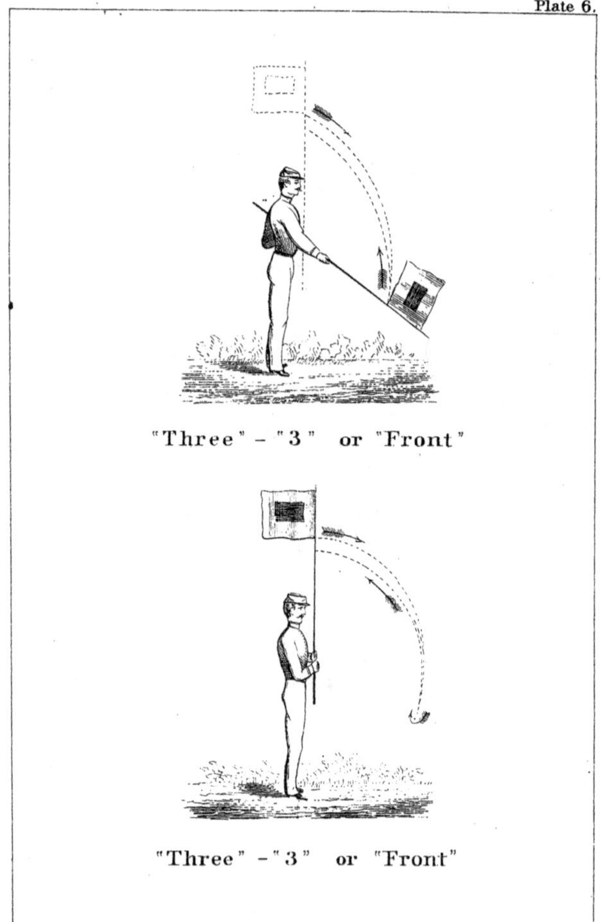

"Three" - "3" or "Front"

"Three" - "3" or "Front"

Bureau of Navigation 1868.

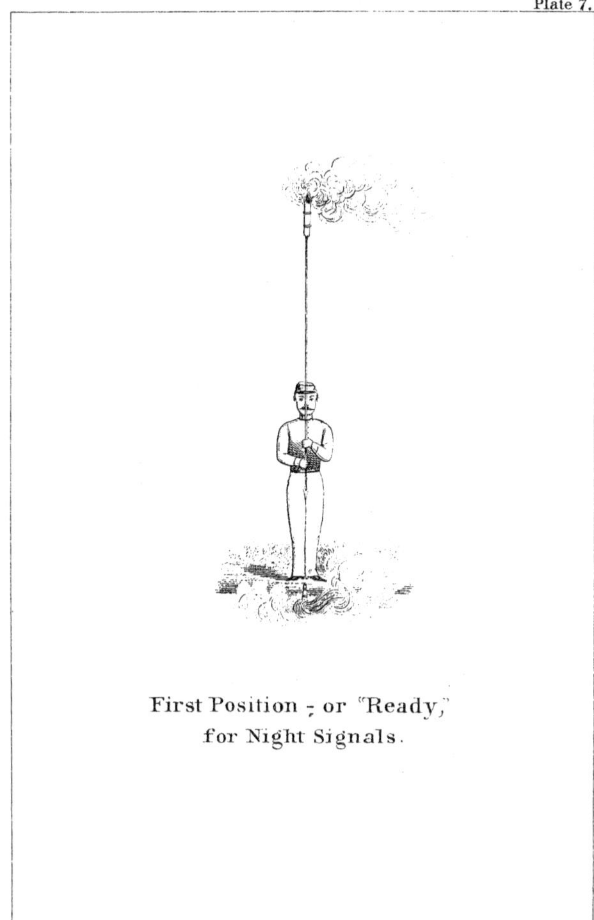

First Position ; or "Ready,"
for Night Signals.

Bureau of Navigation 1868.

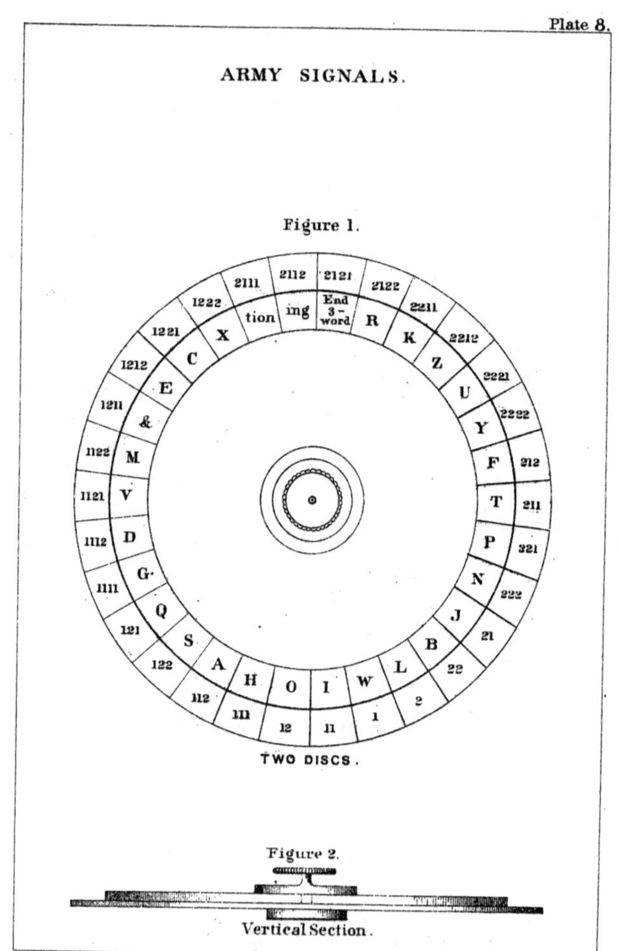


Bureau of Navigation 1868.

# FLOTILLA AND BOAT SQUADRON CODE.

## ALPHABET.

| Nos. | A | Nos. | Z |
|---|---|---|---|
| 1 | A or An. | 14 | N. |
| 2 | B. | 15 | O. |
| 3 | C. | 16 | P. |
| 4 | D. | 17 | Q. |
| 5 | E. | 18 | R. |
| 6 | F. | 19 | S. |
| 7 | G. | 20 | T. |
| 8 | H. | 21 | U. |
| 9 | I. | 22 | V. |
| 10 | J. | 23 | W. |
| 11 | K. | 24 | X. |
| 12 | L. | 25 | Y. |
| 13 | M. | 26 | Z. |

## COMPASS SIGNALS.*

| Nos. | POINTS. | Nos. | POINTS. |
|---|---|---|---|
| 27 | North. | 43 | South. |
| 28 | North by East. | 44 | South by West. |
| 29 | North North East. | 45 | South South West. |
| 30 | North East by North. | 46 | South West by South. |
| 31 | North East. | 47 | South West. |
| 32 | North East by East. | 48 | South West by West. |
| 33 | East North East. | 49 | West South West. |
| 34 | East by North. | 50 | West by South. |
| 35 | East. | 51 | West. |
| 36 | East by South. | 52 | West by North. |
| 37 | East South East. | 53 | West North West. |
| 38 | South East by East. | 54 | North West by West. |
| 39 | South East. | 55 | North West. |
| 40 | South East by South. | 56 | North West by North. |
| 41 | South South East. | 57 | North North West. |
| 42 | South by East. | 58 | North by West. |

* The signal will be dipped ONCE and hoisted again for a quarter of a oint, TWICE for half a point, and THREE TIMES for three-quarters of a point, lways counting to the right.

| Nos. | ABA |
|---|---|
| 59 | Aback. |
| 60 | Abandon-ed-ing-s. |
| 61 | Has, or have, abandoned. |
| 62 | Has, or have not, abandoned. |
| 63 | Do not abandon the. |
| 64 | Shall I, or we, aband'n the? |
| 65 | Abaft. |
| 66 | Abaft the beam. |
| 67 | Abaft the foremast. |
| 68 | Abaft the smoke stack. |
| 69 | Abeam-abreast. |
| 70 | Form line abreast. |
| 71 | Keep bright looko't abeam. |
| 72 | Land seen on port beam. |
| 73 | Land seen on starboard beam. |
| 74 | Stranger-s, seen on port beam. |
| 75 | Stranger-s, seen on starboard beam. |
| 76 | Take station on port beam. |
| 77 | Take station on starboard beam. |
| 78 | Able-ly. |
| 79 | Aboard. |
| 80 | All aboard, come immediately. |
| 81 | All are aboard. |
| 82 | All are not aboard. |
| 83 | Aboard, come. |
| 84 | Aboard of the vessel designated by number or pendant, go. |
| 85 | About. |
| 86 | About ship. |
| 87 | About dark. |
| 88 | About daylight. |
| 89 | About dusk. |
| 90 | About midnight. |
| 91 | About noon. |
| 92 | About sunrise. |
| 93 | About sunset. |
| 94 | Above. |
| 95 | Absent-ed-tee-s. |
| 96 | Absence. |
| 97 | During my absence. |
| 98 | In the absence of. |
| 99 | Abstain-ed-ing-s. |
| 100 | Abundant-ance-ly. |
| 1 | Abuse-ed-ing-ive-ly. |
| 102 | Abuses. |

| Nos. | ACT |
|---|---|
| 103 | Accede-d-ing-s. |
| 4 | Accelerate-d-ing-ion. |
| 5 | Accept-ed-ing-s. |
| 6 | Accession-s. |
| 7 | Accident-s. |
| 8 | Accidental-ly. |
| 9 | Accommodate-d-ing-ion. |
| 110 | Accompany-ied-ies-ing-ment. |
| 1 | Accompany me, or the vessel underway. |
| 2 | Accompany the stranger to the anchorage. |
| 3 | Accompany the prize-s. |
| 4 | Accompany the stranger needing assistance. |
| 5 | Accomplish-ed-ing. |
| 6 | Have you accomplished? |
| 7 | Has, or have, accomplished. |
| 8 | Has, or have not, accomplished. |
| 9 | May be easily accomplished. |
| 120 | Account-ed-ing. |
| 1 | Cannot account for. |
| 2 | Can you account for? |
| 3 | On no account. |
| 4 | Send me a full account of the. |
| 5 | Accounts. |
| 6 | Has, or have, received accounts. |
| 7 | Has, or have not, received accounts. |
| 8 | Accoutre-d-ments. |
| 9 | Accumulate-d-ing-ion-s. |
| 130 | Accurate-acy-ly. |
| 1 | Accuse-d-ing-ation-s. |
| 2 | Accustom-ed. |
| 3 | Acknowledge-d-ing-ment-s. |
| 4 | Acquaint-ed. |
| 5 | Acquiesce-d-ing. |
| 6 | Acquiescence. |
| 7 | Acquire-d-ing. |
| 8 | Acquisition-s. |
| 9 | Acquit-ted-ing. |
| 140 | Acquittal. |
| 1 | Across-athwart. |
| 2 | Act-ed-ing. |
| 3 | Action. |
| 144 | Commence the action. |

| Nos. | ACT |
|---|---|
| 145 | Do not commence the action. |
| 6 | Continue the action. |
| 7 | Discontinue the action. |
| 8 | Ready, are you, for action? |
| 9 | Ready, I am, for action. |
| 150 | Ready, I am not, for action. |
| 1 | Renew the action, I intend to. |
| 2 | Prepare for action immediately. |
| 3 | Withdraw from action in good order. |
| 4 | Active-ly-ity. |
| 5 | Actual-ly. |
| 6 | Adapt-ed-ing. |
| 7 | Not well adapted to the. |
| 8 | Is well adapted to the. |
| 9 | Adaptation. |
| 160 | Add. |
| 1 | Addition-al-ly. |
| 2 | Address-ed-ing. |
| 3 | Adhere-ed-ing-s. |
| 4 | Adherence. |
| 5 | Adjacent-ly–adjoin-ed-ing. |
| 6 | Adjourn-ed. |
| 7 | Adjust-ed-ing-ment. |
| 8 | Admiral. |
| 9 | Admit-ted-ting-s. |
| 170 | Admission-s. |
| 1 | Admonish-ed-ing. |
| 2 | Admonition-s. |
| 3 | Adrift. |
| 4 | Boat adrift. |
| 5 | Advance-d-ing. |
| 6 | Advance in the present order. |
| 7 | Advance in the prescribed order to the attack. |
| 8 | Advance and open on the enemy. |
| 9 | Advance in line ahead according to numerical order or promotion. |
| 180 | Advance in line abreast. |
| 1 | Advance in two lines, or columns of lines ahead. |
| 2 | Advance in three divisions each in line ahead. |
| 183 | Advance in do'ble echelon. (Second ord. of steaming.) |

| Nos. | AFT |
|---|---|
| 184 | Advance on bow and quarter line to port of the leaders. |
| 5 | Advance on bow and quarter line to starboard of the leaders. |
| 6 | Advance, form the, on the senior officer, or the one whose pendant is shown. |
| 7 | Advance in close order. |
| 8 | Advance in open order. |
| 9 | Advance, keep a bright lookout in the. |
| 190 | Advance, close up, on the. |
| 1 | Adv'ce will slacken speed. |
| 2 | Adv. will increase speed. |
| 3 | Advance, the vessel-s, designated will. |
| 4 | Advantage-ous-ly. |
| 5 | Take advantage of the. |
| 6 | Has, or have, gained considerable advantage. |
| 7 | Is there any advantage likely to be gained by? |
| 8 | No possible advantage can be hoped for, by. |
| 9 | Adventurer-s. |
| 200 | Adverse-ly. |
| 1 | Adversary-ies. |
| 2 | Advice-s. |
| 3 | Advise-d-ing-able. |
| 4 | It would be advisable to. |
| 5 | It would not be adv'able to. |
| 6 | Affair-s. |
| 7 | Brilliant affair. |
| 8 | Sad affair. |
| 9 | Afford-ed-ing. |
| 210 | Afford all the assistance you can. |
| 1 | Has, or have, afforded all the assistance possible. |
| 2 | Afloat. |
| 3 | Am, or are, afloat. |
| 4 | Am, or are not, afloat. |
| 5 | Afloat abaft. |
| 6 | Afloat forward. |
| 7 | Hope to be at next high tide. |
| 8 | Afraid. |
| 9 | After-afterwards. |
| 220 | After dark. |
| 221 | After daylight. |

| Nos. | AFT |
|---|---|
| 222 | Afternoon. |
| 3 | After sunrise. |
| 4 | After sunset. |
| 5 | After midnight. |
| 6 | After the moon goes down. |
| 7 | After the moon rises. |
| 8 | After flood tide makes. |
| 9 | After ebb tide makes. |
| 230 | After high water. |
| 1 | After low water. |
| 2 | Again. |
| 3 | Against. |
| 4 | Aggravate-d-ing. |
| 5 | Aggravation-s. |
| 6 | Aggressor-s. |
| 7 | Aggrieve-d. |
| 8 | Ago. |
| 9 | How long ago? |
| 240 | A long time ago. |
| 1 | Not very long ago. |
| 2 | Agree-d-ing. |
| 3 | Agreement-s. |
| 4 | Aground. |
| 5 | Ahead. |
| 6 | Danger ahead. |
| 7 | Keep farther ahead. |
| 8 | Keep more directly ahead. |
| 9 | Land is seen ahead. |
| 250 | Stranger-s seen ahead. |
| 1 | Not so far ahead, keep. |
| 2 | Go ahead. |
| 3 | Go ahead fast-er. |
| 4 | Go ahead, and keep a bright lookout. |
| 5 | Go ahead slow-er. |
| 6 | Go ahead, and sound as you go. |
| 7 | Aid-ed-ing. |
| 8 | Aide-de-Camp-s. |
| 9 | Aim-ed-ing. |
| 260 | Aim higher. |
| 1 | Aim lower. |
| 2 | Aim more to the left. |
| 3 | Aim more to the right. |
| 4 | Aim in the direction shown by compass signal. |
| 5 | Alarm-ed-ing. |
| 6 | Alert. |
| 7 | Be on the alert. |
| 8 | Alien-s. |
| 9 | Alienate-ed-ing. |
| 270 | Alive. |

| Nos. | AMM |
|---|---|
| 271 | All. |
| 2 | Along shore, keep close. |
| 3 | Along shore, is or are keeping. |
| 4 | Alongside, come or go. |
| 5 | Alongside, send a boat. |
| 6 | Allow-ed-ing. |
| 7 | Allowable. |
| 8 | Allowance-s. |
| 9 | What allowance are you on? |
| 280 | Shut allowance off. |
| 1 | Ally-ies. |
| 2 | Almost. |
| 3 | Aloft. |
| 4 | Alone. |
| 5 | Aloof. |
| 6 | Keep aloof. |
| 7 | Already. |
| 8 | Also. |
| 9 | Alter-ed-ing. |
| 290 | Alter course to that now shown. |
| 1 | Altered course to that now shown. |
| 2 | Do not alter course without orders. |
| 3 | Alteration-s. |
| 4 | What alteration-s necessary? |
| 5 | Alternate-ly-ing. |
| 6 | Altitude-s. |
| 7 | Meridian altitude-s. |
| 8 | Altitude-s for time. |
| 9 | Am. |
| 300 | Am I, or are we? |
| 1 | Am I, or are we not? |
| 2 | If I am, or we are not to. |
| 3 | If I am, or we are to. |
| 4 | Ambush-ed. Ambuscade-d-s. |
| 5 | American-s. |
| 6 | Amicable-y. |
| 7 | Amity. |
| 8 | Amiss. |
| 9 | Amnesty-ies. |
| 310 | Among. Amongst. |
| 1 | Ample-y. |
| 2 | Amputate-d-ing. |
| 3 | Amputation-s. |
| 4 | Amuse-d-ing. |
| 5 | The enemy. |
| 316 | Ammunition. |

| Nos. | AMM |
|---|---|
| 317 | My ammunition is nearly exhausted. |
| 8 | Want ammunition for 24-pdr. howitzers, smooth bore. |
| 9 | Want ammunition for 24-pdr. howitzers, rifled. |
| 320 | Want ammunition for 12-pdr. howitzers, smooth bore. |
| 1 | Want ammunition for 12-pdr. howitzers, rifled. |
| 2 | Want ammunition for regulation muskets. |
| 3 | Want ammunition for regulation pistols. |
| 4 | Want ammunition for revolvers. |
| 5 | Want ammunition for carbines. |
| 6 | Want ammunition for all small arms. |
| 7 | Want ammunition for all arms. |
| 8 | I can spare ammunition. |
| 9 | I cannot spare ammunit'n. |
| 330 | Anchor-s. |
| 1 | Anchor-ed-ing-s. |
| 2 | At anchor. |
| 3 | Must anchor. |
| 4 | Shall endeav'r to anchor in the bay or place in view, or that pointed out by compass signal. |
| 5 | Anchor immediately. |
| 6 | Anchor as soon as you can. |
| 7 | Anchor on bearings shown from me. |
| 8 | Anchor in line of battle. |
| 9 | Anchor in first order of steaming. |
| 340 | Anchor in second order of steaming. |
| 1 | Anchor in third order of steaming. |
| 2 | Anchor close in shore. |
| 3 | Anchor in close order. |
| 4 | Anchor in open order. |
| 5 | Anchor, preserving the present order or format'n. |
| 346 | Weigh anchor and stand out or off. |

| Nos. | ARR |
|---|---|
| 347 | Anchorage-s. |
| 8 | Anchorage is good. |
| 9 | Anchorage is unsafe. |
| 350 | And. |
| 1 | Annoy-ed-ing-s. |
| 2 | Annul-led-ling-s. |
| 3 | Annulling signal. |
| 4 | Another. |
| 5 | Answer-ed-ing-s. |
| 6 | Not received an answer. |
| 7 | Received an answer. |
| 8 | A. M. Ante-Meridian. |
| 9 | Anticipate-d-ing-s. |
| 360 | Anticipation-s. |
| 1 | Anxious-ly. |
| 2 | Anxiety-ies. |
| 3 | Any. |
| 4 | Any body. |
| 5 | Any one. |
| 6 | Any thing. |
| 7 | Any where. |
| 8 | Appear-ed-ing-s. |
| 9 | Appearance-s. |
| 370 | Has the appearance of. |
| 1 | Has not the appearance of. |
| 2 | Apply-ied-ing-ies. |
| 3 | Application-s. |
| 4 | Apprehend-ed-ing. |
| 5 | Apprehension-s. |
| 6 | Apprentice-s. |
| 7 | Naval Apprentice-s. |
| 8 | Approach-ed-ing-es. |
| 9 | Approve-d-ing-s. |
| 380 | Approbation. |
| 1 | Apron-s. |
| 2 | Arbitrary-ily. |
| 3 | Ardor. |
| 4 | Arduous-ly. |
| 5 | Are. |
| 6 | Around. |
| 7 | Arm-ed-ing. |
| 8 | Arms. |
| 9 | With arms. |
| 390 | Without arms. |
| 1 | With side arms only. |
| 2 | Well armed. |
| 3 | With small arms. |
| 4 | With all arms. |
| 5 | Arm chest-s. |
| 6 | Armistice-s. |
| 7 | Army-ies. |
| 398 | Arrange-d-ing. |

| Nos. | ARR |
|---|---|
| 399 | Arrangement-s. |
| 400 | Make your arrangements for an early move. |
| 1 | Make your arrangements for attacking the enemy. |
| 2 | Arrest-ed-ing-s. |
| 3 | You will place under arrest. |
| 4 | Has or have been arrested. |
| 5 | Report all arrests. |
| 6 | Arrive-d-ing-s. |
| 7 | When did you arrive? |
| 8 | A vessel has just arrived from. |
| 9 | Arrival-s. |
| 410 | What is the latest arrival from home? |
| 1 | What is the latest arrival from the Command'r-in-Chief? |
| 2 | Articles. |
| 3 | Artificer-s. |
| 4 | What artificer-s have you? |
| 5 | Send artificer-s to. |
| 6 | Artillery. |
| 7 | Heavy artillery. |
| 8 | Light artillery. |
| 9 | As. |
| 420 | As soon as. |
| 1 | As soon as you are ready. |
| 2 | As soon as you report. |
| 3 | As soon as possible. |
| 4 | Ascertain-ed-ing-s. |
| 5 | Cannot ascertain. |
| 6 | Did you ascertain? |
| 7 | Endeavor to ascertain. |
| 8 | Has it been ascertained? |
| 9 | Ashore. Aground. |
| 430 | Go ashore. |
| 1 | Send ashore. |
| 2 | Do not allow any communication with the shore. |
| 3 | Ask-ed-ing-s. |
| 4 | Will you ask? |
| 5 | Assault-ed-ing. |
| 6 | Assault the place. |
| 7 | Attempt to carry the place by assault. |
| 8 | Was carried by assault. |
| 9 | Assemble-d-ing. |
| 440 | Assent-ed-ing. Yes. |
| 441 | Assign-ed-ing-ment. |

| Nos. | AUT |
|---|---|
| 442 | Assist-ed-ing. |
| 3 | Can you assist? |
| 4 | Can you assist me with? |
| 5 | Cannot assist you with. |
| 6 | Assistance. |
| 7 | Do not need any assistance. |
| 8 | Assistance is greatly needed. |
| 9 | Do you need any assistance? |
| 450 | Give immediate assistance. |
| 1 | Vessels or boats needing it, give every possible assistance to. |
| 2 | Astern. |
| 3 | Astern of the line. |
| 4 | Astern of the Commander-in-Chief. |
| 5 | Drop astern. |
| 6 | Keep astern. |
| 7 | At. |
| 8 | At the time. |
| 9 | At what time? |
| 460 | Attack-ed-ing-s. |
| 1 | Shall I, or we, attack? |
| 2 | Begin the attack. |
| 3 | Defer the attack. |
| 4 | Will attack as soon as possible. |
| 5 | Do not commence the attack without orders. |
| 6 | Atrocious-ly. |
| 7 | Atrocity-ies. |
| 8 | Attempt-ed-ing-s. |
| 9 | Shall I, or we, make the attempt? |
| 470 | Made the attempt but failed. |
| 1 | Attend-ed-ing. |
| 2 | Attendance. |
| 3 | Auger-s. |
| 4 | Auspicious-ly. |
| 5 | Authentic-al-ly. |
| 6 | Author-s. |
| 7 | Authority. |
| 8 | On what, or whose, authority? |
| 9 | On the authority of. |
| 480 | Without authority. |
| 1 | Authorities. |
| 2 | The civil authorities of the. |
| 483 | The military authorities. |

| Nos. | AUT |
|---|---|
| 484 | The naval authorities. |
| 5 | Auxiliary-ies. |
| 6 | Avail-ed-ing. |
| 7 | Will avail myself, or ourselves, of the. |
| 8 | Available. |
| 9 | Average-d-ing. |
| 490 | Averse. |
| 1 | Aversion. |
| 2 | Avoid-ed-ing-s. |
| 3 | Avoid, if possible, being seen by the. |
| 4 | Avoid all strange boats and vessels. |
| 5 | Aweigh. |
| 6 | Awning-s. |
| 7 | Furl awning-s. |
| 8 | Spread awning-s. |
| 9 | Axe-s. |
| 500 | Axletree-s. |
| 1 | Azimuth. |
| 2 | Azimuth Compass-es. |
| 3 | Bad-ly. |
| 4 | Very bad. |
| 5 | Baffle-d-ing. |
| 6 | Baffling wind-s. |
| 7 | Bag-s. |
| 8 | Bread bags. |
| 9 | Clothes bags. |
| 510 | Baggage. |
| 1 | Send baggage on board ship. |
| 2 | Send baggage to the rear. |
| 3 | Pack up baggage for a move. |
| 4 | Heavy baggage leave on board ship. |
| 5 | Reduce baggage to the smallest quantity practicable. |
| 6 | Ballast-ed-ing. |
| 7 | What kind of ballast have you in? |
| 8 | Pay particular attention to the stowage of ballast. |
| 9 | Ball cartridge-s. |
| 520 | Bandage-d-ing. |
| 1 | Bandages. |
| 2 | Bandages wanted. |
| 3 | Bank-ed-ing-s. |
| 4 | Bank fires. |
| 525 | Bar-s. |

| Nos. | BAY |
|---|---|
| 526 | Bar can be crossed. |
| 7 | Bar cannot be crossed. |
| 8 | Bar is dangerous at this time. |
| 9 | When can the bar be safely crossed? |
| 530 | Barge-s. |
| 1 | Recall the barge. |
| 2 | Send the barge. |
| 3 | Barometer-s. |
| 4 | Anaroid Barometer need'd. |
| 5 | Barrel-s. |
| 6 | Barricades-ed-ing. |
| 7 | Bathe-ed-ing. |
| 8 | Can the people be allowed to bathe? |
| 9 | Let the people bathe. |
| 540 | Battalion-s. |
| 1 | Land Marine battalion-s. |
| 2 | Land Blue Jacket battalion-s. |
| 3 | Recall battalion-s. |
| 4 | Battery-ies. |
| 5 | Are there any batteries? |
| 6 | What is the state of the batteries? |
| 7 | There are no batteries. |
| 8 | There are batteries. |
| 9 | The batteries can be taken. |
| 550 | The batteries are very strong. |
| 1 | Hold possession of the batteries. |
| 2 | Can you hold the batteries? |
| 3 | The enemy is erecting batteries. |
| 4 | The enemy's batteries are destroyed. |
| 5 | Destroy the batteries and return. |
| 6 | Battle, a signal for. |
| 7 | Prepare for battle. |
| 8 | Are you ready for battle? |
| 9 | Battle rages fiercely on shore. |
| 560 | Battle-axes. |
| 1 | Bay-s. |
| 2 | In the bay. |
| 3 | Proceed down the bay. |
| 4 | Proceed across the bay. |
| 5 | Proceed up the bay. |
| 566 | Bayonet-s. |

| Nos. | BAY |
|---|---|
| 567 | I am, or we are, in need of bayonets. |
| 8 | I, or we, have no bayonets. |
| 9 | Bayonets are indispen'ble. |
| 570 | Send all bayonets that can be spared. |
| 1 | Be-being-been. |
| 2 | Beach-ed. |
| 3 | Beach is difficult to land upon. |
| 4 | Beach is good for landing. |
| 5 | Beam-abeam. |
| 6 | Abaft the beam. |
| 7 | Before the beam. |
| 8 | Lee beam. |
| 9 | Port beam. |
| 580 | Starboard beam. |
| 1 | Weather beam. |
| 2 | Bear-s-ing-s. |
| 3 | Bear up together. |
| 4 | Bear up in succession. |
| 5 | Bear up and steer as shown by compass signal. |
| 6 | Bear, how does the? |
| 7 | Bed-s-bedding-s. |
| 8 | Air beds-bedding. |
| 9 | Stow bedding. |
| 590 | Beef-beeves. |
| 1 | Cannot get fresh beef. |
| 2 | Endeavor to get fresh beef. |
| 3 | Send for fresh beef. |
| 4 | Before. |
| 5 | Begin-ning began. |
| 6 | Behind. |
| 7 | Behind hand. |
| 8 | Behind the point. |
| 9 | Believe-d-ing-lief. |
| 600 | Belong-s. |
| 1 | Below. |
| 2 | Bend-ing. |
| 3 | Bend sails. |
| 4 | Bending sails. |
| 5 | Bend cable-s. |
| 6 | Bend sheet cable-s. |
| 7 | Benefit-ed-ing-s. |
| 8 | Berth-s. |
| 9 | A good berth. |
| 610 | A bad berth. |
| 1 | The best berth. |
| 2 | Shift your berth further in. |
| 613 | Shift your berth further out. |

| Nos. | BOI |
|---|---|
| 614 | Besiege-d-ing-ers. |
| 5 | Best. |
| 6 | Better. |
| 7 | Between. |
| 8 | Between decks. |
| 9 | Between wind and water. |
| 620 | Beyond. |
| 1 | Bight-ed-s. |
| 2 | Bilge-s. |
| 3 | Bilge pump-s. |
| 4 | Clean bilges. |
| 5 | Bind-ing. |
| 6 | Bitt-s. |
| 7 | Black-ed-ing. |
| 8 | Black paint. |
| 9 | Blame-d-ing. |
| 630 | Blameable. |
| 1 | Blank-s. |
| 2 | Blanket-s. |
| 3 | Bleed-ing. |
| 4 | Bled. |
| 5 | Blend-ed-ing. |
| 6 | Block-s. |
| 7 | Blockade-d-ing. |
| 8 | Blockade runner-s. |
| 9 | Blockading vessel-s. |
| 640 | Board-ed-ing. |
| 1 | Boarding nettings. |
| 2 | Boarding pistols. |
| 3 | Boarding pikes. |
| 4 | Come on board. |
| 5 | Remain on board. |
| 6 | Return on board. |
| 7 | Board the stranger. |
| 8 | Boards. |
| 9 | Oak boards. |
| 650 | Pine boards. |
| 1 | Boat-s. |
| 2 | Cannot send boat-s. |
| 3 | Send me boat-s. |
| 4 | Will send boat-s. |
| 5 | Lost boat-s. |
| 6 | Boat is adrift. |
| 7 | Pick up the boat-s. |
| 8 | Boats. |
| 9 | Boats to assemble near the flag ship. |
| 660 | |
| 1 | Boats to be in readiness for service fully armed and equipped. |
| 2 | |
| 3 | |
| 4 | Boiler-s. |
| 665 | Boilers are leaky. |

| Nos. | BOI |
|---|---|
| 666 | Boilers need repairs. |
| 7 | Bold-ly. |
| 8 | Both. |
| 9 | Bottom. |
| 670 | Hard bottom. |
| 1 | Muddy bottom. |
| 2 | Rocky bottom. |
| 3 | Sandy bottom. |
| 4 | Soft bottom. |
| 5 | Sticky bottom. |
| 6 | Bound. |
| 7 | Where bound? |
| 8 | Brackish. |
| 9 | Water is brackish. |
| 680 | Brave-ly. |
| 1 | Bravery. |
| 2 | Breach-ed. |
| 3 | A practicable breach. |
| 4 | Repaired the breach. |
| 5 | Bread, biscuit. |
| 6 | Can you spare me bread? |
| 7 | Break-broken. |
| 8 | Breakers. |
| 9 | Breakers ahead. |
| 690 | Breakers on lee bow. |
| 1 | Breakers on lee beam. |
| 2 | Breakers on the weather bow. |
| 3 | Breakers on the weather beam. |
| 4 | Lookout for breakers. |
| 5 | Ice breakers. |
| 6 | Do you see breakers? |
| 7 | Breakfast. |
| 8 | Will you take breakfast with me? |
| 9 | Let the people have their breakfasts. |
| 700 | The men have had breakfast. |
| 1 | Breastwork-s. |
| 2 | Bridge-s. |
| 3 | Bring. |
| 4 | Bring to. |
| 5 | Bring to on the port tack. |
| 6 | Bring to on the starboard tack. |
| 7 | Bring off beef and vegetables. |
| 8 | Bring off letters and papers. |
| 709 | Bring off sand. |

| Nos. | CAP |
|---|---|
| 710 | Bring off provisions. |
| 1 | Bring off officers and men. |
| 2 | Bringoff working party-ies. |
| 3 | Brush-es. |
| 4 | Bucket-s. |
| 5 | Fire buckets. |
| 6 | Water buckets. |
| 7 | Bury-ied-ing-s. |
| 8 | Burn-ing. |
| 9 | Burnt. |
| 720 | Burst-ing. |
| 1 | Bursting charge-s. |
| 2 | Busy-ied-ing. |
| 3 | But. |
| 4 | Butcher-s. |
| 5 | Butchers land and kill the cattle. |
| 6 | Butter. |
| 7 | Buy-ing, bought. |
| 8 | By. |
| 9 | By-and-bye. |
| 730 | Cable-s. |
| 1 | Cable's length. |
| 2 | Cannot veer more cable. |
| 3 | Lost a cable. |
| 4 | Veer cable. |
| 5 | Calamity-ies. |
| 6 | Calibre-s. |
| 7 | Calm. |
| 8 | If it should be calm. |
| 9 | When it is calm. |
| 740 | Camp-s. |
| | Camp equipage. |
| 1 | Can. |
| 2 | Can he, she, or they? |
| 3 | Can you? |
| 4 | Can I, or we? |
| 5 | Can there be? |
| 6 | I am sure I, or we, can. |
| 7 | I think I, or we, can. |
| 8 | Canal-s. |
| 9 | Cancel-led-ling-s. |
| 750 | Candle-s. |
| 1 | In need of candles. |
| 2 | Cannon-ade-ed-ing. |
| 3 | Distant cannonade heard. |
| 4 | Cannot. |
| 5 | Canteen-s. |
| 6 | Canvas. |
| 7 | Caps. |
| 8 | Musket caps. |
| 759 | Pistol caps. |

| Nos. | CAP |
|---|---|
| 760 | Cape. |
| 1 | Around the cape. |
| 2 | Capitulate-d-ing. |
| 3 | Capitulation. |
| 4 | Captain-s. |
| 5 | Captain or commanding officer to repair on board the senior officer's vessel. |
| 6 | Capture-d-ing. |
| 7 | Care. |
| 8 | Careful-ly. |
| 9 | Careless-ness. |
| 770 | Cargo-es. |
| 1 | Carpenter-s. |
| 2 | Carry-ied-ing-ies. |
| 3 | Cartouch box-es. |
| 4 | Cartridges. |
| 5 | Ball cartridges for rifle muskets needed. |
| 6 | Ball cartridges for smooth-bore muskets wanted. |
| 7 | Ball cartridges for carbines wanted. |
| 8 | Caulk-ed-ing. |
| 9 | Do you need caulking? |
| 780 | In need of caulking. |
| 1 | Caulkers. |
| 2 | Have you any caulkers? |
| 3 | Send caulkers. |
| 4 | Cast. |
| 5 | Cast off. |
| 6 | Cast to port. |
| 7 | Cast to starboard. |
| 8 | Cast away. |
| 9 | Catch-ing, caught. |
| 790 | Cattle. |
| 1 | Caution. |
| 2 | Cautious-ly. |
| 3 | Cannot be too cautious. |
| 4 | Not sufficiently cautious. |
| 5 | Caution your people. |
| 6 | Cavalry. |
| 7 | Cease-ed. |
| 8 | Cease firing. |
| 9 | Cease chasing. |
| 800 | Cease work. |
| 1 | Celebrate-ed-ing-ion. |
| 2 | Celebrate the day. |
| 3 | Censure-d-ing. |
| 4 | Censurable-ly. |
| 5 | Centre-ed-ing-s. |
| 806 | Certain-ly-ty. |

| Nos. | CHE |
|---|---|
| 807 | Certify-ied-ies. |
| 8 | Chafe-d-ing. |
| 9 | Chain-s. |
| 810 | Chain cables. |
| 1 | Chance-d. |
| 2 | Change-d-ing. |
| 3 | Change of moon. |
| 4 | Change of tide. |
| 5 | Change of wind. |
| 6 | Change of weather. |
| 7 | Channel-s. |
| 8 | In the channel, |
| 9 | Acquainted with the channel. |
| 820 | Not acquainted with the channel. |
| 1 | Channel is broad. |
| 2 | Channel is crooked. |
| 3 | An easy channel. |
| 4 | A straight channel. |
| 5 | Out of the channel. |
| 6 | The channel is very narrow. |
| 7 | Stake out the channel. |
| 8 | Channel is well marked. |
| 9 | Charge-d-ing. |
| 830 | Take charge of the prisoners. |
| 1 | Take charge of the prize-s. |
| 2 | Chase-d-ing. |
| 3 | Chase as per compass signal. |
| 4 | Chase to windward. |
| 5 | Chase the stranger-s. |
| 6 | Endeavor to cut off the chase from the land. |
| 7 | Are you overhauling the chased vessel? |
| 8 | Chasing boats will keep on different tacks. |
| 9 | Bring the chased vessel to by firing at her. |
| 840 | Chart-s. |
| 1 | Need a chart of this locality. |
| 2 | Have you a chart of this locality to spare? |
| 3 | I have no chart-s of this locality. |
| 4 | I will send a chart. |
| 5 | Check-ed-ing. |
| 6 | Check the enemy. |
| 7 | Enemy has been checked. |

| Nos. | CHE |
|---|---|
| 849 | Cheer-ed-ing. |
| 850 | Cheer ship. |
| 1 | Cheerful-ly-ness. |
| 2 | Chief-ly. |
| 3 | Chisel-s. |
| 4 | Cold chisels. |
| 5 | Choke-d-ing. |
| 6 | Pumps choked. |
| 7 | Cholera. |
| 8 | Choose. Chosen. |
| 9 | Christian-s. |
| 860 | Christmas day. |
| 1 | Chronometer-s. |
| 2 | Chronometer stopped. |
| 3 | Church-es. |
| 4 | Cipher-s. |
| 5 | Circumspect-ion. |
| 6 | Circumstances. |
| 7 | All the circumstances. |
| 8 | Under the circumstances. |
| 9 | City-ies. |
| 870 | Citizen-s. |
| 1 | Civil-ity-ities. |
| 2 | Civil authorities. |
| 3 | Civil service. |
| 4 | Civilian-s. |
| 5 | Claim-ed-ing. |
| 6 | Claims. |
| 7 | Clamor. |
| 8 | Clamorous-ly. |
| 9 | Clandestine-ly. |
| 880 | Class-ed-ing. |
| 1 | Clean-ly. |
| 2 | Cleanliness. |
| 3 | Clear-ly. |
| 4 | The coast is clear. |
| 5 | Should the weather become clear. |
| 6 | Clemency. |
| 7 | Clerk-s. |
| 8 | Clever-ly. |
| 9 | Clew-s. |
| 890 | Clew up and furl sails. |
| 1 | Cliff-s. |
| 2 | Climate. |
| 3 | Clinch-ed-ing. |
| 4 | Clinker-built boat. |
| 5 | Close-ly. |
| 6 | Close order. |
| 7 | Close as soon as possible. |
| 8 | Close hauled. |
| 899 | Too close. |

| Nos. | COL |
|---|---|
| 900 | Close around the commanding officer or vessel designated. |
| 1 | Cloth. Clothes. |
| 2 | Blue cloth-clothes. |
| 3 | Clothing. |
| 4 | Summer clothing. |
| 5 | Winter clothing. |
| 6 | Warm clothing. |
| 7 | Cloud-y-s. |
| 8 | Clue. |
| 9 | Clump-s. |
| 910 | Coal-s. |
| 1 | In want of coal. |
| 2 | How many days' coal on hand? |
| 3 | Cannot get coal. |
| 4 | Go into port and fill up with coal as rapidly as possible. |
| 5 | Coal heavers. |
| 6 | Coamings. |
| 7 | Coast-s. |
| 8 | On the coast. |
| 9 | Off the coast. |
| 920 | Along the coast. |
| 1 | A dangerous coast. |
| 2 | Acquainted with the coast. |
| 3 | Unacquainted with the coast. |
| 4 | Clear of the coast. |
| 5 | With the coast. |
| 6 | Coast chart-s. |
| 7 | Coast, line of the. |
| 8 | Coasting-er-s. |
| 9 | Coasting vessel-s. |
| 930 | Coasting trade. |
| 1 | Cocoa. |
| 2 | Cocoa nuts. |
| 3 | Cocoa nut trees. |
| 4 | Code. |
| 5 | Boat Signal Code. |
| 6 | Naval Signal Code. |
| 7 | Coffin-s. |
| 8 | Coil-s-ed-ing. |
| 9 | Coke. |
| 940 | Cold-er-est. |
| 1 | Collect-ed-ing. |
| 2 | Collect all the information you can in regard to the movements of the enemy. |
| 943 | Collect news and report it. |

| Nos. | COL |
|---|---|
| 944 | Collision-s. |
| 5 | Color-s. |
| 6 | Do not show any colors. |
| 7 | Show false colors. |
| 8 | What colors did the stranger show? |
| 9 | Column-s. |
| 950 | Form into two columns. |
| 1 | Form into three columns. |
| 2 | Columns advance. |
| 3 | Columns take distance in close order. |
| 4 | Columns take distance in open order. |
| 5 | Combine-d-ing. |
| 6 | Combination-s. |
| 7 | Combustible-s. |
| 8 | Come-ing. |
| 9 | Come alongside. |
| 960 | Come aboard. |
| 1 | Come ashore. |
| 2 | Coming in. |
| 3 | Coming out. |
| 4 | Comfort-s. |
| 5 | Comfortable-y. |
| 6 | For the comfort of the people. |
| 7 | Command-ed-ing. |
| 8 | Commander-s. |
| 9 | Commander-in-Chief. |
| 970 | Commander of the flotilla. |
| 1 | Command'r of the division. |
| 2 | Commands. |
| 3 | Commemorate the day. |
| 4 | Commemoration. |
| 5 | Commence-ment. |
| 6 | Commence the action. |
| 7 | Commence the evolution. |
| 8 | Commence the exercise-s. |
| 9 | Commend-ed-ing. |
| 980 | Commendation-s. |
| 1 | Commerce. |
| 2 | Commercial-ly. |
| 3 | Commit-ted-ting. |
| 4 | Commitment-s. |
| 5 | Commodore. |
| 6 | Commodious-ly. |
| 7 | Common-ly. |
| 8 | Communicate-d-ing. |
| 989 | Communication is allowed with. |

| Nos. | COM |
|---|---|
| 990 | Communication is not allowed with. |
| 1 | Has had communication with. |
| 2 | Has not had communication with. |
| 3 | Wishes to communicate with. |
| 4 | Communication-s. |
| 5 | Compact-ly-ness. |
| 6 | Company-ies. |
| 7 | In company with. |
| 8 | Keep company with. |
| 9 | Was or were in company with. |
| 1000 | Was or were not in company with. |
| 1 | Compass-es. |
| 2 | Need a compass. |
| 3 | By compass. |
| 4 | How do you head by your compass? |
| 5 | Compel-led-ling. |
| 6 | Will be compelled to. |
| 7 | Compel them to. |
| 8 | Compensate-d-ing. |
| 9 | Compensation-s. |
| 1010 | Competent. |
| 1 | Is he competent? |
| 2 | Fully competent. |
| 3 | Not competent. |
| 4 | Complain-ed-ing-s. |
| 5 | Complaint-s. |
| 6 | Make-s complaint. |
| 7 | Cause of complaint-s. |
| 8 | Complete-d-ing. |
| 9 | Are you complete with? |
| 1020 | Can you complete? |
| 1 | Complete your water and provisions as soon as possible. |
| 2 | When will you complete your fitments? |
| 3 | Compliment-s. |
| 4 | Complement-s. |
| 5 | What is your complement of men and officers? |
| 6 | Complement is complete. |
| 7 | Comply-ied-ing-ies. |
| 8 | Cannot comply with. |
| 9 | Comply with the. |
| 1030 | Shall be complied with. |

| Nos. | COM |
|---|---|
| 1031 | Compliance. |
| 2 | In compliance with. |
| 3 | Compose-d-ing. |
| 4 | To be composed of. |
| 5 | Who compose the? |
| 6 | Composition. |
| 7 | Comprehend-ed-ing-s. |
| 8 | Do you comprehend? |
| 9 | Comprehend-s the signal perfectly. |
| 1040 | Do not comprehend the signals. |
| 1 | Comprehension. |
| 2 | Compromise-d-ing. |
| 3 | Compulsion. |
| 4 | Compute-d-ing. |
| 5 | Computation-s. |
| 6 | Conceal-ed-ing. |
| 7 | Concealment-s. |
| 8 | Concede-d-ing. |
| 9 | Concession-s. |
| 1050 | Conceive-d-ing. |
| 1 | Conception. |
| 2 | Concern-ed-ing. |
| 3 | Concert-ed-ing. |
| 4 | Act in concert. |
| 5 | Act without concert. |
| 6 | Conciliate-d-ing. |
| 7 | Conciliation. |
| 8 | Conclude-d-ing. |
| 9 | Conclusion-s. |
| 1060 | Conclusive. |
| 1 | Concur-red-ring. |
| 2 | Concurrence. |
| 3 | Condemn-ed. |
| 4 | Condemnation-s. |
| 5 | Condense-d-ing. |
| 6 | Condenser-s. |
| 7 | Condenser is out of order. |
| 8 | Condenser is under repair. |
| 9 | Condition-al-ly. |
| 1070 | In what condition? |
| 1 | In very bad condition. |
| 2 | In very good condition. |
| 3 | Conditions. |
| 4 | What are the conditions? |
| 5 | Upon what conditions? |
| 6 | Conduce-d-ing. |
| 7 | Conducive. |
| 8 | Conduct-ed-ing. |
| 9 | Confer-red-ring. |
| 1080 | Confess-ed-ing. |

| Nos. | CON |
|---|---|
| 1081 | Confession-s. |
| 2 | Confide-d-ing. |
| 3 | Confidence. |
| 4 | Confine-d-ing. |
| 5 | Confinement. |
| 6 | Keep in close confinement. |
| 7 | Confirm-ed-ing. |
| 8 | Confirmation-s. |
| 9 | Conflagration. |
| 1090 | Conform-ed. |
| 1 | Conform to the. |
| 2 | Confuse-d-ing. |
| 3 | Confusion. |
| 4 | Congratulate-d-ing. |
| 5 | Congratulation-s. |
| 6 | Congress-ional. |
| 7 | Conjecture-d-ing-al. |
| 8 | Connect-ed-ing. |
| 9 | Connexion-s. |
| 1100 | Connive-d-ing. |
| 1 | Connivance. |
| 2 | Conquer-ed-ing. |
| 3 | Conqueror-s. |
| 4 | Conscience. |
| 5 | Conscientious-ly. |
| 6 | Consent-ed-ing. |
| 7 | Consequence-s. |
| 8 | Of great consequence. |
| 9 | Of no consequence. |
| 1110 | In consequence of. |
| 1 | The consequence will be. |
| 2 | What was the consequ'nce? |
| 3 | Consider-ed-ing. |
| 4 | Consideration-s. |
| 5 | Consist-ed-ing-s. |
| 6 | Consistent-ly. |
| 7 | Consort-s. |
| 8 | Conspicuous-ly. |
| 9 | Conspire-d-ing. |
| 1120 | Conspirator-s. |
| 1 | Constant-ly. |
| 2 | Constitute-d-ing. |
| 3 | Constitution-al. |
| 4 | Constitution of the U. States. |
| 5 | Construct-ed-ing. |
| 6 | Construction. |
| 7 | A right construction. |
| 8 | A wrong construction. |
| 9 | Consul-s. |
| 1130 | United States Consul. |
| 1 | United States Vice-consul. |
| 1132 | Consulate. |

| Nos. | CON |
|---|---|
| 1133 | Consult-ed-ing-s. |
| 4 | Wish-es to consult. |
| 5 | Consultation-s. |
| 6 | Consume-d-ing. |
| 7 | Consumption. |
| 8 | Contact. |
| 9 | Contagion. |
| 1140 | Contagious. |
| 1 | Contagious disease-s. |
| 2 | Disease is not contagious. |
| 3 | Contain-ed-ing-s. |
| 4 | Contemplate-d-ing-s. |
| 5 | Contempt-s. |
| 6 | Contemptuous-ly-ness. |
| 7 | Contemptible-y-ness. |
| 8 | Contend-s-ing. |
| 9 | Content-ed. |
| 1150 | Contentment. |
| 1 | Contents. |
| 2 | Contest-s. |
| 3 | Continue-d-ing. |
| 4 | Continuation. |
| 5 | Continually. |
| 6 | Contraband. |
| 7 | Contraband articles. |
| 8 | Contraband trade. |
| 9 | Contraband of war. |
| 1160 | Contract-ed-ing. |
| 1 | Contracts. |
| 2 | Contractor-s. |
| 3 | Contractor for fresh provisions. |
| 4 | Contradict-ed-ing-s. |
| 5 | Has been contradicted. |
| 6 | Has not been contradicted. |
| 7 | Contradictory. |
| 8 | Contradictory reports in circulation. |
| 9 | Contradictory statements made. |
| 1170 | Contrary. |
| 1 | Contrary to orders. |
| 2 | Contrary winds. |
| 3 | Contribute-d-ing-s. |
| 4 | Contrive-d-ing-s. |
| 5 | Contrivance-s. |
| 6 | Control-led-ling-s. |
| 7 | Convalesce-ing. |
| 8 | Convalescent-s. |
| 9 | Convenient-ly. |
| 1180 | Convenience-s. |

| Nos. | COU |
|---|---|
| 1181 | It will be a great convenience. |
| 2 | Conversation-s. |
| 3 | Convey-ed-ing-s. |
| 4 | Convict-ed-ing. |
| 5 | Convict-s. |
| 6 | Convince-d-ing-s. |
| 7 | Convoy-ed-ing-s. |
| 8 | When will the convoy? |
| 9 | When did the convoy? |
| 1190 | Where is the convoy? |
| 1 | Cook-s. |
| 2 | Mess cook-s. |
| 3 | Ship's cook-s. |
| 4 | Cooper-s. |
| 5 | Cooper's adze. |
| 6 | Cooper's tools. |
| 7 | Coöperate-d-ing-s. |
| 8 | Coöperate with the army. |
| 9 | Coöperate with the barges. |
| 1200 | Coöperate with the launches. |
| 1 | Coöperate with the flotilla. |
| 2 | Coöperate with the small steamers. |
| 3 | A hearty coöperation is expected. |
| 4 | A zealous coöperation will ensure success. |
| 5 | Correct-ed-ing-s. |
| 6 | Correspond-ed-ing-s. |
| 7 | Correspondence. |
| 8 | Corroborate-d-ing-s. |
| 9 | Cost-ly. |
| 1210 | Cot-s. |
| 1 | Cotton. |
| 2 | Could. |
| 3 | Counsel. |
| 4 | Count-ed-ing-s. |
| 5 | Count the enemy's guns, and report the number. |
| 6 | Count the enemy's vessels, and report the number. |
| 7 | Countermand-ed-ing-s. |
| 8 | Countersign. |
| 9 | Courage-ous-ly. |
| 1220 | Courier-s. |
| 1 | Court-s. |
| 2 | Court of Inquiry. |
| 3 | Court martial. |
| 4 | Civil court-s. |
| 1225 | Military court-s. |

| Nos. | COU |
|---|---|
| 1226 | Course-s. |
| 7 | Alter course together as per compass signal, preserving relative bearings and distances. |
| 8 | Alter course in succession as per compass signal, preserving relative bearings and distances. |
| 9 | Shall shape a course for. |
| 1230 | Steer the course indicated by compass signal. |
| 1 | Steer the same course as the commanding officer. |
| 2 | Cove-s. |
| 3 | Go into the cove. |
| 4 | Look into the cove. |
| 5 | Cover-ed-ing-s. |
| 6 | Cover the landing of the. |
| 7 | Under cover of the. |
| 8 | Cockswain-s. |
| 9 | Craft. |
| 1240 | Crank-s. |
| 1 | Crank pin-s. |
| 2 | Credible-ibility. |
| 3 | Credit. |
| 4 | Creditable-y. |
| 5 | Creek-s. |
| 6 | Crew-s. |
| 7 | Crime-s. |
| 8 | Criminal-s. |
| 9 | Cripple-d-ing. |
| 1250 | Crowbar-s. |
| 1 | Cruel-ly-ties. |
| 2 | Cruise-d-ing. |
| 3 | Where did you cruise? |
| 4 | On a cruise. |
| 5 | During the cruise. |
| 6 | Cruise off and on. |
| 7 | Cruise along the coast. |
| 8 | Cruise off the entrance to the bay. |
| 9 | Cruise off the bar. |
| 1260 | Cruise among the islands. |
| 1 | Enemy's cruiser-s. |
| 2 | Culpable-bility. |
| 3 | Culprit-s. |
| 4 | Currents. |
| 5 | Strong current with us. |
| 6 | Strong current against us. |
| 7 | Strong current setting out. |
| 1268 | Strong current setting in. |

| Nos. | DAY |
|---|---|
| 1269 | Cannot stem the current. |
| 1270 | Custody. |
| 1 | Custom-house. |
| 2 | Custom-house official-s. |
| 3 | Cut-ting. |
| 4 | Cut off the. |
| 5 | Cut out the. |
| 6 | Cut up the. |
| 7 | Cutlass-es. |
| 8 | Cutlasses needed for boats. |
| 9 | Cutlasses send to the boats. |
| 1280 | Cutter-s. |
| 1 | First cutter-s. |
| 2 | Second cutter-s. |
| 3 | Third cutter-s. |
| 4 | Fourth cutter-s. |
| 5 | Cwt.-hundred weight. |
| 6 | Cylinder-s. |
| 7 | Cylinder head-s. |
| 8 | Damage-d-ing. |
| 9 | Damage may be repaired soon. |
| 1290 | Have you received any damage? |
| 1 | Have not received any damage. |
| 2 | Repair damage immediately. |
| 3 | Withdraw and repair damage. |
| 4 | Damage repaired. |
| 5 | Damp-ness. |
| 6 | Danger-s. |
| 7 | Dangerous-ly. |
| 8 | You are running into danger. |
| 9 | There is no danger. |
| 1300 | It is very dangerous navigation. |
| 1 | Dare-d-ing. |
| 2 | Dark-en-ed. |
| 3 | After dark. |
| 4 | Before dark. |
| 5 | Dash. |
| 6 | Make a dash at the enemy. |
| 7 | Date-ed-ing-s. |
| 8 | What is the date of? |
| 9 | Day-s. |
| 1310 | To-day. |
| 1 | Day after. |
| 2 | Day before. |
| 1313 | Daylight. |

| Nos. | DAY | Nos. | DIK |
|---|---|---|---|
| 1314 | How many days? | 1366 | Military Department. |
| 5 | What day? | 7 | Navy Department. |
| 6 | Day of the month. | 8 | Treasury Department. |
| 7 | Day of the week. | 9 | Depend-ed-ing-s. |
| 8 | Day of the year. | 1370 | Deplore-d-ing-s. |
| 9 | Dead-ly. | 1 | Depot-s. |
| 1320 | Deal-ings. | 2 | Depredation-s. |
| 1 | Dear. | 3 | Depress-ed-ing-s. |
| 2 | Dearest. | 4 | Deprive-d-ing. |
| 3 | Debility. | 5 | Describe-d-ing-s. |
| 4 | Decay-ed-ing. | 6 | Desert-ed-ing. |
| 5 | Deceive-d-ing. | 7 | Deserter-s. |
| 6 | Deception-s. | 8 | Desertion-s. |
| 7 | December. | 9 | Deserve-d-ing. |
| 8 | Decide-d-ing. | 1380 | Design-ed-ing-s. |
| 9 | Decipher-ed-ing. | 1 | Desire-d-ing-s. |
| 1330 | Deck-s. | 2 | Desist-ed-ing-s. |
| 1 | Decline-d-ing-s. | 3 | Desolate-d-ing. |
| 2 | Decoy-ed-ing. | 4 | Desolation. |
| 3 | Deep-ly. | 5 | Despair-ed-ing-s. |
| 4 | Deepest. | 6 | Destination-s. |
| 5 | Defame-d-ing. | 7 | Destroy-ed-ing. |
| 6 | Defamation. | 8 | Can you destroy? |
| 7 | Default. | 9 | Cannot destroy. |
| 8 | Defeat-ed-ing. | 1390 | Destroy prize-s if necess'ry. |
| 9 | Defect-s. | 1 | Have destroyed. |
| 1340 | Can make good my defects. | 2 | Shall I destroy? |
| 1 | Make good your defects. | 3 | You will destroy. |
| 2 | What are your defects? | 4 | Detach-ed-ing. |
| 3 | Defend-ed-ing-s. | 5 | Detachment-s. |
| 4 | Defense. | 6 | Detachment of Marines. |
| 5 | Defensive, | 7 | Detachment of Seamen. |
| 6 | Defer-red-ring. | 8 | Detail-ed-ing. |
| 7 | Deficient-cy. | 9 | Details. |
| 8 | Define-d-ing. | 1400 | Detain-ed-ing. |
| 9 | Defraud-ed-ing. | 1 | Detect-ed-ing-s. |
| 1350 | Defray-ed-ing. | 2 | Deter-red-ring. |
| 1 | Defy-ied-ing-ies. | 3 | Determine-d-ing. |
| 2 | Degrade-d-ing-s. | 4 | Determination. |
| 3 | Degradation. | 5 | Detriment-al. |
| 4 | Degree-s. | 6 | Deviate-d-ing. |
| 5 | Delay-ed-ing-s. | 7 | Deviation-s. |
| 6 | Delinquent-s. | 8 | Deviat'n of the compass-es. |
| 7 | Delirious-ium. | 9 | Devise-d-ing. |
| 8 | Delirium tremens. | 1410 | Devolve-d. |
| 9 | Deliver-ed-ing-s. | 1 | Devote-d-ing. |
| 1360 | Demand-ed ing-s. | 2 | Did. |
| 1 | Demolish-ed-ing-es. | 3 | Diet-ed-ing. |
| 2 | Denote-d-ing-s. | 4 | Differ-ing-s. |
| 3 | Deny-ied-ing-ies. | 5 | Difference-s. |
| 4 | Depart-ed-ing-s. | 6 | Difficult-y-ies. |
| 1365 | Department-s. | 1417 | Dike-s. |

| Nos. | DIL |
|---|---|
| 1418 | Dilatory-iness. |
| 9 | Diligent-ly. |
| 1420 | Dimension-s. |
| 1 | Dine. Dinner. |
| 2 | After dinner. |
| 3 | Boats' crews get dinner. |
| 4 | Before dinner. |
| 5 | Have the people dined? |
| 6 | Dinner, send, with people going on service. |
| 7 | Send the peoples' dinner. |
| 8 | Peoples' dinner has not been sent. |
| 9 | Dingy, send the. |
| 1430 | Direct-ed-ing-ly. |
| 1 | Direction-s. |
| 2 | Director-s. |
| 3 | Disable-d-ing. |
| 4 | Disability-ies. |
| 5 | Disadvantage. |
| 6 | Disaffected. |
| 7 | Disaffection. |
| 8 | Disagree-d-ing-s. |
| 9 | Disappear-ed-ing. |
| 1440 | Disappoint-ed-ing. |
| 1 | Disapprove-d-ing. |
| 2 | Disarm-ed-ing. |
| 3 | Disaster-s-ous. |
| 4 | Disband-ed-ing. |
| 5 | Disbelieve-d. |
| 6 | Disbelief. |
| 7 | Discern-ed-ing-ment. |
| 8 | Discharge-d-ing. |
| 9 | Discipline-d-ing. |
| 1450 | Disconcert-ed-ing. |
| 1 | Disconnect-ed. |
| 2 | Discontinue-d-ing. |
| 3 | Discover-ed-ing. |
| 4 | Have discovered the enemy. |
| 5 | Have not discovered anything. |
| 6 | Have you discovered that which you have been in search of? |
| 7 | Discovered, what have you? |
| 8 | Discourage-d-ing-ment-s. |
| 9 | Discredit-ed-ing. |
| 1460 | Discreditable-y. |
| 1 | Discretion. Discreet-ly. |
| 1462 | Act very discreetly. |

| Nos. | DIS |
|---|---|
| 1463 | Act at your own discretion. |
| 4 | At his, your, or their discretion. |
| 5 | Disease-s. |
| 6 | Disease is contagious. |
| 7 | Disease is not contagious. |
| 8 | Disease is epidemic. |
| 9 | Disease is spreading. |
| 1470 | Disembark-ed-ing. |
| 1 | Get ready to disemb'rk the. |
| 2 | Have disembarked. |
| 3 | Have not disembarked. |
| 4 | Will not disembark the. |
| 5 | Disengage-d. |
| 6 | Disgrace-d-ing. |
| 7 | Disgraceful-ly. |
| 8 | Disguise-d-ing-s. |
| 9 | Dishearten-ed-ing. |
| 1480 | Dishonest-y-ly. |
| 1 | Dishonor-able-y. |
| 2 | Disingenuous-ly-ness. |
| 3 | Disinterested-ness. |
| 4 | Dislike-d-ing. |
| 5 | Dislocate-d. |
| 6 | Dislodge-d-ing. |
| 7 | Dislodge the enemy. |
| 8 | Dislodged, the enemy is. |
| 9 | Dislodged, the enemy cannot be, with present force. |
| 1490 | Dismantle-d-ing. |
| 1 | Dismast-ed. |
| 2 | Dismiss-ed. |
| 3 | Dismissal. |
| 4 | Dismount-ed-ing. |
| 5 | Disobey-ed-ing. |
| 6 | Your orders. |
| 7 | Disorder. |
| 8 | In great disorder. |
| 9 | Dispensary-ies. |
| 1500 | Dispense-d-ing. |
| 1 | Can you dispense with? |
| 2 | Cannot dispense with. |
| 3 | Disperse-d. |
| 4 | Boats and vessels of the flotilla will disperse and rendezvous as previously directed. |
| 5 | Display-ed-ing. |
| 6 | Displease-d-ing. |
| 7 | Displeasure. |
| 1508 | Dispose-d-ing. |

| Nos. | DIS |
|---|---|
| 1509 | Disposition-s. |
| 1510 | Dispossess-ed-ing. |
| 1 | Disprove-d-ing. |
| 2 | Dispute-d-ing-s. |
| 3 | Disqualify-ied-ing-ies. |
| 4 | Disqualification-s. |
| 5 | Disregard-ed-ing. |
| 6 | Disregard my movements. |
| 7 | Disregard all signals until further orders. |
| 8 | Disrepute-able. |
| 9 | Dissolve-d-ing. |
| 1520 | Dissolution. |
| 1 | Dissuade-d-ing. |
| 2 | Distance-s. |
| 3 | Keep within signal distance. |
| 4 | Take positions at proper distance. |
| 5 | Too great a distance. |
| 6 | You are at the proper distance. |
| 7 | Distinct-ly. |
| 8 | Distinction-s. |
| 9 | Distinctness. |
| 1530 | Distinguish-ed-ing-able. |
| 1 | Can plainly distinguish. |
| 2 | Cannot distinguish. |
| 3 | Can you distinguish? |
| 4 | Distinguishing pendants, show your. |
| 5 | Distinguishing lights, carry your. |
| 6 | Distress-ed-ing. |
| 7 | Assist the distressed. |
| 8 | In distress, and in need of immediate assistance. |
| 9 | Signal of distress, this is a. |
| 1540 | Stay by the distressed party-ies. |
| 1 | Distribute-d-ing. |
| 2 | To be distributed. |
| 3 | Distribution. |
| 4 | Make an equal distribut'n. |
| 5 | Distrust-ed-ing. |
| 6 | Disunite-d-ing. |
| 7 | Disunion. |
| 8 | Ditch-es. |
| 9 | Dive-d-ing. |
| 1550 | Diver-s. |
| 1 | Diving bell-s. |
| 1552 | Diving apparatus and crew. |

| Nos. | DOW |
|---|---|
| 1553 | Divert-ed-ing. |
| 4 | Diversion-s. |
| 5 | Make a diversion. |
| 6 | The movement is intended to be a diversion. |
| 7 | Divide-d-ing. |
| 8 | Divide your command. |
| 9 | Division-s. |
| 1560 | First division. |
| 1 | Second division. |
| 2 | Third division. |
| 3 | Reserve division. |
| 4 | Divine service. |
| 5 | Divulge-d-ing. |
| 6 | Do not divulge your information or orders. |
| 7 | Do. Does. |
| 8 | Do not. |
| 9 | Do they? |
| 1570 | Do we? |
| 1 | Do you? |
| 2 | Done. |
| 3 | Can anything be done for you? |
| 4 | Can it be done? |
| 5 | If it can be done. |
| 6 | If it cannot be done. |
| 7 | Dock-ed-ing-s. |
| 8 | Go into dock. |
| 9 | In need of docking. |
| 1580 | Dockyard-s. |
| 1 | Dockyard establishment. |
| 2 | From the dockyard. |
| 3 | Set fire to the dockyard. |
| 4 | Send for working party-ies at the dockyard. |
| 5 | Send working party-ies to the dockyard. |
| 6 | Doing. |
| 7 | Dollar-s. |
| 8 | Dollars worth. |
| 9 | Mexican dollars. |
| 1590 | Spanish dollars. |
| 1 | Double-d-ing. |
| 2 | Double on the enemy. |
| 3 | Enemy is trying to double |
| 4 | on you. |
|  | Doubt-ed-ing-s. |
| 5 | Doubtful-ly. |
| 6 | Doubtless. |
| 7 | Down. |
| 1598 | Downwards. |

| Nos. | DOZ |
|---|---|
| 1599 | Dozen-s. |
| 1600 | Drag-ged-ging. |
| 1 | I am dragging. |
| 2 | Drag rope-s. |
| 3 | Drag net-s. |
| 4 | Draught. |
| 5 | Lessen your draught of water as much as possible. |
| 6 | What is your draught of water? |
| 7 | Your draught of water is too great. |
| 8 | Draw-ing. |
| 9 | Draw your charges. |
| 1610 | Draw your charges and reload your guns. |
| 1 | Draw the enemy's fire. |
| 2 | Draw off from the. |
| 3 | Drawing off, the enemy is. |
| 4 | Dread-ed-ing-s. |
| 5 | Dreadful. |
| 6 | Dredge-d-ing-s. |
| 7 | Dress-ed-ing. |
| 8 | Full dress uniform. |
| 9 | Full dress ship-s. |
| 1620 | Undress uniform. |
| 1 | Undress ship-s. |
| 2 | Drill-ed-ing. |
| 3 | Drill your men at great guns. |
| 4 | Drill with small arms. |
| 5 | Drill with all arms. |
| 6 | Drink-ing. |
| 7 | Drinking water. |
| 8 | Drive-n-ing. Drove. |
| 9 | Drive the enemy from his position. |
| 1630 | Have driven the enemy off. |
| 1 | I cannot drive the enemy away. |
| 2 | Drown-ed-ing. |
| 3 | Man drowned. |
| 4 | Officer drowned. |
| 5 | Drum-s. |
| 6 | Drum and fife. |
| 7 | Drum head-s. |
| 8 | Drummer-s. |
| 9 | Drunk-en. |
| 1640 | Drunkenness. |
| 1641 | Dry-ied-ing. |

| Nos. | EFF |
|---|---|
| 1642 | Duck-s. |
| 3 | Duplicate-d-ing-s. |
| 4 | Duplicity. |
| 5 | During. |
| 6 | Duration. |
| 7 | Dusk. |
| 8 | Dusk of the evening. |
| 9 | Duty-ies. |
| 1650 | Dysentery. |
| 1 | Each. |
| 2 | Each of us or our. |
| 3 | Each of you or your. |
| 4 | Each of their. |
| 5 | Each of the. |
| 6 | Each other. |
| 7 | Eager-ly-ness. |
| 8 | Early-ier-iest. |
| 9 | Earnest-ly-ness. |
| 1660 | Earth-ly-y. |
| 1 | Ease-y-ily. |
| 2 | Not easily done. |
| 3 | With the greatest ease. |
| 4 | Ebb-ed-ing. |
| 5 | Do not wait for the ebb-tide. |
| 6 | Ebb-tide will make at. |
| 7 | Ebb-tide will cease at. |
| 8 | Take advantage of the ebb-tide. |
| 9 | Wait for the ebb-tide. |
| 1670 | Economy. |
| 1 | Practice the strictest economy. |
| 2 | Economical-ly. |
| 3 | Eddy-ies. |
| 4 | Eddy currents. |
| 5 | Eddy winds. |
| 6 | Get into the eddies. |
| 7 | Keep out of the eddies. |
| 8 | Edge-d-ing-s. |
| 9 | Edge of the bank. |
| 1680 | Edge of the channel. |
| 1 | Edge of the shoal. |
| 2 | Edition-s. |
| 3 | Editor-s. |
| 4 | Educate-d-ing. |
| 5 | Education. |
| 6 | Effect-s-ed. |
| 7 | Can you effect? |
| 8 | Can be effected by. |
| 9 | If you can effect. |
| 1690 | The effect of. |

| Nos. | EFF |
|---|---|
| 1691 | Cannot be effected. |
| 2 | Effective-ly. |
| 3 | Get within effective range. |
| 4 | Not within effective range. |
| 5 | You are in effective range. |
| 6 | Effectual-ly. |
| 7 | Efficacious. |
| 8 | Efficient-ly. |
| 9 | Effort-s. |
| 1700 | Employ all your efforts. |
| 1 | My efforts are unavailing. |
| 2 | Unsuccessful, my efforts have been. |
| 3 | Egress. |
| 4 | Eight-h-ly. |
| 5 | Eighteen-th. |
| 6 | Either. |
| 7 | Either of the. |
| 8 | Either of us, or of our. |
| 9 | Either of your, or of their. |
| 1710 | Either of them. |
| 1 | Elapse-d-ing. |
| 2 | Elastic-ity. |
| 3 | Elate-d. |
| 4 | Electric-al. |
| 5 | Electric telegraph. |
| 6 | Electricity. |
| 7 | Elements. |
| 8 | Elevate-d-ing. |
| 9 | Elevate your guns more. |
| 1720 | Elevation-s. |
| 1 | Elevatory screw is broken. |
| 2 | Eleven-th. |
| 3 | Eligible-ity. |
| 4 | Else. |
| 5 | Elsewhere. |
| 6 | Nothing else. |
| 7 | What else? |
| 8 | Elude-d-ing. |
| 9 | Elude the pursuing ves'el-s if possible. |
| 1730 | Embargo-es. |
| 1 | Embark-ed-ing. |
| 2 | Cannot embark the. |
| 3 | Could not be embarked. |
| 4 | Embark the marines and troops. |
| 5 | Embark the howitzers and field pieces. |
| 6 | Embark the seamen. |
| 1737 | Embark all arms. |

| Nos. | ENC |
|---|---|
| 1738 | Enemy's troops are embarking. |
| 9 | Enemy's troops have embarked. |
| 1740 | Our troops are embarked. |
| 1 | Shall I embark our forces? |
| 2 | Ready be to embark at once. |
| 3 | Embarcation. |
| 4 | Cover the embarcation of the forces. |
| 5 | Embarcation is completed. |
| 6 | Embarrass-ed-ing-ment-s. |
| 7 | Embrace-d-ing. |
| 8 | Embrasure-s. |
| 9 | Emerge-d-ing. |
| 1750 | Eminent-ly. |
| 1 | Emissary-ies. |
| 2 | Emolument-s. |
| 3 | Employ-ed-ing-ment-s. |
| 4 | I am, or we are, employed. |
| 5 | Not to be employed. |
| 6 | Empower-ed. |
| 7 | Is he, or are they, empowered to? |
| 8 | He is, or they are, not empowered. |
| 9 | Empty. |
| 1760 | Is, or are, empty. |
| 1 | How many empty casks? |
| 2 | Send empty casks to the. |
| 3 | Emulate-d-ing. |
| 4 | Emulation. |
| 5 | Enable-d-ing. |
| 6 | Enact-ed-ing. |
| 7 | Encamp-ed-ing. |
| 8 | Is encamped. |
| 9 | Was encamped. |
| 1770 | Encampment-s. |
| 1 | Enclose-d-ing. |
| 2 | Enclosure-s. |
| 3 | Encomium-s. |
| 4 | Encounter-ed-ing. |
| 5 | Encourage-d-ing. |
| 6 | Encouragement-s. |
| 7 | For the greater encouragement. |
| 8 | Every encouragement must be held out to. |
| 9 | Encroach-ed-ing. |
| 1780 | Encroachment-s. |

| Nos. | ENC |
|---|---|
| 1781 | Encumber-ed-ing. |
| 2 | Encumbrance-s. |
| 3 | End-ed-ing. |
| 4 | At the end of the. |
| 5 | Before the end of the. |
| 6 | Ended with the. |
| 7 | The latter end of the. |
| 8 | Endanger-ed-ing, |
| 9 | Endeavor-ed-ing-s. |
| 1790 | Notwithstanding his, my, or our, endeavors. |
| 1 | Has, or have, been endeavoring to. |
| 2 | In endeavoring to. |
| 3 | Shall I, or we, endeavor to? |
| 4 | Shall endeavor to. |
| 5 | Use your utmost endeavors to. |
| 6 | Endure-d-ing. |
| 7 | Endurance. |
| 8 | Enemy-ies. |
| 9 | Attack the enemy. |
| 1800 | Attack the enemy's van. |
| 1 | Attack the enemy's rear. |
| 2 | Attack the enemy's centre. |
| 3 | Anchor inside the enemy and engage him. |
| 4 | Anchor outside the enemy and engage him. |
| 5 | Enemy is coming out. |
| 6 | Enemy is going on. |
| 7 | Enemy is at sea. |
| 8 | Enemy's boats or ves'ls are. |
| 9 | Enemy is advancing. |
| 1810 | Enemy is retreating. |
| 1 | Enemy appears to be ready for sea. |
| 2 | Enemy is in sight. |
| 3 | Enemy's vessels are at anchor. |
| 4 | Dash at the enemy's line. |
| 5 | Keep the enemy in sight if possible. |
| 6 | Take stations for mutual support, and engage the enemy as he comes within effective range. |
| 7 | Weather gage get of the enemy. |
| 1818 | When the enemy. |

| Nos. | ENT |
|---|---|
| 1819 | Should the enemy. |
| 1820 | Should the enemy not. |
| 1 | Energetic-al-ly. |
| 2 | Enforce-d-ing. |
| 3 | Enfilade-d-ing. |
| 4 | Engage-d-ing. |
| 5 | Engage the enemy. |
| 6 | Have been engaged with the enemy. |
| 7 | Engagement-s. |
| 8 | Close engagement. |
| 9 | Discontinue the engagement. |
| 1830 | Partial engagement. |
| 1 | Severe engagement. |
| 2 | The last engagement. |
| 3 | Engine-s. |
| 4 | Engine-s disabled. |
| 5 | Engine room-s. |
| 6 | Fire engine-s. |
| 7 | Engineer-s. |
| 8 | I am in need of Engineers. |
| 9 | Have you as many Engineers as you require? |
| 1840 | Chief Engineer-s. |
| 1 | First Assistant Engineer-s. |
| 2 | Second Assis't Engineer-s. |
| 3 | Third Assis't Engineer-s. |
| 4 | English-man-men. |
| 5 | Enjoin-ed-ing. |
| 6 | Enjoy-ed-ing. |
| 7 | Enjoyment-s. |
| 8 | Enlarge-d-ing. |
| 9 | Enlargement. |
| 1850 | Enmity-ies. |
| 1 | Enormous-ly. |
| 2 | Enough. |
| 3 | Has, or have, enough. |
| 4 | Has, or have not, enough. |
| 5 | Have you enough? |
| 6 | Will be enough. |
| 7 | Enrage-d-ing. |
| 8 | Enrich-ed-ing. |
| 9 | Enrol-led-ling. |
| 1860 | Enrolment-s. |
| 1 | Ensign-s. |
| 2 | Entangle-d-ing. |
| 3 | Enter-ed-ing. |
| 4 | Has, or have, entered into. |
| 5 | Try to enter the. |
| 1866 | Should he, or they, enter the. |

| Nos. | ENT |
|---|---|
| 1867 | Should he, or they, try to enter the. |
| 8 | Entrance-s. |
| 9 | At the entrance. |
| 1870 | Near the entrance. |
| 1 | Outside of the entrance. |
| 2 | Inside the entrance. |
| 3 | Enterprise-s. |
| 4 | Entertain-ed-ing. |
| 5 | Entertainment-s. |
| 6 | Enthusiasm. |
| 7 | Entice-d-ing. |
| 8 | Endeavor to entice the. |
| 9 | Was, or were, enticed into. |
| 1880 | Entire-ly. |
| 1 | Entitle-d-ing. |
| 2 | He is, or they are, entitled to. |
| 3 | He is, or they are, not entitled to. |
| 4 | Entreat-ed-ing. |
| 5 | Entreaty-ies. |
| 6 | Enumerate-d-ing. |
| 7 | Enumeration. |
| 8 | Envelope-ed-ing. |
| 9 | Envoy-s. |
| 1890 | Envoy-s Extraordinary. |
| 1 | Envy-ious. |
| 2 | Epaulettes. |
| 3 | Epidemic-s. |
| 4 | Equal-ly. |
| 5 | At equal distances. |
| 6 | Equality. |
| 7 | Equinox-es-ial. |
| 8 | Autumnal equinox. |
| 9 | Vernal equinox. |
| 1900 | Equip-ped-ping. |
| 1 | Equipment-s. |
| 2 | Equipage. |
| 3 | Leave equipage on board ship. |
| 4 | Equity. |
| 5 | Equitable-ly. |
| 6 | Equivalent-s. |
| 7 | Equivocate-d-ing. |
| 8 | Equivocation-s. |
| 9 | Eradicate-ed-ing. |
| 1910 | Erase-ed-sure-s. |
| 1 | Erect-ed-ing. |
| 2 | Erection-s. |
| 3 | Error-s. |
| 1914 | Erroneous-ly. |

| Nos. | EXA |
|---|---|
| 1915 | Eruption-s. |
| 6 | Escalade-d-ing. |
| 7 | Prepare to escalade the enemy's works. |
| 8 | Escape-d-ing. |
| 9 | Have, or has, escaped. |
| 1920 | When did they escape ? |
| 1 | Escort-ed-ing. |
| 2 | Especial-ly. |
| 3 | Essential-ly. |
| 4 | It is essential. |
| 5 | It is not essential. |
| 6 | Establish-ed-ing. |
| 7 | Establishment-s. |
| 8 | Esteem-ed-ing. |
| 9 | Estimate-d-ing. |
| 1930 | Estimation. |
| 1 | In my estimation. |
| 2 | In your estimation. |
| 3 | Etiquette. |
| 4 | Evacuate-d-ing. |
| 5 | Has, or have, evacuated. |
| 6 | Is, or are, about to evacuate. |
| 7 | Have not yet evacuated. |
| 8 | Evade-d-ing. |
| 9 | Evasion-s. |
| 1940 | Evasive-ly. |
| 1 | Evaporate-d-ing. |
| 2 | Evaporation. |
| 3 | Even-ly-ness. |
| 4 | Evening-s. |
| 5 | Every evening. |
| 6 | In the evening. |
| 7 | Last evening. |
| 8 | To-morrow evening. |
| 9 | Ever. |
| 1950 | Have you ever ? |
| 1 | Every. |
| 2 | Every day. |
| 3 | Every one. |
| 4 | Everything. |
| 5 | Every where. |
| 6 | Evidence-s. |
| 7 | Evident-ly. |
| 8 | Evil-ly-s. |
| 9 | Evolution-s. |
| 1960 | Evolutionary exercises, prepare for. |
| 1 | Evolutionary exercises, commence. |
| 1962 | Exact-ed-ing. |

| Nos. | EXA |
|---|---|
| 1963 | Exaction-s. |
| 4 | Exactly. |
| 5 | Exactly at the time and place. |
| 6 | Exactly at the. |
| 7 | Exaggerate-d-ing-s. |
| 8 | Exaggeration-s. |
| 9 | Examine-d-ing. |
| 1970 | Examination-s. |
| 1 | Examine stranger-s. |
| 2 | Have you examined? |
| 3 | Have examined. |
| 4 | Have not examined. |
| 5 | Shall I examine? |
| 6 | You will examine. |
| 7 | Example-d-s. |
| 8 | I have made an example of. |
| 9 | Make an example of. |
| 1980 | Set a good example. |
| 1 | Exceed-ed-ing-ly. |
| 2 | Excel-led-ling. |
| 3 | Excellent-ly. |
| 4 | Except-ed-ing. |
| 5 | Exception-al. |
| 6 | Excess. |
| 7 | Excesses. |
| 8 | Exchange-d ing. |
| 9 | An exchange has been effected. |
| 1990 | Exclaim-ed-ing. |
| 1 | Exclamation. |
| 2 | Exclude-d-ing. |
| 3 | Exclusion. |
| 4 | Excuse-d-ing. |
| 5 | Cannot excuse you. |
| 6 | Excuse me. |
| 7 | Excusable-y. |
| 8 | Very excusable. |
| 9 | Execute-d-ing. |
| 2000 | Could not execute. |
| 1 | Has, or have executed. |
| 2 | Has, or have not executed. |
| 3 | Has been well executed. |
| 4 | Has been badly executed. |
| 5 | Execution-s. |
| 6 | In the execution of. |
| 7 | Did, or does great execution. |
| 8 | Execution has been very great. |
| 9 | Executive. |
| 2010 | Executive Officer-s. |

| Nos. | EXP |
|---|---|
| 2011 | Executive of the United States. |
| 2 | Executive Department-s. |
| 3 | Executive of the State-s. |
| 4 | Executive of the city. |
| 5 | Exemplary. |
| 6 | Exemplary conduct. |
| 7 | Exempt-ed-ing. |
| 8 | Exemption-s. |
| 9 | Exercise-d-ing-s. |
| 2020 | Exercise at great guns. |
| 1 | Exercise with small arms. |
| 2 | Exercise, general, with all arms. |
| 3 | Exercise crews frequently. |
| 4 | Exercises to be short, and during the coolest periods of the day. |
| 5 | Exercise your discretion. |
| 6 | Do not exercise during the heat of the day. |
| 7 | May I exercise my crew? |
| 8 | Exert-ed-ing. |
| 9 | Exertion-s. |
| 2030 | Great exertion is necessary. |
| 1 | Use every exertion in your power. |
| 2 | Exhaust-ed-ing. |
| 3 | Men and officers are greatly exhausted. |
| 4 | Exhaustion. |
| 5 | Exhort-ed-ing. |
| 6 | Exhortation-s. |
| 7 | Exigence-y-ies. |
| 8 | Exigencies of the service will not permit. |
| 9 | Exigencies of the service must be duly considered. |
| 2040 | Exigencies of the service must not be disregarded. |
| 1 | Exile-d-s. |
| 2 | Exist-ed-ing. |
| 3 | Existence. |
| 4 | Exonerate-d-ing. |
| 5 | Exoneration. |
| 6 | Exorbitant-ly. |
| 7 | Expand-ed-ing. |
| 8 | Expansion-s. |
| 9 | Expansive-ly. |
| 2050 | Expect-ed-ing. |
| 1 | Did not expect. |
| 2052 | Do you expect? |

| Nos. | EXP |
|---|---|
| 2053 | Expected from. |
| 4 | Expected to. |
| 5 | Daily expected. |
| 6 | Hourly expected. |
| 7 | Has, or have been expected. |
| 8 | Will expect. |
| 9 | Expectation-s. |
| 2060 | Expedient-s. |
| 1 | Expedience. |
| 2 | Expedition-s. |
| 3 | An expedition against the enemy is in contemplation. |
| 4 | Have you received any tidings or news of the expedition? |
| 5 | Is the expedition safe? |
| 6 | The expedition has sailed. |
| 7 | The expedition has returned safely. |
| 8 | The expedition has not been heard from. |
| 9 | The expedition must start at the time now or hereafter indicat'd by signal. |
| 2070 | Part of the expedition. |
| 1 | With great expedition. |
| 2 | Secret expedition-s. |
| 3 | Night expedition-s. |
| 4 | Expeditious-ly. |
| 5 | Be as expeditious as possible. |
| 6 | Expedite-d-ing. |
| 7 | Expedite the movement-s. |
| 8 | Expedite the work. |
| 9 | Expel-led-ling. |
| 2080 | Expend-ed-ing. |
| 1 | Expenditure-s. |
| 2 | Expense-s-ive-ly. |
| 3 | Experience-d-ing. |
| 4 | Has, or have experienced. |
| 5 | Has, or have not experienced. |
| 6 | Have you experienced? |
| 7 | In the course of your experience. |
| 8 | What has been been your experience? |
| 9 | Experiment-ed-ing. |
| 2090 | Experiment-s. |
| 2091 | For experiment-s. |

| Nos. | EXT |
|---|---|
| 2092 | Tried the experiment-s. |
| 3 | Try the experiment. |
| 4 | Will not try the experiment. |
| 5 | Would not try the experiment. |
| 6 | Unsafe experiment-s. |
| 7 | Experimental-ly. |
| 8 | Experimental squadron-s. |
| 9 | Expert-s. |
| 2100 | Experts are required to. |
| 1 | Experts must be consulted. |
| 2 | Expire-d-ing. |
| 3 | Expiration-s. |
| 4 | Explain-ed-ing. |
| 5 | Explanation-s. |
| 6 | Cannot explain the. |
| 7 | Cannot be explained. |
| 8 | Can be explained satisfactorily. |
| 9 | Will explain fully. |
| 2110 | Has been satisfactorily explained. |
| 1 | Has not been satisfactorily explained. |
| 2 | Will you explain? |
| 3 | Requires full explanation. |
| 4 | Explicit-ly-ness. |
| 5 | Explode-d-ing. |
| 6 | Explosion-s. |
| 7 | Exploit-s. |
| 8 | Explore-d-ing. |
| 9 | Exploration-s. |
| 2120 | Export-ed-ing-s. |
| 1 | Exportation-s. |
| 2 | Expose-d-ing. |
| 3 | Exposure-s. |
| 4 | Expostulate-d-ing-s. |
| 5 | Expostulation-s. |
| 6 | Express-ed-ing. |
| 7 | An express is going to. |
| 8 | An express has arrived from. |
| 9 | Has, or have expressed. |
| 2130 | Should he, or they express. |
| 1 | Expression-s. |
| 2 | Expressive-ly. |
| 3 | Expressly. |
| 4 | Expulsion-s. |
| 5 | Extend-ed-ing. |
| 6 | Extension-s. |
| 2137 | Extensive-ly. |

| Nos. | EXT |
|---|---|
| 2138 | Exterior-ly. |
| 9 | Exterminate-d-ing. |
| 2140 | External-ly. |
| 1 | Extinguish-ed-ing. |
| 2 | Cannot extinguish the fire. |
| 3 | Fire is not extinguished. |
| 4 | Fire has been extinguish'd. |
| 5 | Extort-ed-ing. |
| 6 | Extortion-s. |
| 7 | Extortioner-s. |
| 8 | Extortionate. |
| 9 | Extract-ed-ing. |
| 2150 | Extraordinary-ily. |
| 1 | Extravagant-ly. |
| 2 | Extravagance. |
| 3 | Extreme-ly. |
| 4 | Extremity-ies. |
| 5 | At the extremity-ies. |
| 6 | In the extremity. |
| 7 | To the last extremity. |
| 8 | Extricate-d-ing. |
| 9 | Exult-ed-ing. |
| 2160 | Exultation-s. |
| 1 | Eye-d-ing. |
| 2 | Eyes. |
| 3 | Fabricate-d-ing. |
| 4 | Fabrication-s. |
| 5 | Face-d-ing-s. |
| 6 | Facilitate-d-ing. |
| 7 | Facility-ies. |
| 8 | Fact-s. |
| 9 | It is a fact that. |
| 2170 | It is not a fact that. |
| 1 | Faction-s. |
| 2 | Factious-ly-ness. |
| 3 | Factory-ies, |
| 4 | Fail-ed-ing, |
| 5 | Cannot fail to. |
| 6 | Do not fail to. |
| 7 | Do not risk the chance of failing. |
| 8 | Is likely to fail. |
| 9 | If it fail. |
| 2180 | Failure-s. |
| 1 | Fair. |
| 2 | Fair weather. |
| 3 | Fair tide. |
| 4 | Fair wind-s. |
| 5 | Fairly-ness. |
| 6 | Faithful-ly-ness. |
| 7 | Fall-en-ing-fell. |
| 2188 | Have you fallen in with? |

| Nos. | FAV |
|---|---|
| 2189 | Have they fallen in with? |
| 2190 | Should you fall in with. |
| 1 | Should you not fall in with. |
| 2 | Falling off. |
| 3 | Falling to leeward. |
| 4 | False-ly. |
| 5 | Falsehood-s. |
| 6 | Fame. |
| 7 | Famous-ly. |
| 8 | Familiar-ly-ity. |
| 9 | Family-ies. |
| 2200 | Famine. |
| 1 | Famish-ed-ing. |
| 2 | Fancy-ies. |
| 3 | Fanciful-ly. |
| 4 | Far. |
| 5 | Farther. |
| 6 | As far as. |
| 7 | A little farther. |
| 8 | Far from. |
| 9 | Not far from. |
| 2210 | Not far enough. |
| 1 | How far. |
| 2 | Too far. |
| 3 | Fare-d-ing. |
| 4 | Farewell. |
| 5 | Farm-s. |
| 6 | Fascines. |
| 7 | Fascines needed. |
| 8 | Fascines send to. |
| 9 | Fascines, send for. |
| 2220 | Fascinate-d-ing. |
| 1 | Fascination-s. |
| 2 | Fasten-ed ing-s. |
| 3 | As fast as possible. |
| 4 | Not very fast. |
| 5 | Very fast. |
| 6 | Faster. |
| 7 | Fastest. |
| 8 | Father. |
| 9 | Fathom-s. |
| 2230 | How many fathoms water have you? |
| 1 | How many fathoms cable out? |
| 2 | Fatigue-d-ing. |
| 3 | Not fatigued. |
| 4 | Very much fatigued. |
| 5 | Very fatiguing operation-s. |
| 6 | Fault-s. |
| 7 | Fault finding. |
| 2238 | Favor-ed-ing. |

| Nos. | FAV |
|---|---|
| 2239 | Favor me with your. |
| 2240 | In favor of the. |
| 1 | It will be a favor to. |
| 2 | Favorable-y. |
| 3 | Appears to be favorable. |
| 4 | Is favorable. |
| 5 | Is not favorable. |
| 6 | Should it be favorable. |
| 7 | Should it not be favorable. |
| 8 | Fear-ed-ing. |
| 9 | Need not fear. |
| 2250 | Without fear. |
| 1 | Fearful-ly. |
| 2 | Feasible. |
| 3 | February. |
| 4 | Feeble-y-ness. |
| 5 | Feeling-s. |
| 6 | Felt. |
| 7 | Feign-ed-ing. |
| 8 | Feint-s. |
| 9 | Have made a feint. |
| 2260 | Make a feint. |
| 1 | Only intended as a feint. |
| 2 | Fell. |
| 3 | Female-s. |
| 4 | Fence-s. |
| 5 | Fencing. |
| 6 | Ferocious-ly-ness. |
| 7 | Ferry-ies. |
| 8 | Ferry boat-s. |
| 9 | Ferry man-men. |
| 2270 | Festival-s. |
| 1 | Festivity-ies. |
| 2 | Fetch-ed-ing. |
| 3 | Can fetch. |
| 4 | Can you fetch in? |
| 5 | Try to fetch in. |
| 6 | Fever-s-ish. |
| 7 | Fever is contagious. |
| 8 | Fever is not contagious. |
| 9 | Fever is epidemic. |
| 2280 | Have fever on board. |
| 1 | Typhoid fever. |
| 2 | Typhus fever. |
| 3 | Yellow fever. |
| 4 | Few. |
| 5 | Fewer. |
| 6 | Fickle-ness. |
| 7 | Fid-ded-ding. |
| 8 | Fiddle-s. |
| 9 | Fiddler-s. |
| 2290 | Fiddle strings. |

| Nos. | FIR |
|---|---|
| 2291 | Field. |
| 2 | Field piece-s. |
| 3 | Have you any field pieces? |
| 4 | Put a field piece into the boat-s. |
| 5 | Send with field pieces. |
| 6 | Send without field pieces. |
| 7 | Fierce-ly. |
| 8 | Fife-s. |
| 9 | Fifer-s. |
| 2300 | Fifteen-th. |
| 1 | Fifty-ieth. |
| 2 | Fight-ing. |
| 3 | A running fight. |
| 4 | Would not fight. |
| 5 | File-s. |
| 6 | Handsaw files. |
| 7 | Rank and file. |
| 8 | Rat-tail files. |
| 9 | Fill-ed-ing. |
| 2310 | Fill powder. |
| 1 | Fill shells. |
| 2 | Fill up with water. |
| 3 | Fill up with provisions. |
| 4 | Filth-y-iness. |
| 5 | Find-ing-found. |
| 6 | Cannot find. |
| 7 | Could not find. |
| 8 | Did you find? |
| 9 | Should you find. |
| 2320 | Has, or have, found. |
| 1 | Has, or have, not found. |
| 2 | Was, or were, found. |
| 3 | Has, or have, been found. |
| 4 | Has, or have, not been found. |
| 5 | Fine-s. |
| 6 | Finger-s. |
| 7 | Finish-ed-ing. |
| 8 | Cannot finish. |
| 9 | Have you finished? |
| 2330 | When will you finish? |
| 1 | Will be finished. |
| 2 | Will not be finished. |
| 3 | Fire-ing. |
| 4 | Cease firing. |
| 5 | Commence firing. |
| 6 | Concentrate fire. |
| 7 | Do not fire until the signal is made to commence action. |
| 2338 | Exercise without firing. |

| Nos. | FIR |
|---|---|
| 2339 | Fire from the. |
| 2340 | Fire direct to the. |
| 1 | Fire for ricochet. |
| 2 | Firing, you are, too low. |
| 3 | Firing, you are, too high. |
| 4 | Firing, you are, effective-ly. |
| 5 | Fire more deliberately. |
| 6 | Fire as you come within range. |
| 7 | Fire at the stranger-s. |
| 8 | Fire is extinguished. |
| 9 | Fire is not extinguished. |
| 2350 | Hear firing at a distance. |
| 1 | Is on fire. |
| 2 | Is the fire? |
| 3 | No firing allowed without orders. |
| 4 | Prepare to fire with blank cartridge-s. |
| 5 | Prepare to fire at a mark. |
| 6 | Reserve your fire. |
| 7 | There is a fire. |
| 8 | The vessel is on fire and needs assistance. |
| 9 | The enemy has open'd fire. |
| 2360 | What was the cause of the firing? |
| 1 | Set fire to the enemy's vessel-s. |
| 2 | Set fire to the place. |
| 3 | Fire more to the left. |
| 4 | Fire more to the right. |
| 5 | Fires. |
| 6 | Bank fires. |
| 7 | Haul fires. |
| 8 | Light fires. |
| 9 | Fire engine-s. |
| 2370 | Fire-ship-s. |
| 1 | Boats to tow off fire-ships. |
| 2 | Cover the fire-ships. |
| 3 | Do your best to destroy the fire-ships. |
| 4 | Enemy's fire-ships. |
| 5 | Fire-ships are coming in. |
| 6 | Fire-ships are destroyed. |
| 7 | Fire-ships are at anchor. |
| 8 | Fire-ships are coming out. |
| 9 | Fire-ships to proceed on service as ordered. |
| 2380 | Send in the fire-ships. |
| 2381 | Tow off the fire-ships. |

| Nos. | FLE |
|---|---|
| 2382 | Sink the fire-ships. |
| 3 | Fireman-men. |
| 4 | Are you in need of firemen? |
| 5 | Am in need of firemen. |
| 6 | Fire-works. |
| 7 | In need of fire-works. |
| 8 | Firm-ly-ness. |
| 9 | First. |
| 2390 | Fish-ing. |
| 1 | Fishing boat-s. |
| 2 | Fishing hooks. |
| 3 | Fishing lines. |
| 4 | Fishing seine-s. |
| 5 | Let the people fish. |
| 6 | Plenty of fish. |
| 7 | Procure fish if possible. |
| 8 | Fishing place, proceed to the. |
| 9 | Fisherman-men. |
| 2400 | Allow all fishermen to pass. |
| 1 | Do not allow fishermen to pass. |
| 2 | Overhaul all fishermen, |
| 3 | Fishery-ies. |
| 4 | Fit-ting-s. |
| 5 | Five. Fifth. |
| 6 | Fix-ed-ing. |
| 7 | Fixture-s. |
| 8 | Flag-s. |
| 9 | Cannot make out the flag. |
| 2410 | Do not show your flag. |
| 1 | Haul down your flag. |
| 2 | Hoist your flag. |
| 3 | Flag-of-truce. |
| 4 | What is the flag? |
| 5 | Strange flag. |
| 6 | Flagrant-ly. |
| 7 | Flame-s. |
| 8 | Flange-s. |
| 9 | Flank-ed-ing. |
| 2420 | Flank movement-s. |
| 1 | Flannel. |
| 2 | Blue flannel. |
| 3 | Red flannel. |
| 4 | White flannel. |
| 5 | Flash-ed-ing-es. |
| 6 | Flat-s. |
| 7 | Flaw-s. |
| 8 | Flaw-s of wind. |
| 9 | Fleet-s. |
| 2430 | Did the fleet? |
| 2431 | Enemy's fleet |

| Nos. | FLE |
|---|---|
| 2432 | Friend's fleet. |
| 3 | Fleet is. |
| 4 | Fleet is not. |
| 5 | Fleet is at sea. |
| 6 | Fleet is in port. |
| 7 | Fleet has returned to port. |
| 8 | Is a fleet of. |
| 9 | Is the fleet? |
| 2440 | In the fleet. |
| 1 | Of the fleet. |
| 2 | Has, or have discovered a strange fleet. |
| 3 | For the fleet. |
| 4 | From the fleet. |
| 5 | To the fleet. |
| 6 | With the fleet. |
| 7 | Where is the fleet? |
| 8 | Flinch-ed-ing. |
| 9 | Flint-s. |
| 2450 | Float-ed-ing. |
| 1 | Flotilla-s. |
| 2 | Enemy's flotilla. |
| 3 | Our flotilla. |
| 4 | Flotilla, prepare to attack the. |
| 5 | Flotilla has been attacked. |
| 6 | Flotilla is seriously damaged. |
| 7 | Flotilla will withdraw. |
| 8 | Flotilla prepare f'r service. |
| 9 | Flotilla will get underway immediately. |
| 2460 | Flour. |
| 1 | Flow-ing-s. |
| 2 | Fluctuate-d-ing. |
| 3 | Flue-s. |
| 4 | Fluke-s. |
| 5 | Fluke of the anchor. |
| 6 | Flush-ed. |
| 7 | Fly. |
| 8 | Foe-s. |
| 9 | Fog-s. Foggy. |
| 2470 | During the fog. |
| 1 | Had fog. |
| 2 | Intend to anchor during the fog. |
| 3 | On account of the fog. |
| 4 | Should it become foggy. |
| 5 | Foil-ed-ing. |
| 6 | Follow-ed-ing. |
| 7 | Can you follow? |
| 2478 | Follow my motions. |

| Nos. | FOR |
|---|---|
| 2479 | Follow and watch the enemy's motions. |
| 2480 | Is, or are to follow. |
| 1 | Shall I follow? |
| 2 | You will follow. |
| 3 | Food. |
| 4 | Foolish-ly. |
| 5 | Foot. Feet. |
| 6 | Foothold. |
| 7 | Footing. |
| 8 | For. |
| 9 | Forbear-s. |
| 2490 | Forbid-den-ding. |
| 1 | Force-d. |
| 2 | Considerable force. |
| 3 | Inferior force. |
| 4 | Has, or have been forced. |
| 5 | Force the passage. |
| 6 | Forced them to. |
| 7 | Their force-s. |
| 8 | What is the force? |
| 9 | Ford-ed-ing. |
| 2500 | Fordable. |
| 1 | Forecastle. |
| 2 | Forefoot. |
| 3 | Foreign-er-s. |
| 4 | Forelock-s. |
| 5 | Foremast-s. |
| 6 | Foretopmast-s. |
| 7 | Foretop-gallant-mast-s. |
| 8 | Foremost. |
| 9 | Forenoon. |
| 2510 | In the forenoon. |
| 1 | Forerunner-s. |
| 2 | Foresee-ing. Foresaw-seen. |
| 3 | Could not be foreseen. |
| 4 | Did not foresee. |
| 5 | Forest-s. |
| 6 | Forfeit-ed-ing. |
| 7 | Forge-s. |
| 8 | Forget-ting. Forgotten. |
| 9 | Do not forget. |
| 2520 | Did you not forget? |
| 1 | Have, or has been forgotten. |
| 2 | Will not forget. |
| 3 | Forgive-n-ing. |
| 4 | Forlorn hope. |
| 5 | Form. |
| 2526 | Form the first order of steaming. |

| Nos. | FOR |
|---|---|
| 2527 | Form the second order of steaming. |
| 8 | Form the third order of steaming. |
| 9 | Form the first order of sailing. |
| 2530 | Form the second order of sailing. |
| 1 | Form the fifth order of sailing. |
| 2 | Form order of battle or line ahead. |
| 3 | Form the order of retreat. |
| 4 | Formal-ly. |
| 5 | Formality-ies. |
| 6 | Formerly. |
| 7 | Formidable. |
| 8 | Forsake-n-ing. |
| 9 | Foretell. Foretold. |
| 2540 | Fort-s. |
| 1 | Are there any forts? |
| 2 | Examine the forts. |
| 3 | For the fort-s. |
| 4 | How many guns in the fort-s? |
| 5 | In the fort. |
| 6 | Is a strong fort. |
| 7 | Is not a strong fort. |
| 8 | Out of range from the fort. |
| 9 | Round the fort-s. |
| 2550 | The fort-s mount-s the number of guns shown by numeral signal. |
| 1 | Forthcoming. |
| 2 | Forthwith. |
| 3 | Fortify-ied-ing-ies. |
| 4 | Fortitude. |
| 5 | Fortnight. |
| 6 | Fortunate-ly. |
| 7 | Have been so fortunate as to. |
| 8 | Have you been fortunate? |
| 9 | Forty-ieth. |
| 2560 | Forward-ness. |
| 1 | Fought. |
| 2 | Foul-ly. |
| 3 | Foul bottom. |
| 4 | Foundation-s. |
| 5 | Has no foundation. |
| 6 | Is without foundation. |
| 7 | Founder-ed-ing. |
| 2568 | Four. |

| Nos. | FUR |
|---|---|
| 2569 | Fourteen-th. |
| 2570 | Fracture-s-ed. |
| 1 | A severe fracture. |
| 2 | Frame-s. |
| 3 | France. Frenchman-men. |
| 4 | Frank-ly-ness. |
| 5 | Frap-ped-ping. |
| 6 | Fraud-s. |
| 7 | Fraudulent-ly. |
| 8 | Free-ly. |
| 9 | Freeze-ing. Frozen. |
| 2580 | Fright-s. |
| 1 | Frequent-ly. |
| 2 | Fresh-en-ing. |
| 3 | Friction. |
| 4 | Friday. |
| 5 | Friend-s. |
| 6 | A friend of. |
| 7 | Friendly. |
| 8 | Not very friendly. |
| 9 | Very friendly. |
| 2590 | Friendship-s. |
| 1 | Frightful-ly. |
| 2 | Frighten-ed-ing. |
| 3 | Frivolous. |
| 4 | Frock-s. |
| 5 | Blue frocks. |
| 6 | White frocks. |
| 7 | From. |
| 8 | Front. |
| 9 | Fruit-s. |
| 2600 | Fruitless-ly. |
| 1 | Frustrate-ed-ing. |
| 2 | Fuel. |
| 3 | No fuel. |
| 4 | Fuel is nearly expended. |
| 5 | Cannot procure fuel. |
| 6 | Procure fuel if possible. |
| 7 | Fugitive-s. |
| 8 | Fulfill. |
| 9 | Not able to fulfill. |
| 2610 | Fumigate-d-ing. |
| 1 | Funeral-s. |
| 2 | Funeral party. |
| 3 | Funnel-s. |
| 4 | Furl-ed-ing. |
| 5 | Furl awnings. |
| 6 | Furl sails. |
| 7 | Furnace-s. |
| 8 | Furnish-ed-ing. |
| 9 | Further. |
| 2620 | Further off, keep. |

| Nos. | FUR |
|---|---|
| 2621 | Furious-ly. |
| 2 | Furious gale-s. |
| 3 | Future. |
| 4 | In the future. |
| 5 | Gabion-s. |
| 6 | Gain-ed-ing. |
| 7 | I am, or we are, gaining. |
| 8 | I am, or we are, not gaining. |
| 9 | He is, or they a-e, gaining on us. |
| 2630 | We do not gain upon him, or them. |
| 1 | Gale-s. |
| 2 | Had a very heavy gale. |
| 3 | Constant gale-s. |
| 4 | After the gale. |
| 5 | Before the gale. |
| 6 | During the gale. |
| 7 | Rode out the gale safely. |
| 8 | Gallantly. |
| 9 | Behaved very gallantly. |
| 2640 | Gallant conduct. |
| 1 | Galley-ies. |
| 2 | Ship's galley-ies. |
| 3 | Gallons. |
| 4 | Gallons of oil. |
| 5 | Gallons of water. |
| 6 | Garboard strake. |
| 7 | Garrison-s. |
| 8 | Bring off the garrison. |
| 9 | Can't relieve the garrison. |
| 2650 | Endeavor to relieve the garrison. |
| 1 | Gather-ed-ing. |
| 2 | Gauge. |
| 3 | Lee gauge. |
| 4 | Weather gauge. |
| 5 | Gear. |
| 6 | Reeve gear. |
| 7 | Unreeve gear. |
| 8 | Running gear. |
| 9 | General. |
| 2660 | General Commanding. |
| 1 | The General wishes. |
| 2 | Generous-ly. |
| 3 | Behaved very generously. |
| 4 | Very generous conduct. |
| 5 | Gentle-ly. |
| 6 | Gentleman-men-like. |
| 7 | Genuine-ness. |
| 2668 | Geographical-ly. |

| Nos. | GON |
|---|---|
| 2869 | Get-ting-Got-gotten. |
| 2670 | Can get. |
| 1 | Cannot get. |
| 2 | Can you get? |
| 3 | Did you get? |
| 4 | Did not get. |
| 5 | Have you gotten? |
| 6 | Have they got? |
| 7 | Will get. |
| 8 | Will you get? |
| 9 | Gig-s. |
| 2680 | Captain's gig. |
| 1 | Send the, or my gig. |
| 2 | Girtlines. |
| 3 | Hammock girtlines. |
| 4 | Give-en-gave. |
| 5 | Can give you. |
| 6 | Cannot give you. |
| 7 | Did you give? |
| 8 | Give him, or them. |
| 9 | Will you give? |
| 2690 | Glad-ly. |
| 1 | Am very glad to. |
| 2 | Shall be very glad to. |
| 3 | Glaring-ly. |
| 4 | Glass-es. |
| 5 | Double glasses. |
| 6 | Single glasses. |
| 7 | Gloom-y. |
| 8 | Glorious-ly. |
| 9 | Glorious news. |
| 2700 | Glue. |
| 1 | Glue pot. |
| 2 | Go-ing. |
| 3 | Am going to. |
| 4 | Am, is, or are, to go. |
| 5 | Are you going? |
| 6 | Do not go. |
| 7 | Is, or are, going to. |
| 8 | Is, or are, not going. |
| 9 | Go to the. |
| 2710 | Let him, or them, go. |
| 1 | Shall I go? |
| 2 | When he, or they, go. |
| 3 | When you go. |
| 4 | When do you go? |
| 5 | Will you go? |
| 6 | Gold-en. |
| 7 | Gone. |
| 8 | He has gone to. |
| 2719 | Where is he, or, are they, gone? |

| Nos. | GON |
|---|---|
| 2720 | They are gone to. |
| 1 | They are not gone. |
| 2 | They have gone to. |
| 3 | Good-ness. |
| 4 | Have the goodness to. |
| 5 | Make good the, or your. |
| 6 | Will be very good news. |
| 7 | Govern-ed-ing. |
| 8 | Government-s. |
| 9 | Governor-s. |
| 2730 | Gracious-ly. |
| 1 | Graceful-ly. |
| 2 | Gradual-ly. |
| 3 | Grain-s. |
| 4 | Grand-ly. |
| 5 | Grapeshot. |
| 6 | Grapnel-s. |
| 7 | In want of a grapnel. |
| 8 | Provide yourself-selves with grapnels. |
| 9 | Grapple-d-ling. |
| 2740 | Grasp-ed-ing. |
| 1 | Gratify-ied-ies. |
| 2 | Grating-s. |
| 3 | Gratuitous-ly. |
| 4 | Gravel-ly. |
| 5 | Gravelly bottom. |
| 6 | Great-ly. |
| 7 | Greater-est. |
| 8 | Grease-d-ing. |
| 9 | Grieve-d-ing-ious-grief. |
| 2750 | Grindstone-s. |
| 1 | Gripes. |
| 2 | Gross-ly. |
| 3 | Groundless. |
| 4 | Group-s. |
| 5 | Grow-ing-s. |
| 6 | Grumble-d-ing-s. |
| 7 | Guard-ed-ing-s. |
| 8 | Be upon your guard. |
| 9 | Officer-s of the guard. |
| 2760 | Relieve the guard on shore. |
| 1 | Row guard during the night. |
| 2 | Guardship-s. |
| 3 | Guess-warp-s. |
| 4 | Guide-s-ance. |
| 5 | Under your guidance. |
| 6 | Guilt-y. |
| 7 | Not guilty. |
| 8 | Gulf of Mexico. |
| 2769 | Gulf Stream. |

| Nos. | HAI |
|---|---|
| 2770 | Gum-my. |
| 1 | Gun-s. |
| 2 | Exercise great guns by firing at a mark. |
| 3 | Gun boat-s. |
| 4 | Gun carriage-s. |
| 5 | Load guns with round shot. |
| 6 | Load guns with shell. |
| 7 | Load guns with canister. |
| 8 | Load guns with shrapnel shell. |
| 9 | Guns, double shot your. |
| 2780 | Guns, get on board your. |
| 1 | Guns, throw overboard your. |
| 2 | With hawser and buoys attached to them. |
| 3 | Guns, recover your. |
| 4 | Guns, depress your, more. |
| 5 | Guns, elevate your, more. |
| 6 | Gunner-s. |
| 7 | Gunner's mate-s. |
| 8 | Gunner's crew. |
| 9 | Quarter gunner-s. |
| 2790 | Gunsmith-s. |
| 1 | Gunwales. |
| 2 | Gunwharf-ves. |
| 3 | Gust-s. |
| 4 | Gusts of wind. |
| 5 | Guy-s-ed-ing. |
| 6 | Habeas corpus, writ of. |
| 7 | Habitual-ly. |
| 8 | In the habit of. |
| 9 | Habitable. |
| 2800 | Habitation-s. |
| 1 | Had. |
| 2 | Could have had. |
| 3 | Could not have had. |
| 4 | Had not. |
| 5 | Have you had? |
| 6 | Has, or have, had. |
| 7 | Has, or have not, had. |
| 8 | Should have had. |
| 9 | To be had. |
| 2810 | Not to be had. |
| 1 | Would have had. |
| 2 | Hail-ed-ing. |
| 3 | Hail the passing boat, or vessel. |
| 4 | Hail, pass within. |
| 5 | I wish to pass within hail. |
| 2816 | Can I pass within hail? |

| Nos. | HAI |
|---|---|
| 2817 | Did you pass within hail? |
| 8 | You cannot pass within hail. |
| 9 | Half. |
| 2820 | Halfway. |
| 1 | Halliards. |
| 2 | Halt-ed-ing. |
| 3 | Hammer-s. |
| 4 | Claw Hammer-s. |
| 5 | Hammers and nails. |
| 6 | Sledge hammer-s. |
| 7 | Hammocks. |
| 8 | Hammock cloths. |
| 9 | Scrub hammocks. |
| 2830 | Pipe down hammocks. |
| 1 | Pipe up hammocks. |
| 2 | Sling clear hammocks. |
| 3 | Hamper-ed-ing. |
| 4 | Hand-s. |
| 5 | In need of hands. |
| 6 | Hand-irons needed. |
| 7 | Handle-d-ing. |
| 8 | Handsome-ly. |
| 9 | Handsomely done. |
| 2840 | Handspikes. |
| 1 | Hang-ing. |
| 2 | Hanging lamp-s. |
| 3 | Happen-ed-ing. |
| 4 | When did it happen? |
| 5 | How did it happen? |
| 6 | Should it happen again. |
| 7 | It happened on the. |
| 8 | Should it so happen that. |
| 9 | Happy-ily. |
| 2850 | Shall or will be very happy. |
| 1 | Was very happy to. |
| 2 | Harass-ed-ing. |
| 3 | Harass the enemy as much as possible. |
| 4 | Harbor-s. |
| 5 | A bad harbor. |
| 6 | A good harbor. |
| 7 | Am going into harbor. |
| 8 | Can you see inside the harbor? |
| 9 | Have been in the harbor. |
| 2860 | Proceed into the harbor. |
| 1 | Go off the harbor. |
| 2 | In the harbor of. |
| 2863 | Reconnoitre the harbor and report by signal what you see. |

| Nos. | HAV |
|---|---|
| 2864 | Vessels at anchor in the harbor. |
| 5 | Vessel-s coming out of harbor. |
| 6 | Hardship-s. |
| 7 | Harm-ed. |
| 8 | Harmless-ness. |
| 9 | Harpoon-s. |
| 2870 | Harsh-ly. |
| 1 | Harshness. |
| 2 | Haste-ily. |
| 3 | In great haste. |
| 4 | Hasten-ed-ing. |
| 5 | Hat-s. |
| 6 | Black hat-s. |
| 7 | Straw hat-s. |
| 8 | Tarpaulin hat-s. |
| 9 | White hat-s. |
| 2880 | Hat covers. |
| 1 | Hatchet-s. |
| 2 | Hatchways. |
| 3 | Hate-d-ing. |
| 4 | Hateful-ly. |
| 5 | Haul-ed-ing. |
| 6 | Haul aft your sheets. |
| 7 | Haul your fenders in. |
| 8 | Haul off shore. |
| 9 | Haul out of the line. |
| 2890 | Haul your wind. |
| 1 | Have-ing. |
| 2 | Am to have. |
| 3 | Am not to have. |
| 4 | Have not. |
| 5 | Have done. |
| 6 | Have not done. |
| 7 | Have they? |
| 8 | Have you? |
| 9 | Let them have. |
| 2900 | Let him have. |
| 1 | May not have. |
| 2 | May have. |
| 3 | Shall, or will, have. |
| 4 | Shall, or will not, have. |
| 5 | Would have. |
| 6 | Would not have. |
| 7 | You cannot have. |
| 8 | You can have. |
| 9 | You may have. |
| 2910 | Haversack-s. |
| 1 | With their haversacks. |
| 2 | Without haversacks. |
| 2913 | Havoc. |

| Nos. | HAW |
|---|---|
| 2914 | Hawse. |
| 5 | Athwart hawse. |
| 6 | Clear hawse. |
| 7 | Hawse hole-s. |
| 8 | Hawse pipe-s. |
| 9 | In the hawse of. |
| 2920 | Hawse is clear. |
| 1 | Hawse is not clear. |
| 2 | Hawser-s. |
| 3 | In want of hawser-s. |
| 4 | Large hawser-s. |
| 5 | Small hawser-s. |
| 6 | Light hawser-s. |
| 7 | Hazard-ous. |
| 8 | Hazard-ed-ing. |
| 9 | Haze-y-iness. |
| 2930 | Hazy weather. |
| 1 | He. |
| 2 | He can. |
| 3 | He cannot. |
| 4 | He is. |
| 5 | He is not. |
| 6 | He did. |
| 7 | He did not. |
| 8 | He will. |
| 9 | He will not. |
| 2940 | He does. |
| 1 | He does not. |
| 2 | He should. |
| 3 | He should not. |
| 4 | He must. |
| 5 | He must not. |
| 6 | If he. |
| 7 | When he. |
| 8 | Head-ed-ing. |
| 9 | Head-s. |
| 2950 | Cut heads. |
| 1 | Knight heads. |
| 2 | Mast heads. |
| 3 | Trim by the head. |
| 4 | Trims by the head. |
| 5 | Too much by the head. |
| 6 | Headland-s. |
| 7 | Headquarters. |
| 8 | Headstrong. |
| 9 | Heal-ed-ing. |
| 2960 | Health-y-iness. |
| 1 | In good health. |
| 2 | In bad health. |
| 3 | Is quite healthy. |
| 4 | Is not healthy. |
| 2965 | Hear-d-ing. |

| Nos. | HES |
|---|---|
| 2966 | Have heard. |
| 7 | Have not heard. |
| 8 | Has he, or have they heard? |
| 9 | Have you heard? |
| 2970 | Heart. |
| 1 | Heartily. |
| 2 | Heat-ed-ing. |
| 3 | During the heat. |
| 4 | Heave-s-ing. |
| 5 | Cannot heave up my anchor. |
| 6 | Heave short your cable. |
| 7 | Heave to. |
| 8 | Heave up your anchor. |
| 9 | Shall I heave to? |
| 2980 | When you heave to. |
| 1 | Heavy-ily. |
| 2 | Heaviest. |
| 3 | Heaviest anchor. |
| 4 | Heal-ed-ing. |
| 5 | Height-en-ed. |
| 6 | Heinous-ness. |
| 7 | Heinous offence-s. |
| 8 | Heinous conduct. |
| 9 | Helm-s. |
| 2990 | Port your helm-s. |
| 1 | Starboard your helm-s. |
| 2 | Helmsman-men. |
| 3 | Help-ed-ing. |
| 4 | Do-es not want any help. |
| 5 | Is greatly in need of help. |
| 6 | With the help of. |
| 7 | Without the help. |
| 8 | Helpless-ness. |
| 9 | Hemp-en. |
| 3000 | Hemp cable-s. |
| 1 | Hemp hawser-s. |
| 2 | Hemp rope. |
| 3 | Henceforth. |
| 4 | Her-s-self. |
| 5 | Herd-s. |
| 6 | Herds of cattle. |
| 7 | Herds of sheep. |
| 8 | Here. |
| 9 | Is, or are here. |
| 3010 | Is, or are not here. |
| 1 | Herewith. |
| 2 | Hero-es. |
| 3 | Heroic. |
| 4 | Heroic conduct. |
| 5 | Heroism. |
| 3016 | Hesitate-d-ing. |

| Nos. | HES |
|---|---|
| 3017 | Hesitation. |
| 8 | With great hesitation. |
| 9 | Without hesitation. |
| 3020 | Hide-ing. Hidden. |
| 1 | Hide-s. |
| 2 | Hide rope. |
| 3 | Raw hide-s. |
| 4 | High-ly. |
| 5 | High and dry. |
| 6 | High tide-s. |
| 7 | High water. |
| 8 | Higher. |
| 9 | Higher up, go. |
| 3030 | Higher up, do not go. |
| 1 | Highest. |
| 2 | Go to the highest point you can reach with your boat-s or vessel-s. |
| 3 | Hill-s-y. |
| 4 | Him-self. |
| 5 | Hinder-ed-ing. |
| 6 | Hindrance-s. |
| 7 | Hinge-s. |
| 8 | Hoist-ed-ing. |
| 9 | Hoist up all boats. |
| 3040 | Hoist your colors. |
| 1 | Hoist false colors. |
| 2 | Hoist your number. |
| 3 | Hoist your private signal. |
| 4 | Hoist your distinguishing flag or pendant. |
| 5 | Hoist out all boats. |
| 6 | Hoist in all boats. |
| 7 | Hire-d-ing. |
| 8 | Hit-s-ting. |
| 9 | Hitherto. |
| 3050 | Hog-ged. |
| 1 | Hogshead-s. H. H. D. |
| 2 | Hold-ing. Held. |
| 3 | Cut away your masts and hold on to the last as it is your only chance for safety. |
| 4 | Hold on as long as possible. |
| 5 | Hold out as long as possible. |
| 6 | I fear I cannot hold on much longer. |
| 7 | Hole-s. |
| 8 | Hollow-s. |
| 3059 | Home-s. |

| Nos. | HOT |
|---|---|
| 3060 | Homeward. |
| 1 | Going home. |
| 2 | Homeward bound. |
| 3 | Not going home. |
| 4 | Honest-y-ly. |
| 5 | Honor-s. |
| 6 | Do me the honor to. |
| 7 | Will do myself the hon'r to. |
| 8 | Honorable-y. |
| 9 | It was very honorable. |
| 3070 | Honorable discharge-s. |
| 1 | Honorably discharge. |
| 2 | Hook-s. |
| 3 | Fishing hooks. |
| 4 | Hoop-s. |
| 5 | Hope-s. |
| 6 | Have, or has great hopes. |
| 7 | Have, or has no hope. |
| 8 | Hope you are. |
| 9 | Hope you will. |
| 3080 | Hope you will not. |
| 1 | Hopeful-ly. |
| 2 | Hopeless-ness. |
| 3 | Horizon. |
| 4 | Horizontal-ly. |
| 5 | Horrible-y. |
| 6 | Horse-s. |
| 7 | Horse-power. |
| 8 | Hose. |
| 9 | Fire hose. |
| 3090 | Suction hose. |
| 1 | Watering hose. |
| 2 | Hospital-s. |
| 3 | From the hospital. |
| 4 | In, or at the hospital. |
| 5 | Send to the hospital. |
| 6 | Hospitable-lity-ies. |
| 7 | Hostage-s. |
| 8 | Hostile-ly. |
| 9 | In a hostile manner. |
| 3100 | Appear to be hostile. |
| 1 | Do not appear to be hostile. |
| 2 | Hostility-ies. |
| 3 | Hostilities have ceased. |
| 4 | Hostilities have commenced. |
| 5 | Hot-ly. |
| 6 | Hot work, had, with the enemy. |
| 7 | Hotly contested action. |
| 8 | Hotly pressed, I have been. |
| 3109 | Hottest. |

| Nos. | HOU | Nos. | IF |
|---|---|---|---|
| 3110 | Hounds of the mast-s. | 3156 | Husband-ed-ing. |
| 1 | Hour-s-ly. | 7 | Hydrography-ic-al-ly. |
| 2 | At what hour? | 8 | Hydrographic Office. |
| 3 | At the indicated hour precisely. | 9 | Hydrographic survey-s. |
| 4 | Hour of the day next shown. | 3160 | I am. |
| 5 | Hour of the night next shown. | 1 | I am not. |
| 6 | In an hour. | 2 | I can. |
| 7 | In half an hour. | 3 | I cannot. |
| 8 | Within twelve hours. | 4 | I could. |
| 9 | Within twenty-four hours. | 5 | I could not. |
| 3120 | Within forty-eight hours. | 6 | I might. |
| 1 | House-d-s. | 7 | I might not. |
| 2 | Hover-ed-ing. | 8 | I should. |
| 3 | How. | 9 | I should not. |
| 4 | How are you? | 3170 | I would. |
| 5 | How do you? | 1 | I would not. |
| 6 | How are they? | 2 | Ice-y. |
| 7 | How do-es the? | 3 | Ice blink-s. |
| 8 | How did? | 4 | Iceberg-s. |
| 9 | How will? | 5 | Ice floe-s. |
| 3130 | How could? | 6 | Ice field-s. |
| 1 | How would? | 7 | Idea-s. |
| 2 | However. | 8 | Ideal-ly. |
| 3 | Howitzer-s. | 9 | Identical-ly. |
| 4 | Howitzer-s, 24 pdr. smooth. | 3180 | Idle-y. |
| 5 | Howitzer-s, 12 pdr. smooth. | 1 | Idler-s. |
| 6 | Howitzer-s, rifled. | 2 | Idleness. |
| 7 | Exercise howitzers. | 3 | If. |
| 8 | Prepare howitzers for immediate service. | 4 | If I can. |
| 9 | Send howitzer battery on shore. | 5 | If I cannot. |
| 3140 | Send howitzer ammunition to. | 6 | If he does. |
| 1 | Hulks. | 7 | If he does not. |
| 2 | Sheer hulk-s. | 8 | If he can. |
| 3 | Hull-ed-ing-s. | 9 | If he cannot. |
| 4 | Humane-ly. | 3190 | If he had. |
| 5 | Humanity. | 1 | If he had not. |
| 6 | Humble-y. | 2 | If they are. |
| 7 | Humiliation. | 3 | If they are not. |
| 8 | Hundred-s-th-s. | 4 | If they were. |
| 9 | Hunger-ry. | 5 | If they were not. |
| 3150 | Hurricane-s. | 6 | If it should. |
| 1 | Hurry-ied-ing. | 7 | If it should not. |
| 2 | Hurry up the boats. | 8 | If it is so. |
| 3 | Hurt. | 9 | If it is not. |
| 4 | Not much hurt. | 3200 | If the. |
| 3155 | Hurter-s. | 1 | If you can. |
| | | 2 | If you cannot. |
| | | 3 | If you could. |
| | | 4 | If you could not. |
| | | 5 | If you do. |
| | | 6 | If you do not. |
| | | 3207 | If you are. |

| Nos. | IF | Nos. | IMP |
|---|---|---|---|
| 3208 | If you are not. | 3259 | Impede-d-ing. |
| 9 | If we, or our. | 3260 | Impediment-s. |
| 3210 | If we are. | 1 | Impel-led-ling. |
| 1 | If we are not. | 2 | Impenetrable-ilty. |
| 2 | If we do. | 3 | Imperceptible-y. |
| 3 | If we do not. | 4 | Imperfect-ly. |
| 4 | Ignite-d-ing. | 5 | Impertinent-ly. |
| 5 | Ignition. | 6 | Impertinence. |
| 6 | Ignominy-ies. | 7 | Impetuous-ly. |
| 7 | Ignorant-ly. | 8 | Impetuosity. |
| 8 | Ignorance. | 9 | Implement-s. |
| 9 | Ill-s. | 3270 | Implicate-d-ing. |
| 3220 | Illness. | 1 | Implication-s. |
| 1 | Has been ill. | 2 | Implicit-ly. |
| 2 | Has not been ill. | 3 | Implicitness. |
| 3 | Is ill. | 4 | Implore-d-ing. |
| 4 | Illegal-ity-ies. | 5 | Imply-ied-ing-ies. |
| 5 | Illegible-y. | 6 | Impolitic. |
| 6 | Illuminate-d-ing. | 7 | Import-s. |
| 7 | Illumination-s. | 8 | Important-ance. |
| 8 | Illustrate-d-ing. | 9 | Is of little importance. |
| 9 | Illustration-s. | 3280 | Is of the greatest import- |
| 3230 | Illustrious. | | ance. |
| 1 | Imagine-d ing. | 1 | Is not of much importance. |
| 2 | Imagination-s. | 2 | Do you attach importance |
| 3 | Imbecile-ity. | | to? |
| 4 | Imitate-d-ing. | 3 | Impose-d-ing. |
| 5 | Immaterial-ly. | 4 | Imposition-s. |
| 6 | Immediate. | 5 | Impossible. |
| 7 | Immediately. | 6 | Impossibility-ies. |
| 8 | Do it immediately. | 7 | Imposter-s. |
| 9 | Not immediately. | 8 | Imposture-s. |
| 3240 | Proceed immediately to. | 9 | Impracticable. |
| 1 | Return immediately. | 2290 | Impracticability. |
| 2 | Immense-ity. | 1 | Is impracticable. |
| 3 | Immensely. | 2 | Is not impracticable. |
| 4 | Immersion-s. | 3 | Impregnable-y. |
| 5 | Imminent-ly. | 4 | Impregnability. |
| 6 | Imminent danger. | 5 | The enemy seems to be |
| 7 | Not in imminent danger. | | impregnably fortified. |
| 8 | Immoderate. | 6 | Impress-ed. |
| 9 | Immortal-ity. | 7 | Impression-s. |
| 3250 | Immovable-y. | 8 | Impressive-ly. |
| 1 | Impart-ed-ing. | 9 | Impressiveness. |
| 2 | Impartial-ly. | 3300 | Imprison-ed-ing. |
| 3 | Impartiality. | 1 | Imprisonment-s. |
| 4 | Observe the strictest im- | 2 | Improbable. |
| 5 | partiality. | 3 | Improbabilities. |
| | Impassable. | 4 | Improper-ly. |
| 6 | Impatient-ly. | 5 | Is very improper. |
| 7 | Impatience. | 6 | Would it be improper? |
| 3258 | Impeach-ed-ment. | 3307 | Would it not be improper? |

| Nos. | IMP |
|---|---|
| 3308 | Improve-d-ing. |
| 9 | Improvement-s. |
| 3310 | Does he improve? |
| 1 | Does it improve? |
| 2 | Has improved. |
| 3 | Has not improved. |
| 4 | Will improve. |
| 5 | Will not improve. |
| 6 | Imprudent-ly. |
| 7 | Imprudence-s. |
| 8 | Very imprudently. |
| 9 | Impunity. |
| 3320 | In. |
| 1 | Intelligence. |
| 2 | Bring intelligence. |
| 3 | Brought intelligence from. |
| 4 | Communicate intelligence by signal. |
| 5 | Has any intelligence been? |
| 6 | Has no intelligence. |
| 7 | Has intelligence to communicate. |
| 8 | Have received intelligence of, or from. |
| 9 | Have you any intelligence? |
| 3330 | With intelligence that. |
| 1 | Obtain all the intelligence you can. |
| 2 | You must ask for intelligence in regard to. |
| 3 | Inability. |
| 4 | Inaccessible. |
| 5 | Inaccuracy-ies. |
| 6 | Inactive-ity. |
| 7 | Inadequate-ly. |
| 8 | Inadmissible-y. |
| 9 | Inattention. |
| 3340 | Great inattention. |
| 1 | Inattentive-ly. |
| 2 | Incapacity. |
| 3 | Incapable-ity. |
| 4 | Incautious-ly. |
| 5 | Incessant-ly. |
| 6 | Inch-es. |
| 7 | Incident-s. |
| 8 | Incidental-ly. |
| 9 | Incline-d-ing. |
| 3350 | Inclination-s. |
| 1 | I am, he is, or they are, inclined to. |
| 3352 | Not inclined to. |

| Nos. | IND |
|---|---|
| 3353 | Include-d-ing. |
| 4 | Do you include? |
| 5 | Is, or are, included. |
| 6 | Is, or are not, included. |
| 7 | Incompetent-ence-cy. |
| 8 | Incomplete-d. |
| 9 | Incomprehensible-ly. |
| 3360 | Inconsiderate-ly. |
| 1 | Inconsistent-ly. |
| 2 | Inconsistency-ies. |
| 3 | Incontestable-y. |
| 4 | Inconvenient-ly. |
| 5 | Inconvenience-s. |
| 6 | Incorrect-ly. |
| 7 | Incorrigible-y. |
| 8 | Increase-d-ing. |
| 9 | Incredible-y. |
| 3370 | Incredibility. |
| 1 | Incur-red-ring-s. |
| 2 | Incurable-y. |
| 3 | Indebted-ness. |
| 4 | Indeed. |
| 5 | Indefatigable-y. |
| 6 | Indefensible-y. |
| 7 | Indemnify-ied-ies. |
| 8 | Indemnification-s. |
| 9 | Indenture-s. |
| 3380 | Independence. |
| 1 | Independent-ly. |
| 2 | Index-indices. |
| 3 | India. |
| 4 | Indian-s. |
| 5 | Indian allies. |
| 6 | Indian allies of the enemy. |
| 7 | Indian enemies. |
| 8 | Indicate-d-ing. |
| 9 | Indication-s. |
| 3390 | Indifference. |
| 1 | Indifferent-ly. |
| 2 | Indignant-ly. |
| 3 | Indignation. |
| 4 | Indiscreet-ly. |
| 5 | Indiscretion. |
| 6 | Indispensable-y. |
| 7 | Indispensably necessary. |
| 8 | Indisposed. |
| 9 | Indisposition. |
| 3400 | Indisputable-y. |
| 1 | Individual-s. |
| 2 | Individuality-ies. |
| 3 | Indolent-ly. |
| 3404 | Indolence. |

| Nos. | IND |
|---|---|
| 3405 | Indraught-s. |
| 6 | Induce-d-ing-ment-s. |
| 7 | I am induced to. |
| 8 | Was, or were induced to. |
| 9 | Indulge-d-ing-s. |
| 3410 | Industry-ies. |
| 1 | Industrious-ly. |
| 2 | Ineffective-ly. |
| 3 | Ineffectual-ly. |
| 4 | Inequality-ies. |
| 5 | Inestimable-y. |
| 6 | Inevitable-y. |
| 7 | Inexcusable-y. |
| 8 | Inexperience-d. |
| 9 | Inexplicable-y. |
| 3420 | Infallible-y. |
| 1 | Infallibility. |
| 2 | Infamy-ies. |
| 3 | Infamous-ly. |
| 4 | Infant-s. |
| 5 | Infantry. |
| 6 | The enemy's infantry is advancing. |
| 7 | The enemy's infantry is retreating. |
| 8 | The enemy's infantry is numerous. |
| 9 | Infect-ed-ing. |
| 3430 | Infection-s. |
| 1 | Infectious. |
| 2 | Is infectious. |
| 3 | Is not infectious. |
| 4 | Inferior-s. |
| 5 | Inferiority. |
| 6 | Infest-ed-ing. |
| 7 | Infinite-ly. |
| 8 | Infirm. |
| 9 | Infirmity-ies. |
| 3440 | Infirmary-ies. |
| 1 | Inflame-d-ing. |
| 2 | Inflammation. |
| 3 | Inflammatory. |
| 4 | Inflexible-y. |
| 5 | Inflict-ed-ing. |
| 6 | Infliction-s. |
| 7 | Influence-d-s-ing. |
| 8 | Influential. |
| 9 | Influx. |
| 3450 | Inform-ed-ing. |
| 1 | Are informed of, or that. |
| 2 | Can you inform me? |
| 3453 | Cannot inform you. |

| Nos. | INQ |
|---|---|
| 3454 | Inform him, or them that. |
| 5 | Information. |
| 6 | For your information. |
| 7 | For the information of the. |
| 8 | Private information. |
| 9 | Infringe-d-ing-s. |
| 3460 | Infringement-s. |
| 1 | Ingenious-ly. |
| 2 | Ingenuity-ies. |
| 3 | Ingenuous-ly-ness. |
| 4 | Ingratitude. |
| 5 | Ingredient-s. |
| 6 | Inhabit-s. |
| 7 | Inhabit-ed-ing. |
| 8 | Inhospitable-y. |
| 9 | Inhuman-ly. |
| 3470 | Inhumanity. |
| 1 | Inject-ed-ing. |
| 2 | Injudicious-ly. |
| 3 | Injure-d-ing. |
| 4 | Injurious-ly. |
| 5 | Much injury has been done. |
| 6 | No injury has been done. |
| 7 | Very little injury has been done. |
| 8 | It is very injurious to. |
| 9 | Injustice. |
| 3480 | Ink. |
| 1 | Ink-stand-s. |
| 2 | Inland. |
| 3 | Inland water-s. |
| 4 | Inlet-s. |
| 5 | Inner. |
| 6 | Innermost. |
| 7 | Innocent-ly. |
| 8 | Innocence. |
| 9 | Innovate-d-ing. |
| 3490 | Innovation-s. |
| 1 | Innumerable. |
| 2 | Inoffensive-ness. |
| 3 | Inoffensively. |
| 4 | Inquest-s. |
| 5 | Inquire-d-ing. |
| 6 | Inquiry-ies. |
| 7 | Court of Inquiry. |
| 8 | Did you inquire about the? |
| 9 | Have you made inquiries in regard to the. |
| 3500 | Inquire into, or about the. |
| 1 | I have made diligent inquiries in regard to the. |
| 3502 | Inquisitive-ly-ness. |

| Nos. | INC |
|---|---|
| 3503 | Incursion-s. |
| 4 | Inroad-s. |
| 5 | Insane. |
| 6 | Insanity. |
| 7 | Insecure-ity. |
| 8 | Insecurely. |
| 9 | Insensible-ility-ilities. |
| 3510 | Inseparable-y. |
| 1 | Insert-ed-ing. |
| 2 | Not to be inserted in the. |
| 3 | To be inserted in the. |
| 4 | Inside. |
| 5 | Inside of the bar. |
| 6 | Inside of the bay. |
| 7 | Inside of the harbor. |
| 8 | Insignificant. |
| 9 | Insignificance. |
| 3520 | Insincere-ly. |
| 1 | Insincerity. |
| 2 | Insist-ed-ing. |
| 3 | Insist-s upon. |
| 4 | You will insist upon. |
| 5 | Insolence. |
| 6 | Insolent-ly. |
| 7 | Inspect-ed-ing. |
| 8 | Inspection-s. |
| 9 | Flag or senior officer will inspect. |
| 3530 | Prepare for general inspection. |
| 1 | Have you inspected the? |
| 2 | Inspire-d-ing. |
| 3 | Inspiration-s. |
| 4 | Instal-led-ling. |
| 5 | Instalment-s. |
| 6 | Instance-s. |
| 7 | Is there an instance? |
| 8 | Instant-ly. |
| 9 | It must be done instantly. |
| 3540 | Instantaneous-ly. |
| 1 | Instead. |
| 2 | Instigate-d-ing. |
| 3 | Instigation-s. |
| 4 | Institute-d-ing. |
| 5 | Institution-s. |
| 6 | Instruct-ed-ing. |
| 7 | Instructive. |
| 8 | Instruction-s. |
| 9 | For further instructions. |
| 3550 | Give instructions to the. |
| 3551 | Have you any instructions for? |

| Nos. | INT |
|---|---|
| 3552 | Has, or have no instructions for. |
| 3 | You will receive instructions from. |
| 4 | Your instructions are to. |
| 5 | Your instructions will be sent to you. |
| 6 | Secret instructions will be given to you. |
| 7 | Your secret instr'ctions will be your guide. |
| 8 | When will you be ready to carry out your instructions? |
| 9 | Instrument. |
| 3560 | Instruments. |
| 1 | Instrumental-ly-ity. |
| 2 | Insufficient-ly. |
| 3 | Insufficiency. |
| 4 | Insult-ed-ing-s. |
| 5 | Insupportable-y. |
| 6 | Insurmount-ed-ing. |
| 7 | Insurmountable-y. |
| 8 | Insurrection-s. |
| 9 | The insurrection. |
| 3570 | There has been an insurrection. |
| 1 | There is an insurrection. |
| 2 | Integrity. |
| 3 | Intellect. |
| 4 | Intellectual-ly. |
| 5 | Intelligible-y. |
| 6 | Intend-ed-ing. |
| 7 | Do you intend to? |
| 8 | Do not intend to. |
| 9 | I intend to. |
| 3580 | Intercede-d-ing-s. |
| 1 | Intercession-s. |
| 2 | Intercept-ed-ing. |
| 3 | Endeavor to intercept the. |
| 4 | Has, or have been intercepted. |
| 5 | Intercourse. |
| 6 | Intercourse is allowed with the. |
| 7 | Intercourse is allowed with the shore. |
| 8 | No intercourse is allowed with the. |
| 9 | No intercourse is to be allowed with the shore. |
| 3590 | Interest-ed-ing. |

| Nos. | INT | Nos. | IRO |
|---|---|---|---|
| 3591 | Nothing interesting to communicate. | 3638 | Introductory. |
| | | 9 | Intrust-ed-ing. |
| 2 | Nothing to his interest. | 3640 | Invade-d-ing. |
| 3 | To his, or their, interest-s. | 1 | Invasion-s. |
| 4 | Interfere-d-ing. | 2 | Invalid-ed-ing. |
| 5 | Shall, or will, interfere. | 3 | Invalids. |
| 6 | Shall, or will, not interfere. | 4 | A survey will be held upon all invalids on board. |
| 7 | Interference-s. | | |
| 8 | Interior. | 5 | Send all invalids to the hospital. |
| 9 | Intermediate. | | |
| 3600 | Internal-ly. | 6 | Invalidate-d-ing. |
| 1 | Interpose-d-ing. | 7 | Invaluable. |
| 2 | Interposition-s. | 8 | Invariable-y. |
| 3 | Interpret-ed-ing. | 9 | Invent-ed-ing. |
| 4 | Interpretation-s. | 3650 | Invention-s. |
| 5 | Interpreter-s. | 1 | Inventory-ies. |
| 6 | Can you get an interpreter? | 2 | Invert-ed-ing. |
| 7 | Have you an interpreter? | 3 | Invert the present order. |
| 8 | Procure an interpreter, if possible. | 4 | Invest-ed-ing. |
| | | 5 | Invest the place. |
| 9 | Interrogate-d-ing. | 6 | The place is invested. |
| 3610 | Interrogate the prisoner-s. | 7 | The place is not invested. |
| 1 | Interrogate the stranger-s. | 8 | Investigate-d-ing. |
| 2 | Interrupt-ed-ing. | 9 | Has, or have, investigated the. |
| 3 | Interruption-s. | | |
| 4 | Interval-s. | 3660 | Has, or have not, investigated the. |
| 5 | Intervene-d-ing. | | |
| 6 | Intervention-s. | 1 | Is, or are, investigating the. |
| 7 | Interview-s. | 2 | Investigation-s. |
| 8 | Have had interview-s with. | 3 | For an investigation. |
| 9 | Have not had any int'rview. | 4 | Inveterate-ly. |
| 3620 | Seek an interview with the authorities on shore. | 5 | Invincible-y. |
| | | 6 | Inviolable-y. |
| 1 | Intimidate-d ing. | 7 | Invite-d-ing. |
| 2 | Intimidation-s. | 8 | Invitation-s. |
| 3 | Into. | 9 | Invoice-s-d. |
| 4 | Intolerable-y. | 3670 | Involve-d-ing. |
| 5 | Intrench-ed-ing. | 1 | Involuntary-ily. |
| 6 | Intrenching tools. | 2 | Inundate-d-ing. |
| 7 | Intrenchment-s. | 3 | Inundation-s. |
| 8 | Intrepid-ly-idity. | 4 | Inure-d-ing. |
| 9 | Intricate. | 5 | In want of canvas. |
| 3630 | Intricacy-ies. | 6 | Of rope. |
| 1 | The channel or passage is very intricate. | 7 | Of provisions. |
| | | 8 | Of water. |
| 2 | The navigation is very intricate. | 9 | Of coal. |
| | | 3680 | Of oil. |
| 3 | Intrigue-s. | 1 | Irish-Ireland. |
| 4 | Intrigue-d-ing. | 2 | Irishman-men. |
| 5 | Intriguer. | 3 | Irish potatoes. |
| 6 | Introduce-d-ing. | 4 | Iron. |
| 3637 | Introduction. | 3685 | Irons. |

| Nos. | IRO |
|---|---|
| 3686 | Hand-irons. |
| 7 | Feet-irons. |
| 8 | Caulking irons. |
| 9 | Irrecoverable-y. |
| 3690 | Irregular-ly. |
| 1 | Irregularity-ies. |
| 2 | Irregular conduct. |
| 3 | Irregular troops. |
| 4 | Irreparable-y. |
| 5 | Irresistible-y. |
| 6 | Irresolute-ly. |
| 7 | Irresolution. |
| 8 | Irritable. |
| 9 | Irritate-d-ing. |
| 3700 | Irritation-s. |
| 1 | Irruption-s. |
| 2 | Is. |
| 3 | Is he, she, or it? |
| 4 | Is it? |
| 5 | Is it not? |
| 6 | Is there? |
| 7 | Is there not? |
| 8 | Is the? |
| 9 | Is to. |
| 3710 | Is not to. |
| 1 | Is well. |
| 2 | Is not well. |
| 3 | Is sick. |
| 4 | Is not sick. |
| 5 | Island-s. |
| 6 | Island-s of. |
| 7 | From the Island. |
| 8 | On the Island. |
| 9 | To the Island. |
| 3720 | Issue-d-ing. |
| 1 | Issues. |
| 2 | Isthmus. |
| 3 | Isthmus Darien. |
| 4 | Isthmus of Suez. |
| 5 | Isthmus Tehuantepec. |
| 6 | It. |
| 7 | It can. |
| 8 | It cannot. |
| 9 | It does. |
| 3730 | It does not. |
| 1 | It has. |
| 2 | It has not. |
| 3 | It has been. |
| 4 | It has not been. |
| 5 | It may. |
| 6 | It may not. |
| 3737 | It may be. |

| Nos. | JOI |
|---|---|
| 3738 | It may not be. |
| 9 | It is to be. |
| 3740 | It is not to be. |
| 1 | It is as well. |
| 2 | It should be. |
| 3 | It should not be. |
| 4 | It would. |
| 5 | It would not. |
| 6 | It was to. |
| 7 | It was not to. |
| 8 | Jack stay-s. |
| 9 | Jack screw-s. |
| 3750 | Elevating jack-s. |
| 1 | Jacket-s. |
| 2 | Cloth jacket-s. |
| 3 | Blue cloth jacket-s. |
| 4 | Linen jacket-s. |
| 5 | White jacket-s. |
| 6 | Jam-med-ming. |
| 7 | Jammed in between. |
| 8 | January. |
| 9 | Jealous-y. |
| 3760 | Is likely to create jealousy-ies. |
| 1 | There did not appear to be any jealousy-ies. |
| 2 | Jeers. |
| 3 | Jeer block-s. |
| 4 | Jetty-ies. |
| 5 | Jetty-head-s. |
| 6 | Jib-s. |
| 7 | Jib boom-s. |
| 8 | Jib stay-s. |
| 9 | Jib halliards. |
| 3770 | Has, or have, carried away jib boom. |
| 1 | In want of flying jib. |
| 2 | In want of flying jib boom. |
| 3 | In want of a jib. |
| 4 | In want of a jib boom. |
| 5 | Jib stay has parted. |
| 6 | Jib is split. |
| 7 | Jigger-s. |
| 8 | Join-ed-ing. |
| 9 | Going to join. |
| 3780 | Has, or have, joined. |
| 1 | Has, or have not, joined. |
| 2 | Is, or are, to join. |
| 3 | When did he, or she, join? |
| 4 | When will he, or they, join? |
| 3785 | When will you join the? |

| Nos. | JOI |
|---|---|
| 3786 | Join company. |
| 7 | Joint-ed-s. |
| 8 | Journal-s. |
| 9 | Journey-ies. |
| 3790 | Joy-s. |
| 1 | Joyful-ly-ness. |
| 2 | Joyous-ness. |
| 3 | Judge-d-ing. |
| 4 | Judgment-s. |
| 5 | Judge Advocate. |
| 6 | Judicious-ly. |
| 7 | July. |
| 8 | Juncture-s. |
| 9 | June. |
| 3800 | Junior-s. |
| 1 | Junior officer-s. |
| 2 | Junior rank-s. |
| 3 | Junk-s. |
| 4 | Junket-ing. |
| 5 | Jurisdiction-s. |
| 6 | Jury-ies. |
| 7 | Jury mast-s. |
| 8 | Under jury masts. |
| 9 | Jury rudder. |
| 3810 | Just-ly. |
| 1 | Justice. |
| 2 | Justice-s of the Peace. |
| 3 | Justify-ied-ing-ies. |
| 4 | Can justify. |
| 5 | Cannot justify. |
| 6 | Can you justify? |
| 7 | Justifiable-y. |
| 8 | Justification-s. |
| 9 | Kedge-ed-ing. |
| 3820 | Kedge off. |
| 1 | Kedge out. |
| 2 | Is kedging off, or out. |
| 3 | Kedge-s. Anchor-s. |
| 4 | In want of kedge anchor-s. |
| 5 | Anchor with kedges. |
| 6 | Send kedges and hawsers. |
| 7 | Keel-s. |
| 8 | Keel boat-s. |
| 9 | Keep-ing. Kept. |
| 3830 | Can keep. |
| 1 | Cannot keep. |
| 2 | Can you keep? |
| 3 | Could not keep. |
| 4 | Have you kept? |
| 5 | Is, or are to be kept. |
| 6 | Shall I keep? |
| 3837 | Shall, or will keep. |

| Nos. | KNO |
|---|---|
| 3838 | Shall, or will not keep. |
| 9 | Keep company. |
| 3840 | Keep nearer to. |
| 1 | Keep away. |
| 2 | Keep on your course. |
| 3 | Keeping away. |
| 4 | Keg-s. |
| 5 | Keelson-s. |
| 6 | Kettle-s. |
| 7 | Camp kettles. |
| 8 | Cooking kettles. |
| 9 | Key-ed-ing. |
| 3850 | Key up. |
| 1 | Keying up. |
| 2 | Key-s. |
| 3 | I am going to change the secret signal key to that which will be shown by numeral signal. |
| 4 | Secret sign'l key, use No. 1. |
| 5 | Secret sign'l key, use No. 2. |
| 6 | Secret sign'l key, use No. 3. |
| 7 | Secret signal key, use the one agreed upon. |
| 8 | Kill-ed-ing. |
| 9 | How many were killed? |
| 3860 | Killed on board the. |
| 1 | Report the numb'r of killed. |
| 2 | The number of killed will be shown by num'l sig. |
| 3 | Many killed. |
| 4 | None killed. |
| 5 | State the number of killed and wounded. |
| 6 | The number of killed and wounded will be shown by numeral signal. |
| 7 | Kind-ly. |
| 8 | Kindness. |
| 9 | King-s. |
| 3870 | Kingdom-s. |
| 1 | Knapsack-s. |
| 2 | Leave knapsacks on board. |
| 3 | With knapsacks. |
| 4 | Without knapsacks. |
| 5 | Knee-s. |
| 6 | Knee deep. |
| 7 | Knife-ves. |
| 8 | Knight-head-s. |
| 9 | Knot-s. |
| 3880 | How many knots are you making? |

| Nos. | KNO |
|---|---|
| 3881 | Know. |
| 2 | Do not know. |
| 3 | Do you know? |
| 4 | Let him, or them know. |
| 5 | Knowledge. |
| 6 | Known. |
| 7 | Label-ed-s. |
| 8 | Labor-s. |
| 9 | Laborer-s. |
| 3890 | Laborious-ly. |
| 1 | Lacerate-d-ing. |
| 2 | Laceration. |
| 3 | Laconic-al-ly. |
| 4 | Ladder-s. |
| 5 | Scaling ladders. |
| 6 | Lade-n-ing. |
| 7 | Is laden with. |
| 8 | What is she laden with? |
| 9 | Bill of lading. |
| 3900 | Lag-s-ged-ging. |
| 1 | Lagging behind. |
| 2 | Lake-s. |
| 3 | Lament-ed-ing. |
| 4 | Lamentable-y. |
| 5 | Lamentation-s. |
| 6 | Lamp-s. |
| 7 | Lance-s. |
| 8 | Land-ed-ing. |
| 9 | Can a landing be effected? |
| 3910 | Cannot land. |
| 1 | Cover the land'g party-ies. |
| 2 | Do not land without arms. |
| 3 | Do not land without orders. |
| 4 | Brigade of seamen, armed for service, are to land immediately. |
| 5 | Brigade of seamen, armed f'r service, are to be held in readiness to land. |
| 6 | Marines and small-arm men are to land; boats' crews to remain by the boats. |
| 7 | Land the troops. |
| 8 | Troops to be held in readiness to land. |
| 9 | Troops to land in light marching order. |
| 3920 | Troops to land with nothing but arms and ammunition. |

| Nos. | LAT |
|---|---|
| 3921 | Troops to land with the number of days' cooked provisions now indicated by numeral signal. |
| 2 | There is too much surf to land. |
| 3 | There is not too much surf to land. |
| 4 | Pull in, open fire, clear the beach of the enemy, cover the landing of the troops and seamen, and then form on the beach as expeditiously as possible. |
| 5 | When did they land? |
| 6 | Land. |
| 7 | Have made the land. |
| 8 | Make the land. |
| 9 | Look out for the land. |
| 3930 | Off the land. |
| 1 | On the land. |
| 2 | Along the land. |
| 3 | What land? |
| 4 | Landing-s. |
| 5 | Very bad landing-s. |
| 6 | Very good landing-s. |
| 7 | Landing has been effected. |
| 8 | Landlocked. |
| 9 | Landmark-s. |
| 3940 | Language-s. |
| 1 | Lantern-s. |
| 2 | Deck lantern-s. |
| 3 | Side lantern-s. |
| 4 | Head lantern-s. |
| 5 | Signal lantern-s. |
| 6 | Lantern, hoist, for absent boat. |
| 7 | Lantern, keep, at mizzen cap during the night. |
| 8 | Lantern, show, fr'm weather bow during the night. |
| 9 | Lanterns, keep, ready to show during the night. |
| 3950 | Lanterns, show no, during the night. |
| 1 | Large-ly. |
| 2 | Largest. |
| 3 | Lash-ed-ing. |
| 4 | Last. |
| 5 | Late-ly. |
| 3956 | Lateen sail-s. |

| Nos. | LAT |
|---|---|
| 3957 | Latest. |
| 8 | Latest news received will be reported by signal. |
| 9 | Latitude-s. |
| 3960 | Latitudes by dead reckoning. |
| 1 | Latitude by observation at noon. |
| 2 | What is your latitude? |
| 3 | Latterly. |
| 4 | Launch-es. |
| 5 | First launch send to. |
| 6 | Second launch send to. |
| 7 | Launches send to. |
| 8 | Launches with howitzers send to. |
| 9 | Lavish-ly. |
| 3970 | Law-s. |
| 1 | Lawful-ly. |
| 2 | Lawless-ness. |
| 3 | Lawsuit-s. |
| 4 | Lay. |
| 5 | Laid. |
| 6 | Lazaretto. |
| 7 | Lazy-ily. |
| 8 | Laziness. |
| 9 | Lead-ing. |
| 3980 | Lead into action. |
| 1 | Lead into the port or place. |
| 2 | Lead-s. |
| 3 | Keep the lead going. |
| 4 | Black lead. |
| 5 | Red lead. |
| 6 | White lead. |
| 7 | Leak-ed-ing-s. |
| 8 | Can stop the leak. |
| 9 | Can you stop the leak? |
| 3990 | Leak is stopped. |
| 1 | Has sprung a leak. |
| 2 | Leaking fast. |
| 3 | Leaking slowly. |
| 4 | Learn-ed-ing. |
| 5 | Cannot learn anything. |
| 6 | Could not learn anything. |
| 7 | Least. |
| 8 | Leather-ed. |
| 9 | Rigging leather. |
| 4000 | Sole leather. |
| 1 | Leave-left. |
| 2 | Did you leave? |
| 3 | When did you leave? |
| 4004 | When did they leave? |

| Nos. | LET |
|---|---|
| 4005 | The people may have leave of absence for the number of hours shown by numeral signal. |
| 6 | Left him, or them. |
| 7 | Left the place. |
| 8 | Left our. |
| 9 | Left the. |
| 4010 | Left us. |
| 1 | Ledge-s. |
| 2 | Dangerous ledge-s. |
| 3 | Lookout for ledge-s. |
| 4 | Rocky ledge-s. |
| 5 | Lee-ward. |
| 6 | Lee beam. |
| 7 | Lee bow. |
| 8 | Lee quarter. |
| 9 | Lee side. |
| 4020 | Lee tide. |
| 1 | Leeway. |
| 2 | To leeward. |
| 3 | Leeches. |
| 4 | Leg-s. |
| 5 | Legal-ly. |
| 6 | Legality. |
| 7 | Legible-y. |
| 8 | Leisure-ly. |
| 9 | Lemons. |
| 4030 | Lemon syrup. |
| 1 | Lemon juice. |
| 2 | Lend-ing-lent. |
| 3 | Can lend you. |
| 4 | Cannot lend you. |
| 5 | Will lend you. |
| 6 | Will you lend me? |
| 7 | Length-s. |
| 8 | What is the length of? |
| 9 | Lengthen-ed-ing. |
| 4040 | Lenient-ly. |
| 1 | Leniency. |
| 2 | Less-en-ed-ing. |
| 3 | Less than. |
| 4 | Much less than. |
| 5 | Not less than. |
| 6 | Lesson-s. |
| 7 | Let. |
| 8 | Letting. |
| 9 | Letter-s. |
| 4050 | An opportunity offers for sending letters home. |
| 4051 | An opportunity offers for sending letters into port. |

| Nos. | LET |
|---|---|
| 4052 | Bring off all letteıs and papers. |
| 3 | Go for letters and papers. |
| 4 | Has, or have, letters for. |
| 5 | Has, or have, no letters for. |
| 6 | Letters to, or for the mail. |
| 7 | Send boat for letters. |
| 8 | Send letters on board the flag, or vess'l designated, to be forwarded. |
| 9 | Your letters are, or were. |
| 4060 | Letter-s of marque. |
| 1 | Levant. |
| 2 | Levanter-s. |
| 3 | Level-ed-ing. |
| 4 | Lever-s. |
| 5 | Liable-ity-ies. |
| 6 | Liberal-ly. |
| 7 | Liberality. |
| 8 | Liberate-d-ing. |
| 9 | Liberate the prisoners. |
| 4070 | Liberty. |
| 1 | Am I at liberty to? |
| 2 | You are at liberty to. |
| 3 | Lieutenant-s. |
| 4 | Flag Lieutenant. |
| 5 | Junior Lieutenant. |
| 6 | Lieutenant of the watch. |
| 7 | Lieutenant of Marines. |
| 8 | Life-lives. |
| 9 | Life boat-s. |
| 4080 | Life boat, I am in need of a. |
| 1 | Life boat, I have no. |
| 2 | Life boat is injured. |
| 3 | Life boat has been lost. |
| 4 | Life boat, send a. |
| 5 | Lift-ed-ing. |
| 6 | Lifts. |
| 7 | Light-ly-ness. |
| 8 | Lights. |
| 9 | Green light-s. |
| 4090 | Red light-s. |
| 1 | White light-s. |
| 2 | Warning light-s. |
| 3 | Head light-s. |
| 4 | Running light-s. |
| 5 | Top light-s. |
| 6 | Lighter-s. |
| 7 | Lighterage. |
| 8 | Light house-s. |
| 4099 | Light vessel-s. |

| Nos. | LIS |
|---|---|
| 4100 | Light in sight; bearing will be shown by Compass signal. |
| 1 | Lightning-s. |
| 2 | Lightning conductors. |
| 3 | Like-ly. |
| 4 | Is it likely? |
| 5 | Not likely. |
| 6 | Should like to. |
| 7 | Should not like to. |
| 8 | Very likely. |
| 9 | Would you like to? |
| 4110 | Limbers. |
| 1 | Limit-ed-ing. |
| 2 | Limitation-s. |
| 3 | Limits. |
| 4 | Line-s. |
| 5 | Form line ahead, or of battle. |
| 6 | Form line abre'st, or abeam. |
| 7 | Form in two lines, each ahead. |
| 8 | Form in two lines, each abreast. |
| 9 | Form in three lines, each ahead. |
| 4120 | Form in three lines, each abreast. |
| 1 | Form starboard bow and port quarter, line ahead. |
| 2 | Form port bow and starboard quart'r, line ahead. |
| 3 | Keep in the line. |
| 4 | Reform the line-s. |
| 5 | Restore the line-s. |
| 6 | Return to the line-s. |
| 7 | Line of fire. |
| 8 | Line of march. |
| 9 | Line of operations. |
| 4130 | Linen. |
| 1 | Link-s. |
| 2 | Links of chain. |
| 3 | Lint. |
| 4 | Lint needed for wounded. |
| 5 | Lint stock-s. |
| 6 | Liquid-s. |
| 7 | Liquor-s. |
| 8 | List-s. |
| 9 | A list of the. |
| 4140 | Has no list-s of the. |
| 1 | Send a list of the. |
| 4142 | List of killed. |

| Nos. | LIS | Nos. | LUL |
|---|---|---|---|
| 4143 | List of wounded. | 4191 | Look out ahead. |
| 4 | List of deserters or ab- | 2 | Look out for. |
| | sentees. | 3 | Station lookouts. |
| 5 | Literal-ly. | 4 | What does she look like? |
| 6 | Litigation. | 5 | Look into the port and re- |
| 7 | Litigious-ly-ness. | | port. |
| 8 | Little. | 6 | Did you look into the place? |
| 9 | A little more. | 7 | Will look into the place. |
| 4150 | A little worse. | 8 | Look out, vessels will. |
| 1 | As little as. | 9 | Loom-ed-ing-s. |
| 2 | A little faster. | 4200 | Loom of the land. |
| 3 | A little slower. | 1 | Loopholes. |
| 4 | How little? | 2 | Loose-ly. |
| 5 | Living. | 3 | Loose sails to dry. |
| 6 | Liver. | 4 | Lose. Loss. Lost. |
| 7 | Load-ed-ing. Laden. | 5 | Did you lose? |
| 8 | Clear the loaded boats. | 6 | Has, or have lost. |
| 9 | Tow the loaded boats. | 7 | Is, or are lost. |
| 4160 | Loaf-ves. | 8 | What loss sustained? |
| 1 | Loaves of bread. | 9 | With little loss. |
| 2 | Loan-ed-ing. | 4210 | With great loss. |
| 3 | Local-ly. | 1 | With less loss than was |
| 4 | Locality-ies. | | expected. |
| 5 | Lock-ed-ing. | 2 | With very little loss. |
| 6 | Locks. | 3 | Without any loss. |
| 7 | Lockers. | 4 | Loud-ly. |
| 8 | Lodgment-s. | 5 | Loud noise-s. |
| 9 | Lofty. | 6 | Loud report-s of gun-s. |
| 4170 | Log-s. | 7 | Loudest. |
| 1 | Log-book-s. | 8 | Low. |
| 2 | Log-board-s. | 9 | Low ground. |
| 3 | Log-line-s. | 4220 | Low tide. |
| 4 | Log-paper. | 1 | Low water. |
| 5 | Loiter-ed-ing. | 2 | Lower. |
| 6 | Long. | 3 | Lower down, go. |
| 7 | As long as. | 4 | Lowest. Lowermost. |
| 8 | How long? | 5 | Loyal-ly. |
| 9 | Long ago. | 6 | Lubber-ly. |
| 4180 | Not long. | 7 | Luck-ily. |
| 1 | Longer. | 8 | Ludicrous-ly. |
| 2 | Longest. | 9 | Luff. |
| 3 | Longitude-s. | 4230 | Luff all you can. |
| 4 | In what longitude? | 1 | Luff tackle purchase-s. |
| 5 | Difference in longitude. | 2 | Luffs. |
| 6 | Longitude by chronome- | 3 | Luffing. |
| | ter-s. | 4 | Luffing all I can. |
| 7 | Longitude by dead reck- | 5 | Lug-s. |
| | oning. | 6 | Lug sails. |
| 8 | My longitude is as shown | 7 | Luggage. |
| | by numeral signal. | 8 | Lukewarm. |
| 9 | What is your longitude? | 9 | Lull-s. |
| 4190 | Look-ed-ing-s. | 4240 | Wind is likely to lull soon. |

| Nos. | LUL |
|---|---|
| 4241 | When the wind lulls. |
| 2 | Lumber. |
| 3 | Lump-s-y. |
| 4 | Lumpy bottom. |
| 5 | Lunatic-s. |
| 6 | Lunacy. |
| 7 | Lungs. |
| 8 | Lure-d-ing. |
| 9 | Lurk-ed-ing. |
| 4250 | Machine-ry. |
| 1 | Mad-ly. |
| 2 | Madness. |
| 3 | Madden-ed. |
| 4 | Made. |
| 5 | Is, or are made. |
| 6 | Is, or are not made. |
| 7 | To be made. |
| 8 | When will it be made? |
| 9 | Magazine-s. |
| 4260 | Magazine-s of arms. |
| 1 | Magazine-s of ammunit'n. |
| 2 | Magazine-s of provisions. |
| 3 | Magazine-s of powder. |
| 4 | Magazine-s of gen'l stores. |
| 5 | Magistrate-s. |
| 6 | Magnet-s. |
| 7 | Magnetical-ly. |
| 8 | Magnetical instruments. |
| 9 | Magnetism. |
| 4270 | Magnificent-ly. |
| 1 | Magnificence. |
| 2 | Magnify-ed-ing. |
| 3 | Magnitude. |
| 4 | Of great magnitude. |
| 5 | Of small magnitude. |
| 6 | Main. |
| 7 | Mainmast. |
| 8 | Maintop-mast. |
| 9 | Maintop-gallant-mast. |
| 4280 | Mainyard. |
| 1 | Maintopsail-yard. |
| 2 | Maintop-gallant-yard. |
| 3 | Main-royal-mast. |
| 4 | Main-royal-yard. |
| 5 | Mainsail. |
| 6 | Maintopsail. |
| 7 | Maintop-gallant-sail. |
| 8 | Main-royal. |
| 9 | Maintain-ed-ing. |
| 4290 | Maintain your position. |
| 4291 | Maintain, I cannot, my present position. |

| Nos. | MAR |
|---|---|
| 4292 | Maintenance. |
| 3 | Make-s-ing. |
| 4 | Cannot make out. |
| 5 | Make sail. |
| 6 | Shall I make sail? |
| 7 | Will make. |
| 8 | Will you make? |
| 9 | Male-s. |
| 4300 | Malice. |
| 1 | Malicious-ly. |
| 2 | Maliciousness. |
| 3 | Mallet-s. |
| 4 | Sewing mallet-s. |
| 5 | Man-ned-ning. |
| 6 | Every man. |
| 7 | Every man must do his best. |
| 8 | Man-men-of-war. |
| 9 | Men-of-war, have you seen any. |
| 4310 | What men-of-war did you leave out? |
| 1 | Manage-d-ing. |
| 2 | How did you manage to? |
| 3 | Have managed to. |
| 4 | Management. |
| 5 | Manifest-ed-ing. |
| 6 | Manner-s. |
| 7 | In what manner? |
| 8 | In a proper manner. |
| 9 | Manœuvre-s. |
| 4320 | Manœuvreing-s. |
| 1 | Many. |
| 2 | As many as. |
| 3 | How many? |
| 4 | Not many. |
| 5 | Not so many. |
| 6 | Map-s. |
| 7 | Have you a map of the surrounding country. |
| 8 | I have no map of this vicinity. |
| 9 | A map of this vicinity wanted. |
| 4330 | March-ed-ing. |
| 1 | Marines. |
| 2 | Marine battalion-s. |
| 3 | Marine guard-s. |
| 4 | Marine officer-s. |
| 5 | Mark-ed-ing-s. |
| 4336 | Cannot see the leading marks. |

| Nos. | MAR | Nos. | MEM |
|---|---|---|---|
| 4337 | Do you see the leading marks? | 4386 | What is the matter? |
| 8 | The marks are. | 7 | Mattock-s. |
| 9 | What are the marks! | 8 | Mattress-es. |
| 4340 | Market-s. | 9 | Mature-ly. |
| 1 | Do not send market boat-s. | 4390 | Maturity. |
| 2 | How is the market? | 1 | Maul-s. |
| 3 | Is there a market at. | 2 | Topmaul-s. |
| 4 | Send market boat to. | 3 | Maxim-s. |
| 5 | Marline. | 4 | Maximum. |
| 6 | Marline spike-s. | 5 | May. |
| 7 | Marsh-y. | 6 | May I? |
| 8 | Marshal. | 7 | May they? |
| 9 | Provost Marshal. | 8 | May we? |
| 4350 | Martial. | 9 | Mayor. |
| 1 | Court Martial ordered. | 4400 | Me. |
| 2 | Court Martial will convene on board of your vessel. | 1 | Meat-s. |
| 3 | Court Martial will be convened. | 2 | Mean-s. |
| 4 | Court Martial is dissolved. | 3 | By all means. |
| 5 | Court Martial will adjourn. | 4 | By no means. |
| 6 | Martial law. | 5 | By this means. |
| 7 | Martingale-s. | 6 | Do you mean? |
| 8 | Jib martingale. | 7 | Meanwhile. |
| 9 | Mask-ed-ing. | 8 | Measure-d-ing. |
| 4360 | Mask your battery-ies. | 9 | Measurement-s. |
| 1 | Masked battery-ies. | 4410 | Meat-s. |
| 2 | Mason-s. | 1 | Fresh meat. |
| 3 | Masonry. | 2 | Preserved meats. |
| 4 | Mast-s-ing. | 3 | Salt meat. |
| 5 | Foremast is sprung. | 4 | Mechanic-s. |
| 6 | Lower mast-s. | 5 | Medal-s. |
| 7 | Mainmast is sprung. | 6 | Medal-s of honor. |
| 8 | Mizzen mast is sprung. | 7 | Meddle-d-ing. |
| 9 | Step your masts. | 8 | Mediate-ing. |
| 4370 | Step your foremast. | 9 | Mediator-s. |
| 1 | Step your mainmast. | 4420 | Mediation. |
| 2 | Step your mizzen mast. | 1 | Medicine-s. |
| 3 | Strike your masts. | 2 | In need of medicines for sick. |
| 4 | Strike your mainmast. | 3 | Medium. |
| 5 | Strike your foremast. | 4 | Meet-ing-met. |
| 6 | Strike your mizzen mast. | 5 | Did not meet. |
| 7 | Master-ed-ing. | 6 | Did you meet? |
| 8 | Master-at-arms. | 7 | Should you meet. |
| 9 | Mat-s. | 8 | Should you not meet. |
| 4380 | Match-es. | 9 | Melancholy. |
| 1 | Mate-s. | 4430 | Melt-ed-ing. |
| 2 | Material-s. | 1 | Member-s. |
| 3 | Materially. | 2 | Memoranda-um. |
| 4 | Matter-s. | 3 | Memorial-s. |
| 4385 | There is nothi'g the matter. | 4 | Memorialist-s. |
| | | 5 | Memory-ies. |
| | | 4436 | Memorable. |

| Nos. | MEN |
|---|---|
| 4437 | Men. |
| 8 | Have men for. |
| 9 | How are the men? |
| 4440 | How many men? |
| 1 | Sick men. |
| 2 | Wounded men. |
| 3 | Mend-ed-ing. |
| 4 | Mention-ed-ing. |
| 5 | Merchant-s. |
| 6 | Merchantman-men. |
| 7 | Is a merchantman. |
| 8 | What number of merchant-men? |
| 9 | Merchandize. |
| 4450 | Mercury. |
| 1 | Mercy-ful-ly. |
| 2 | Merit-s. |
| 3 | Meritorious-ly. |
| 4 | Mess-es. |
| 5 | Mess-ed-ing. |
| 6 | Messmate-s. |
| 7 | Message-s. |
| 8 | Message to follow this is to be kept secret. |
| 9 | Message is not understood. |
| 1460 | Repeat the message. |
| 1 | Send a message to. |
| 2 | Messenger-s. |
| 3 | Carried away the mes'nger. |
| 4 | Metal-s. |
| 5 | Metallic. |
| 6 | Method-s. |
| 7 | A good method. |
| 8 | A bad method. |
| 9 | Methodical-ly. |
| 470 | Mid-day. |
| 1 | Middle-d-ing. |
| 2 | The middle of the. |
| 3 | Midnight. |
| 4 | Midships. |
| 5 | Midshipman-men. |
| 6 | Midsummer. |
| 7 | Midway. |
| 8 | Might. |
| 9 | Mild-ly. |
| 480 | Mildest. |
| 1 | Mildew. |
| 2 | Mile-s. |
| 3 | About the number of miles shown by numeral sig'l. |
| 484 | How many miles is it to or from? |

| Nos. | MIS |
|---|---|
| 4485 | Miles distant from. |
| 6 | Military. |
| 7 | Military Department. |
| 8 | Military discipline. |
| 9 | Military law-s. |
| 4490 | Militia. |
| 1 | Mill-s. |
| 2 | Million-s. |
| 3 | Mind-ing. |
| 4 | Mindful. |
| 5 | Mines-ing. |
| 6 | Mingle-d-ing. |
| 7 | Minima-mum. |
| 8 | Ministerial-ly. |
| 9 | Minor-s. |
| 4500 | Minority-ies. |
| 1 | Mint-s. |
| 2 | Minute-s. |
| 3 | Minute gun-s. |
| 4 | Minutely-ness. |
| 5 | Misapply-ied-ing-ies. |
| 6 | Misapplication. |
| 7 | Misapprehend-ed-ing. |
| 8 | Misapprehension-s. |
| 9 | Misbehave-d-ing. |
| 4510 | Misbehavior. |
| 1 | Miscarry-ied. |
| 2 | Has, or have, miscarried. |
| 3 | Is, or are, likely to miscarry. |
| 4 | Is, or are, not likely to miscarry. |
| 5 | Mischief. |
| 6 | Mischievous. |
| 7 | Misconduct. |
| 8 | Misery-ies. |
| 9 | Miserable-y. |
| 4520 | Misfortune-s. |
| 1 | Misinformed. |
| 2 | Was, or were, misinformed. |
| 3 | Misinterpret-ed-ing-s. |
| 4 | Misinterpretation-s. |
| 5 | Miss-ed-ing-s. |
| 6 | Are any missing? |
| 7 | Is, or are, missing. |
| 8 | Mistake-ing-s. |
| 9 | There is some mistake. |
| 4530 | Mistaken. |
| 1 | Has, or have, mistaken. |
| 2 | I cannot be mistaken. |
| 3 | Was, or were, mistaken. |
| 4534 | Misunderstand-ing-s. |

| Nos. | MIT |
|---|---|
| 4535 | Mitigate-d-ing. |
| 6 | Is, or are, mitigated. |
| 7 | Mitigation. |
| 8 | Mix-ed-ing. |
| 9 | Mixture-s. |
| 4540 | Mizzen. |
| 1 | Mizzen mast-s. |
| 2 | Mizzen topmast-s. |
| 3 | Mizzen topsail-s. |
| 4 | Moat-s. |
| 5 | Model-s. |
| 6 | Moderate-d-ing. |
| 7 | If moderate weather. |
| 8 | More moderate weather. |
| 9 | Think it will moderate soon. |
| 4550 | Modify-ied-ing-ies. |
| 1 | Molasses. |
| 2 | Molest-ed-ing-s. |
| 3 | Molestation-s. |
| 4 | Moment-s. |
| 5 | Momentary-ily. |
| 6 | Momentous. |
| 7 | Monday-s. |
| 8 | Monday morning. |
| 9 | Monday noon. |
| 4560 | Monday night. |
| 1 | Monday evening. |
| 2 | Money-ies. |
| 3 | Month-s-ly. |
| 4 | A few months. |
| 5 | Moon. |
| 6 | Moonlight. |
| 7 | Full moon. |
| 8 | New moon. |
| 9 | First quarter of the moon. |
| 4570 | Last quarter of the moon. |
| 1 | Moor-ed-ing. |
| 2 | Moor with the hawse open to the. |
| 3 | Shall I moor ship? |
| 4 | When you are moored. |
| 5 | You will moor ship. |
| 6 | You will not moor ship. |
| 7 | Moral-s. |
| 8 | Morally. |
| 9 | Morass. |
| 4580 | More. |
| 1 | Moreover. |
| 2 | Any more. |
| 3 | No more. |
| 4584 | Some more. |

| Nos. | MOU |
|---|---|
| 4585 | Morning-s. |
| 6 | This morning. |
| 7 | To-morrow morning. |
| 8 | Yesterday morning. |
| 9 | Morrow. |
| 4590 | To-morrow. |
| 1 | To-morrow afternoon. |
| 2 | To-morrow night. |
| 3 | Mortal-ly. |
| 4 | Mortally wounded. |
| 5 | Mortality. |
| 6 | Mortar-s. |
| 7 | Mortar beds. |
| 8 | Mortar vessels. |
| 9 | Mortar boats-vessels. |
| 4600 | Mortify-ied-ing-ies. |
| 1 | Most-ly. |
| 2 | Motive-s. |
| 3 | Motion-s. |
| 4 | Disregard Senior officer's motions. |
| 5 | Follow my motions. |
| 6 | Is, or are, in motion. |
| 7 | May I disregard your motions? |
| 8 | Pay particular attention to the Senior officer's motions during the night. |
| 9 | Report the motions of the enemy or stranger. |
| 4610 | Why do you not follow the motions of the Commander-in-chief? |
| 1 | Move-d-ing-s. |
| 2 | Shall I move down? |
| 3 | Shall I move up? |
| 4 | Cannot move at present. |
| 5 | Has, or have, moved. |
| 6 | Has, or have not, moved. |
| 7 | Is, or are, moving. |
| 8 | Is, or are not, moving. |
| 9 | Nothing moving yet. |
| 4620 | Mount-ed-ing. |
| 1 | Mount guns to defend you. |
| 2 | The enemy is mounting guns. |
| 3 | The enemy seems to be ready to mount guns. |
| 4 | Mount your guns as soon as possible. |
| 5 | Mountain-s-ous. |
| 4626 | Mouth-s. |

| Nos. | MOU |
|---|---|
| 4627 | Mouth of the bay. |
| 8 | Mouth of the bayou. |
| 9 | Mouth of the harbor. |
| 4630 | Mouth of the Mississippi. |
| 1 | Mouth of the river. |
| 2 | Much. |
| 3 | As much as. |
| 4 | How much? |
| 5 | How much more? |
| 6 | Much less. |
| 7 | Much more. |
| 8 | Not much. |
| 9 | Not much more. |
| 4640 | Too much. |
| 1 | Not too much. |
| 2 | Muddy. |
| 3 | Muffle-d-ing. |
| 4 | Muffle your oars. |
| 5 | Muffle your drums. |
| 6 | Mule-s. |
| 7 | Multitude-s. |
| 8 | Murder-ed-ing. |
| 9 | Murderous attack. |
| 4650 | Murderer-s. |
| 1 | Murmur-ed-ing. |
| 2 | Music. |
| 3 | Musical-ly. |
| 4 | Musician-s. |
| 5 | Must. |
| 6 | Must be. |
| 7 | Must come. |
| 8 | Must go. |
| 9 | Must not be. |
| 4660 | Must not go. |
| 1 | Musket-s. |
| 2 | In need of muskets. |
| 3 | In need of rifled muskets. |
| 4 | Want muskets sent ashore. |
| 5 | Send me some muskets. |
| 6 | Muster-ed-ing. |
| 7 | Muster book-s. |
| 8 | Muster out. |
| 9 | Muster roll-s. |
| 4670 | Mutilate-d-ing. |
| 1 | Mutilation-s. |
| 2 | Mutiny-ies. |
| 3 | Mutinous. |
| 4 | Mutineer-s. |
| 5 | Crew is mutinous, and am in want of assistance. |
| 6 | Mutton. |
| 4677 | Mutual-ly. |

| Nos. | NAV |
|---|---|
| 4678 | Muzzle-d-ing-s. |
| 9 | Muzzle loaders. |
| 4680 | My. |
| 1 | Myself. |
| 2 | Mine. |
| 3 | Mystery-ies. |
| 4 | Mysterious-ly-ness. |
| 5 | Nail-ed-ing. |
| 6 | Nails. |
| 7 | Nails wanted; size will be indicated by numeral signal. |
| 8 | Name-d-ing-s. |
| 9 | Nameless. |
| 4690 | Narrate-d-ing-s. |
| 1 | Narration-s. |
| 2 | Narrow-s. |
| 3 | Above the narrows. |
| 4 | Below the narrows. |
| 5 | In the narrow part of the. |
| 6 | Is, or are, very narrow. |
| 7 | Is, or are not, very narrow. |
| 8 | In the narrows. |
| 9 | Narrow-ly. |
| 4700 | Narrow escape. |
| 1 | Narrowly escaped. |
| 2 | Nation-s. |
| 3 | National-ly. |
| 4 | Native-s. |
| 5 | Nativity-ies. |
| 6 | Nautical. |
| 7 | Nautical Almanac. |
| 8 | Nautical books. |
| 9 | Navigate-d-ing-ion. |
| 4710 | Can navigate. |
| 1 | Cannot navigate. |
| 2 | Navigation is not safe. |
| 3 | Navigation is very difficult. |
| 4 | Navigation is safe and easy. |
| 5 | Navy-ies. |
| 6 | In the Navy. |
| 7 | Not in the Navy. |
| 8 | Out of the Navy. |
| 9 | Navy list-s. |
| 4720 | Naval. |
| 1 | According to Naval discipline. |
| 2 | Naval battle. |
| 3 | Naval engagement. |
| 4 | Naval skirmish-es. |
| 5 | Naval manœuvres. |
| 4726 | Naval movements. |

| Nos. | NAV |
|---|---|
| 4727 | Not according to Naval discipline. |
| 8 | Navy Yard-s. |
| 9 | Navy Hospital-s. |
| 4730 | Near-ed-ing. |
| 1 | Nearer. |
| 2 | Nearest. |
| 3 | Is, or are, very near. |
| 4 | Is, or are not, very near. |
| 5 | Near enough. |
| 6 | Not near enough. |
| 7 | Too near. |
| 8 | Not too near. |
| 9 | Necessary-ies. |
| 4740 | Is, or are necessary. |
| 1 | Is, or are not necessary. |
| 2 | Will be necessary. |
| 3 | Will not be necessary. |
| 4 | Procure only necessaries. |
| 5 | Necessarily. |
| 6 | Necessity-ies. |
| 7 | Is there any necessity for? |
| 8 | There is a necessity for. |
| 9 | There is no necessity for. |
| 4750 | Necessitate-d-ing. |
| 1 | Necessitous. |
| 2 | Neck-s. |
| 3 | Neck and neck. |
| 4 | Goose neck-s. |
| 5 | Need-ed-ing-s. |
| 6 | In need of supplies. |
| 7 | In need of coal. |
| 8 | In need of provisions. |
| 9 | In need of water. |
| 4760 | In need of. |
| 1 | Not in need of anything. |
| 2 | Not in need of. |
| 3 | Needles. |
| 4 | Sewing needles. |
| 5 | Sail needles. |
| 6 | Palm and needles. |
| 7 | Needless-ly. |
| 8 | Negative. No. Refusal. |
| 9 | Neglect-ed-ing-s. |
| 4770 | Neglectful-ly. |
| 1 | Negligent-ly. |
| 2 | Negligence. |
| 3 | Negotiate-d-ing. |
| 4 | Negotiation-s. |
| 5 | Negotiator-s. |
| 6 | Neither. |
| 4777 | Neither of them. |

| Nos. | NON |
|---|---|
| 4778 | Neither of us. |
| 9 | Net-s. |
| 4780 | Network. |
| 1 | Nettings. |
| 2 | Branding nettings. |
| 3 | Hammock nettings. |
| 4 | Neutral-ly. |
| 5 | Neutrality. |
| 6 | Never. |
| 7 | Nevertheless. |
| 8 | New-ly. |
| 9 | Newest. |
| 4790 | News. |
| 1 | All the news received. |
| 2 | Bad news received. |
| 3 | Good news received. |
| 4 | Have you any news? |
| 5 | Have no news. |
| 6 | Nothing new. |
| 7 | Reliable news has been received. |
| 8 | Reliable, the news is. |
| 9 | Something new. |
| 4800 | Unreliable news. |
| 1 | Newspaper-s. |
| 2 | Next. |
| 3 | Night-s-ly. |
| 4 | A dirty night. |
| 5 | A dark night. |
| 6 | A fine night. |
| 7 | Every night. |
| 8 | In, or during the night. |
| 9 | Keep by me during the night. |
| 4810 | I will remain by you during the night. |
| 1 | Not before night. |
| 2 | Night watch-es. |
| 3 | Nine-th-ly. |
| 4 | Nineteen-th. |
| 5 | Ninety-ieth. |
| 6 | No. Negative. Refusal. |
| 7 | Nobody. |
| 8 | Noise-d-ing. |
| 9 | Noisome. |
| 4820 | Nominal-ly. |
| 1 | Nominate-d-ing. |
| 2 | Nomination-s. |
| 3 | Non-conductor-s. |
| 4 | No one. |
| 5 | None. |
| 4826 | Nonsense-ical. |

| Nos. | NOO | Nos. | OBS |
|---|---|---|---|
| 4827 | Noon. Noonday. | 4877 | Oak timber. |
| 8 | Afternoon. | 8 | Oak wood. |
| 9 | Before noon. | 9 | Oakum. |
| 4830 | Since noon | 4880 | Have you any oakum to spare? |
| 1 | Nor. | 1 | I am in need of oakum. |
| 2 | Not. | 2 | I have no oakum. |
| 3 | Not at all. | 3 | Oars. |
| 4 | Note-d-ing-s. | 4 | I am in want of oars. |
| 5 | Notation-s. | 5 | Lay in your oars. |
| 6 | Nothing. | 6 | Lay on your oars. |
| 7 | Nothing can or will prevent. | 7 | Muffle your oars. |
| 8 | Nothing can or will justify. | 8 | Boat all your oars. |
| 9 | Nothing more at present. | 9 | Oatmeal. |
| 4840 | Nothing less than. | 4890 | Oatmeal for firemen. |
| 1 | Nothing will do but. | 1 | Obedient-ly. |
| 2 | Nothing could be better. | 2 | Obedience. |
| 3 | Nothing could be worse. | 3 | In obedience to orders. |
| 4 | Notice-d-ing-s. | 4 | Obey-ed-ing-s. |
| 5 | Notify-ied-ing-ies. | 5 | Obey orders. |
| 6 | Notification-s. | 6 | Have not obeyed orders. |
| 7 | Notion-s. | 7 | Object-s. |
| 8 | Notoriety-ies. | 8 | Is an object. |
| 9 | Notorious-ly. | 9 | Object is to. |
| 4850 | Notwithstanding. | 4900 | What can be his object? |
| 1 | Nourish-ed-ing-es. | 1 | Without any special object. |
| 2 | Nourishment-s. | 2 | Object-ed-ing. |
| 3 | Novel-ty-ties. | 3 | Has, or have objected. |
| 4 | November. | 4 | Objection-s. |
| 5 | Now. | 5 | There is no objection to. |
| 6 | Now or never. | 6 | What is the objection to? |
| 7 | Now or never; act with vigor. | 7 | Oblige-d-ing-s. |
| 8 | Now is the time to. | 8 | Am, is, or are obliged. |
| 9 | Now it is too late to. | 9 | Has, or have been obliged to. |
| 4860 | Now it is too soon to. | 4910 | Will be obliged to. |
| 1 | Noxious-ness. | 1 | Oblique-ly. |
| 2 | Nozzle-s. | 2 | Turn off obliquely to the left. |
| 3 | Nuisance-s. | 3 | Turn off obliquely to the right. |
| 4 | Number-ed-ing-s. | 4 | Oblong. |
| 5 | National number. | 5 | Obnoxious-ly. |
| 6 | Private number. | 6 | Obscure-d-ing-s. |
| 7 | Regular number. | 7 | Obscurity. |
| 8 | The number of. | 8 | Observe-d-ing-s. |
| 9 | The last number. | 9 | Did not observe. |
| 4870 | Show your number. | 4920 | Has, or have observed. |
| 1 | Numeral-s. | 1 | Have you observed? |
| 2 | Numerical-ly. | 2 | Observation-s. |
| 3 | Nutricious. | 3 | A. M. observations. |
| 4 | Nutriment. | 4924 | P. M. observations. |
| 5 | Oak-en. | | |
| 4876 | Oak boards. | | |

| Nos. | OBS |
|---|---|
| 4925 | Night observations. |
| 6 | Daily observations. |
| 7 | Had no observations. |
| 8 | Obstacle-s. |
| 9 | Should there be no obstacle in the way. |
| 4930 | Should there be any obstacle in the way report immediately. |
| 1 | Obstinate-ly. |
| 2 | Obstruct-ed-ing-s. |
| 3 | Obstruction-s. |
| 4 | Remove the obstruction-s. |
| 5 | The obstructions cannot be removed. |
| 6 | Obtain-ed-ing-s. |
| 7 | Can you obtain? |
| 8 | Cannot obtain. |
| 9 | Has, or have obtained. |
| 4940 | Has, or have not obtained. |
| 1 | Try to obtain. |
| 2 | Make every effort to obtain. |
| 3 | Obviate-d-ing. |
| 4 | Obvious-ly. |
| 5 | Occasion-ed-ing. |
| 6 | Another occasion. |
| 7 | Has, or have had no occasion. |
| 8 | Has, or have had occasion. |
| 9 | On that occasion. |
| 4950 | On any occasion. |
| 1 | The present occasion. |
| 2 | Was, or were occasioned by. |
| 3 | Occupy-ied-ing-ies. |
| 4 | Has, or have occupied. |
| 5 | Has, or have not occupied. |
| 6 | Occur-red-ring-s. |
| 7 | Did not occur. |
| 8 | Occurred on the. |
| 9 | Where did it, or that occur? |
| 4960 | Occurrence-s. |
| 1 | Recent occurrences. |
| 2 | Ocean-s. |
| 3 | Antarctic Ocean. |
| 4 | Arctic Ocean. |
| 5 | Atlantic Ocean. |
| 6 | German Ocean. |
| 7 | Indian Ocean. |
| 4968 | North Pacific Ocean. |

| Nos. | OFF |
|---|---|
| 4969 | South Pacific Ocean. |
| 4970 | South Atlantic Ocean. |
| 1 | October. |
| 2 | Odd-s. |
| 3 | Odd number-s. |
| 4 | Oddly. |
| 5 | Odious-ness. |
| 6 | Odium. |
| 7 | Of. Of him, his, or her. |
| 8 | Of it. |
| 9 | Of that. |
| 4980 | Of the. |
| 1 | Of this. |
| 2 | Of their, or them. |
| 3 | Of you, or your. |
| 4 | Off. |
| 5 | Am, is, or are not off yet. |
| 6 | Blow off steam. |
| 7 | Enemy is cruising off. |
| 8 | Has, or have gotten off. |
| 9 | Off the Navy-yard. |
| 4990 | Off the. |
| 1 | Off the town. |
| 2 | Off and on. |
| 3 | Shall be off as soon as possible. |
| 4 | Off shore. |
| 5 | Off the land. |
| 6 | Offing. |
| 7 | A good offing. |
| 8 | In the offing. |
| 9 | Passed the enemy in the offing. |
| 5000 | The enemy is cruising in the offing. |
| 1 | Offend-ed-ing-s. |
| 2 | Offense. |
| 3 | Be careful not to give offense. |
| 4 | Offensive-ly-ness. |
| 5 | Offender-s. |
| 6 | Offer-ed-ing. |
| 7 | Did he, or they offer to. |
| 8 | Have had an offer. |
| 9 | Have had no offer-s. |
| 5010 | Offer your services to the. |
| 1 | Office-s. |
| 2 | Officer-s. |
| 3 | Army officer-s. |
| 4 | Naval officer-s. |
| 5 | Marine officer-s. |
| 5016 | For an officer. |

| Nos. | OFF |
|---|---|
| 5017 | To the officer-s. |
| 8 | With an officer. |
| 9 | Who is the officer? |
| 5020 | Who was the officer? |
| 1 | What officer-s? |
| 2 | Officer of the deck. |
| 3 | Officer of the day. |
| 4 | Officer of the guard duty. |
| 5 | Officer of the picket guard. |
| 6 | Officer-like. |
| 7 | Officer-like conduct. |
| 8 | Official-ly. |
| 9 | Is, or are official. |
| 5030 | Is, or are not official. |
| 1 | Official business. |
| 2 | Official etiquette. |
| 3 | Official routine. |
| 4 | Officiate-d-ing-s. |
| 5 | Officious-ly. |
| 6 | Very officious conduct. |
| 7 | Often-er. |
| 8 | As often as. |
| 9 | How often? |
| 5040 | Not very often. |
| 1 | Not so often as. |
| 2 | Oil-s. |
| 3 | Lamp oil. |
| 4 | Lamp oil to spare. |
| 5 | Lamp oil needed. |
| 6 | Lamp oil, send, to the. |
| 7 | Lubricating oil needed. |
| 8 | Lubricating oil to spare. |
| 9 | Send some lubricating oil to the. |
| 5050 | Lard oil. |
| 1 | Sperm oil. |
| 2 | Colza oil. |
| 3 | Rock oil. |
| 4 | Neats'-foot oil. |
| 5 | Old-er-est. |
| 6 | Omit-ted-ting. |
| 7 | Do not omit to. |
| 8 | Did you omit to? |
| 9 | I omitted to attend to the duty assigned me. |
| 5060 | On. |
| 1 | On us, or our. |
| 2 | On him, his, or her. |
| 3 | On you, or your. |
| 4 | On them, or their. |
| 5 | On that. |
| 5066 | On this. |

| Nos. | OPT |
|---|---|
| 5067 | On the. |
| 8 | Onward. |
| 9 | One. |
| 5070 | Once. |
| 1 | Onions. |
| 2 | Only. |
| 3 | Onset-s. |
| 4 | Open-ed-ing. |
| 5 | Not to be opened. |
| 6 | Open secret or sealed orders when you. |
| 7 | To be opened. |
| 8 | When it is opened. |
| 9 | When it was opened. |
| 5080 | When was it opened? |
| 1 | Operate-d-ing. |
| 2 | Operation-s. |
| 3 | Operator-s. |
| 4 | Opinion-s. |
| 5 | My opinion is that. |
| 6 | What is your opinion of? |
| 7 | Opinions differ on the subject. |
| 8 | The general opinion seems to be that. |
| 9 | Opiate-s. |
| 5090 | Opium. |
| 1 | Opponent-s. |
| 2 | Opportune-ly. |
| 3 | Opportunity-ies. |
| 4 | Another opportunity, take advantage of, to. |
| 5 | Another opportunity may offer. |
| 6 | Every opportunity. |
| 7 | Few opportunities. |
| 8 | Many opportunities offer. |
| 9 | Next opportunity. |
| 5100 | There is an opportunity. |
| 1 | There will be an opportunity. |
| 2 | Have not had an opportunity. |
| 3 | Oppose-d-ing. |
| 4 | Opposition-s. |
| 5 | There is great opposition to. |
| 6 | There is no opposition to. |
| 7 | Opposite. |
| 8 | Oppress-ed-ing. |
| 9 | Opposition-s. |
| 5110 | Option-al. |

| Nos. | OR |
|---|---|
| 5111 | Or. |
| 2 | Order-s. |
| 3 | Keep in close order. |
| 4 | Keep in closer order by closing upon the centre. |
| 5 | Keep in closer order by closing upon the van. |
| 6 | Keep in open order. |
| 7 | Keep in more open order than you are at present. |
| 8 | Form the first order of steaming. |
| 9 | Form the second order of steaming. |
| 5120 | Form the third order of steaming. |
| 1 | Form the order of battle, or line. |
| 2 | Form the prescribed order of battle. |
| 3 | Form the order of retreat. |
| 4 | Form the first order of sailing. |
| 5 | Form the second order of sailing. |
| 6 | Form the third order of sailing. |
| 7 | Form the fifth order of sailing. |
| 8 | Form the order of sailing in two columns, in lines ahead. |
| 9 | Form the order of sailing in three columns, in lines ahead. |
| 5130 | Order-ed-ing-s. |
| 1 | I am ordered to. |
| 2 | Have received orders to. |
| 3 | Have not received orders. |
| 4 | Have orders for. |
| 5 | Have you any orders for? |
| 6 | My orders are to. |
| 7 | In bad order. |
| 8 | In good order. |
| 9 | It is the order of the. |
| 5140 | Shall I order? |
| 1 | Sailing orders. |
| 2 | Secret orders. |
| 3 | You will order. |
| 4 | Your orders. |
| 5 | Under sailing orders. |
| 5146 | Will you order? |

| Nos. | OUT |
|---|---|
| 5147 | With sealed orders. |
| 8 | Without orders. |
| 9 | Ordinarily. |
| 5150 | Ordnance. |
| 1 | Ordnance outfits. (*See* For boats, in the Ordnance Manual.) |
| 2 | Ordnance stores. |
| 3 | My ordnance supplies are running low. |
| 4 | The enemy is provided with heavy ordnance. |
| 5 | Send ordnance stores to. |
| 6 | Ordnance stores, send for, to. |
| 7 | Organize-d-ing. |
| 8 | Organization-s. |
| 9 | Origin. |
| 5160 | Original-ly-ity. |
| 1 | Oscillate-d-ing. |
| 2 | Oscillation-s. |
| 3 | Oscillations of the barometer. |
| 4 | Ostensible-y. |
| 5 | Ostentation. |
| 6 | Ostentatious-ly. |
| 7 | Other-s. |
| 8 | Otherwise. |
| 9 | Ought. |
| 5170 | They ought to. |
| 1 | They ought not to. |
| 2 | You ought to. |
| 3 | You ought not to. |
| 4 | We ought to. |
| 5 | We ought not to. |
| 6 | Ounce-s. |
| 7 | Our-s. |
| 8 | Ourself-ves. |
| 9 | Our country expects every man to do his whole duty. |
| 5180 | Out-er. |
| 1 | Came out. |
| 2 | Come out. |
| 3 | Coming out. |
| 4 | Go-es, or going, out. |
| 5 | Out of, or from. |
| 6 | Outlaw-ed. |
| 7 | Outlet-s. |
| 8 | Outnumber-ed. |
| 9 | Outrage-d-ing-s. |
| 5190 | Outrageous-ly. |
| 5191 | Outsail-ed-ing-s. |

| Nos. | OUT | Nos. | PAR |
|---|---|---|---|
| 5192 | Outside. | 5243 | Paddle wheels are damaged. |
| 3 | Outward-ly. | 4 | Paddle wheels are not damaged. |
| 4 | Outward bound. | 5 | Paddle wheels. |
| 5 | Outworks. | 6 | Paddles for row-boats. |
| 6 | Overrate-d-ing-s. | 7 | Paddles, use, instead of oars. |
| 7 | Overawe-d-ing-s. | 8 | Page-d-ing-s. |
| 8 | Overbalance-d-ing-s. | 9 | Pain-ed-ing-s. |
| 9 | Overboard. | 5250 | Painful-ly. |
| 5200 | Man-men overboard. | 1 | It is with much pain that. |
| 1 | Overcharge-d-ing-s. | 2 | Painful intelligence has been received from. |
| 2 | Overflow-ed-ing-s. | 3 | Paint-s. |
| 3 | Overhaul-ed-ing-s. | 4 | Black paint. |
| 4 | Overhaul the strange boat, or vessel. | 5 | Green paint. |
| 5 | Overlay-ed-ing-s. | 6 | Red paint. |
| 6 | Overload-ed-ing-s. | 7 | White paint. |
| 7 | Overlook-ed-ing-s. | 8 | Yellow paint. |
| 8 | Overpower-ed-ing-s. | 9 | Paint ship. |
| 9 | Overpress-ed-ing-es. | 5260 | Painting. |
| 5210 | Do not overpress. | 1 | Boat-s. |
| 1 | She is overpressed. | 2 | Ship. |
| 2 | She is not overpressed. | 3 | Painters. |
| 3 | This vessel is overpressed. | 4 | In want of painters. |
| 4 | Overrule-d-ing-s. | 5 | Send painters to. |
| 5 | Overrun-s-ning-ran. | 6 | Pair-s. |
| 6 | Oversight-s. | 7 | Palliate-d-ing-s. |
| 7 | Overtake-took-en-s. | 8 | Palliation-s. |
| 8 | Overthrow-threw-n. | 9 | Palpable-y. |
| 9 | Overture-s. | 5270 | Pamphlet-s. |
| 5220 | Overturn-ed-ing-s. | 1 | Panic-s. |
| 1 | Overwhelm-ed-ing-s. | 2 | Paper-s. |
| 2 | Owe-d-ing-s. | 3 | Bring the papers to me. |
| 3 | What was it owing to? | 4 | Examine her papers. |
| 4 | It was owing to. | 5 | Has false papers. |
| 5 | Own-ed-ing-s. | 6 | Has no papers. |
| 6 | Owner-s. | 7 | Papers are all right. |
| 7 | Pacific. | 8 | Papers look suspicious. |
| 8 | Pacific ocean. | 9 | Some of the papers. |
| 9 | Pacification. | 5280 | Want writing paper. |
| 5230 | Pacify-ied-ies-ing. | 1 | Want official paper. |
| 1 | Pack-s-ing. | 2 | Want cartridge paper. |
| 2 | Pack ice. | 3 | Parade-d-ing-s. |
| 3 | Package-s. | 4 | Paragraph-s. |
| 4 | Packet-s. | 5 | Naval Regulations, paragraph No. |
| 5 | By the packet-s. | 6 | Parallel-s. |
| 6 | Is a packet going to? | 7 | Parallax. |
| 7 | Is a packet from. | 8 | Paralyse-d-ing-s. |
| 8 | Packet has arrived from. | 5289 | Parapet-s. |
| 9 | Packet has sailed for. | | |
| 5240 | Packet will sail for. | | |
| 1 | Paddle-s. | | |
| 5242 | Paddle box. | | |

| Nos. | PAR |
|---|---|
| 5290 | Parbuckle-d-s-ing. |
| 1 | Parcel-s. |
| 2 | Pardon-ed-ing-s. |
| 3 | Parent-s. |
| 4 | Parentage. |
| 5 | Park-s. |
| 6 | Park of artillery. |
| 7 | Parley-ied-ing. |
| 8 | Parole-s. |
| 9 | Parole the prisoners. |
| 5300 | Part-ed-ing-s. |
| 1 | A small part of the. |
| 2 | A large part of the. |
| 3 | Part of the. |
| 4 | The greater part of the. |
| 5 | What part of the? |
| 6 | Part company. |
| 7 | Do not part company. |
| 8 | May I part company? |
| 9 | Has, or have, parted cable-s. |
| 5310 | Am afraid my cable will part. |
| 1 | When did you part company. |
| 2 | Parted company during the night. |
| 3 | If you part your cables, beach your vessel where assistance can be rendered by the people on shore, as shown by compass signal. |
| 4 | Partake-n-ing-took-s. |
| 5 | Partial-ly. |
| 6 | Partiality-ies. |
| 7 | Participate-d-ing. |
| 8 | Participation. |
| 9 | Particular-ly. |
| 5320 | Be very particular to. |
| 1 | In every particular. |
| 2 | Particularize-d-ing-s. |
| 3 | Partisan-s. |
| 4 | Partisan warfare. |
| 5 | Party-ies. |
| 6 | Pass-ed-ing. |
| 7 | Can pass. |
| 8 | Cannot pass. |
| 9 | Pass near me. |
| 5330 | Pass along the line. |
| 1 | Have you ever passed the? |
| 5332 | Have passed. |

| Nos. | PEA |
|---|---|
| 5333 | Have never passed. |
| 4 | Passage-s. |
| 5 | After a passage of. |
| 6 | An intricate passage. |
| 7 | An easy passage. |
| 8 | Can you give passage to? |
| 9 | Is there a passage? |
| 5340 | There is a passage. |
| 1 | There is no passage. |
| 2 | The passage is. |
| 3 | Passenger-s. |
| 4 | Is a passenger. |
| 5 | Send all passengers. |
| 6 | You must not take any passenger-s on board. |
| 7 | Passport-s. |
| 8 | Patch-ed-ing. |
| 9 | Patches. |
| 5350 | Coral patches. |
| 1 | Gulf weed patches. |
| 2 | Patient-ly. |
| 3 | Patience. |
| 4 | Patients. |
| 5 | Patriotic. |
| 6 | Patriotism. |
| 7 | Patrol-led-ling-s. |
| 8 | Call in all patrols. |
| 9 | Send out patrolling party-ies. |
| 5360 | Pattern-s. |
| 1 | Pause-d-ing-s. |
| 2 | Paymaster-s. |
| 3 | Is your paymast'r in funds? |
| 4 | Send paymaster on board. |
| 5 | Paymaster's clerk. |
| 6 | Paymaster's steward. |
| 7 | Paid. |
| 8 | Pay-ed-ing. |
| 9 | Paid on the. |
| 5370 | To be paid. |
| 1 | To be paid off. |
| 2 | When were they paid? |
| 3 | Payment-s. |
| 4 | Peace-ful-ly. |
| 5 | Peace has been restored between the nations whose flags are, or will be, exhibited. |
| 5376 | Peace treaty was signed on the day which will be shown by numeral sig'l. |

| Nos. | PEA |
|---|---|
| 5377 | Every body appears to be peacefully inclined, where I am, or havebeen. |
| 8 | Peak-ed-ing-s. |
| 9 | Peasant-ry. |
| 5380 | Peasantry are arming. |
| 1 | Peasantry are quiet. |
| 2 | Peas. |
| 3 | Peculate-d-ing-s. |
| 4 | Peculation-s. |
| 5 | Peculiar-ly. |
| 6 | Pecuniary. |
| 7 | Pen-s. |
| 8 | Quill pens. |
| 9 | Steel pens. |
| 5390 | Pencils. |
| 1 | Lead pencils. |
| 2 | Slate pencils. |
| 3 | Penalty-ies. |
| 4 | Penetrate-d-ing-s. |
| 5 | Penetration-s. |
| 6 | Peninsula-s. |
| 7 | Penitent-s. |
| 8 | Pension-s. |
| 9 | Pensioner-s. |
| 5400 | People. |
| 1 | Perceive-d-ing. |
| 2 | Perception-s. |
| 3 | Percussion. |
| 4 | Percussion caps. |
| 5 | Percussion locks. |
| 6 | Percussion powder. |
| 7 | Peremptory-ily. |
| 8 | Perfect-ed-ing. |
| 9 | By no means perfect. |
| 5410 | Is it perfect? |
| 1 | The most perfect. |
| 2 | Perfidy-ies. |
| 3 | Perfidious-ly-ness. |
| 4 | Perforate-d-ing-s. |
| 5 | Perforation-s. |
| 6 | Perform-ed-ing. |
| 7 | Performance-s. |
| 8 | Perhaps. |
| 9 | Peril-s. |
| 5420 | Perilous. |
| 1 | A very perilous undertaking. |
| 2 | In a situation of great peril. |
| 3 | Period-s. |
| 4 | Periodical-ly. |
| 5425 | Perish-ed-ing. |

| Nos. | PIE |
|---|---|
| 5426 | Perishable. |
| 7 | Perjure-d-ing-s. |
| 8 | Permanent-ly. |
| 9 | Permit-ted-ting-s. |
| 5430 | Cannot permit. |
| 1 | Will permit. |
| 2 | Will you permit. |
| 3 | Permission-s. |
| 4 | With permission. |
| 5 | Without permission. |
| 6 | Pernicious-ly. |
| 7 | Perpendicular-ly. |
| 8 | Perpetuate-d-ing-s. |
| 9 | Perpetuation-s. |
| 5440 | Perplex-ed-ing-es. |
| 1 | Persecute-d-ing-s. |
| 2 | Persecution-s. |
| 3 | Persevere-d-ing-s. |
| 4 | Perseverance. |
| 5 | Persist-ed-ing-s. |
| 6 | Persistence. |
| 7 | Person-s. |
| 8 | Any person. |
| 9 | Have you any person? |
| 5450 | No person. |
| 1 | Persuade-d-ing-ion-s. |
| 2 | Am persuaded that. |
| 3 | After much persuasion. |
| 4 | Cannot persuade. |
| 5 | Try to persuade. |
| 6 | Peruse-d-ing-s. |
| 7 | Perusal-s. |
| 8 | Pervade-d-ing-s. |
| 9 | Perverse-ly. |
| 5460 | Perversion-s. |
| 1 | Pestilence-tial. |
| 2 | Petition-ed-ing-s. |
| 3 | Petitioner-s. |
| 4 | Pity. |
| 5 | Physical-ly. |
| 6 | Physician-s. |
| 7 | Pick-ed-ing. |
| 8 | Pick up the boat-s adrift. |
| 9 | Pick up a boat in the direction shown by compass signal. |
| 5470 | Pick up my anchor. |
| 1 | Have picked up a boat. |
| 2 | Pickaxe-s. |
| 3 | Pier-s. |
| 4 | Pierhead-s. |
| 5475 | Pierce-d-ing. |

| Nos. | PIG | Nos. | PLU |
|---|---|---|---|
| 5476 | Pig ballast. | 5526 | This place. |
| 7 | Pike-s. | 7 | The place of rendezvous. |
| 8 | Boarding pikes. | 8 | The place decided upon. |
| 9 | Pile-d-ing-s. | 9 | Plain-ly. |
| 5480 | Pillage-d-ing. | 5530 | Plan-ned-ning-s. |
| 1 | Pilot-s. | 1 | A bad plan. |
| 2 | Have you a pilot for? | 2 | A good plan. |
| 3 | Have a pilot for. | 3 | A plan of the harbor. |
| 4 | Have no pilot for. | 4 | A plan of the place. |
| 5 | Send your pilot to the. | 5 | A plan of the city. |
| 6 | Send on shore for pilot-s. | 6 | A plan of the defences. |
| 7 | Send me your coast pilot. | 7 | A plan of attack. |
| 8 | Is your coast pilot capable and reliable. | 8 | A plan of battle. |
| | | 9 | A plan for your consideration. |
| 9 | Will send for a pilot. | | |
| 5490 | A bad pilot. | 5540 | The enemy is evidently planning for an attack. |
| 1 | A good pilot. | | |
| 2 | Pilotage-d-ing. | 1 | Plank-s. |
| 3 | Pilot flag-s. | 2 | In want of plank. |
| 4 | Hoist your pilot flag. | 3 | Plate-d-ing-s. |
| 5 | Haul down your pilot flag. | 4 | Boiler plate-s. |
| 6 | Pint-s. | 5 | Armor plate-s. |
| 7 | Pipe-s. | 6 | Iron-plated vessel-s. |
| 8 | Blow pipe-s. | 7 | Plausible-y. |
| 9 | Copper pipe. | 8 | Play-ed-ing-s. |
| 5500 | Hawse pipe-s. | 9 | Plea-s. |
| 1 | Iron pipe. | 5550 | Plead-ed-ing-s. |
| 2 | Lead pipe-s. | 1 | Pleasant-ly. |
| 3 | Steam pipe-s. | 2 | Please-d-ing-ure. |
| 4 | Water pipe-s. | 3 | I cannot have the pleasure of. |
| 5 | Pirate-s. | | |
| 6 | Are pirates-ical. | 4 | I have had the pleasure of. |
| 7 | Look-s like pirate-s. | 5 | Shall, or may I have the pleasure? |
| 8 | Piracy-ies. | | |
| 9 | Pistol-s. | 6 | With great pleasure. |
| 5510 | In want of boardi'g pistols. | 7 | Pledge-d-ing-s. |
| 1 | In want of revolver pistols. | 8 | Plenty-iful-ly-ness. |
| 2 | In want of pistol ammunition. | 9 | Pliant-ly. |
| | | 5560 | Plomer-block-s. |
| 3 | Send me boarding pistols. | 1 | Plot-ted-ting-s. |
| 4 | Send me revolver pistols. | 2 | Plug-s. |
| 5 | Send me pistol ammunit'n. | 3 | Hawse plugs. |
| 6 | Piston-s. | 4 | Shot plugs. |
| 7 | Piston rod-s. | 5 | Vent plugs. |
| 8 | Pitch-ed-ing-es. | 6 | Plug-ged-ging. |
| 9 | Pitches very badly. | 7 | Holes are all plugged. |
| 5520 | Pity-iable. | 8 | Tubes are all plugged. |
| 1 | Place-d-ing-s. | 9 | Tubes require to be plugged. |
| 2 | At what place? | | |
| 3 | Is, or are placed. | 5570 | Plumber-s. |
| 4 | Not placed. | 1 | Plunder-ed-ing. |
| 5525 | That place. | 5572 | Forbid all plundering. |

| Nos. | PLU | Nos. | POW |
|---|---|---|---|
| 5573 | Do not allow any plundering. | 5618 | Proceed into the nearest port. |
| 4 | Is, or are plundering. | 9 | Reconnoitre the port and report. |
| 5 | Plunderer-s. | 5620 | The nearest port. |
| 6 | Point-ed-ing ly-s. | 1 | What port are you? |
| 7 | Close around the point. | 2 | What port is the vessel? |
| 8 | Not well pointed. | 3 | Portable. |
| 9 | Round the point. | 4 | Portend-s. |
| 5580 | Inside of the point. | 5 | Portion-s. |
| 1 | Outside of the point. | 6 | Position-s. |
| 2 | Poison-ed-ing-s. | 7 | In the same position-s. |
| 3 | Poisonous. | 8 | Not in the same position-s. |
| 4 | Pole-s. | 9 | Take proper positions. |
| 5 | Polar. | 5630 | Take assigned positions. |
| 6 | Police. | 1 | Positive-ly. |
| 7 | Police officer-s. | 2 | Is, or are very positive. |
| 8 | Policy-ies. | 3 | Possess-ed-ing-es. |
| 9 | Polite-ly-ness. | 4 | Do you possess? |
| 5590 | Politic-s. | 5 | Do not possess. |
| 1 | Politician-s. | 6 | Possession-s. |
| 2 | Pompous-ly. | 7 | Do not take possession of the. |
| 3 | Poop. | 8 | In your possession. |
| 4 | Poop-deck-ed. | 9 | Take possession of the. |
| 5 | Poor. | 5640 | Possible-y. |
| 6 | Popular-ity. | 1 | Possibility-ies. |
| 7 | Populace. | 2 | Post. Mail-s. |
| 8 | Population-s. | 3 | To-day's post; mail. |
| 9 | Port-s. | 4 | To-morrow's post; mail. |
| 5600 | Port beam. | 5 | Yesterday's post; mail. |
| 1 | Port bow. | 6 | Post-office-s. |
| 2 | Port side. | 7 | To the post-office. |
| 3 | Port quarter. | 8 | From the post-office. |
| 4 | Port tack-s. | 9 | P. M. Post-meridian. |
| 5 | Port gun-s. | 5650 | Postpone-d-ing-s. |
| 6 | Port fire-s. | 1 | Posture-s. |
| 7 | Port helm. | 2 | Posture of affairs. |
| 8 | Port shore. | 3 | Potatoes. |
| 9 | Port side of the harbor or bay. | 4 | Irish potatoes. |
| 5610 | Are you acquainted with the port? | 5 | Sweet potatoes. |
| 1 | Haul your wind on port tack. | 6 | Poultry. |
| 2 | Heave to on the port tack. | 7 | Pound-s. |
| 3 | Into port, go. | 8 | Pounder-s. |
| 4 | Come out of port. | 9 | Pour-ed-ing-s. |
| 5 | I am acquainted with the port. | 5660 | Poverty. |
| 6 | I am not acquainted with the port. | 1 | Powder. |
| 5617 | Proceed into the port indicated. | 2 | Powder is damaged. |
| | | 3 | Powder magazine is drowned. |
| | | 4 | Powder is expended. |
| | | 5665 | Powder is running short. |

| Nos. | POW |
|---|---|
| 5666 | Can spare you powder. |
| 7 | Cannot spare you powder. |
| 8 | Can you spare me powder? |
| 9 | Short of powder. |
| 5670 | Send for powder. |
| 1 | Power. |
| 2 | Horse power. |
| 3 | Practice. |
| 4 | Practices. |
| 5 | Practicable. |
| 6 | A practicable breach. |
| 7 | Do you think it practicable? |
| 8 | It is practicable. |
| 9 | It is not practicable. |
| 5680 | Should it prove to be practicable. |
| 1 | Praise-d-ing-s. |
| 2 | Praiseworthy. |
| 3 | Pratique. |
| 4 | Granted pratique. |
| 5 | Refused pratique. |
| 6 | Precarious-ly. |
| 7 | Precaution-ary. |
| 8 | Take every precaution. |
| 9 | Great precaution is necessary. |
| 5690 | Precede-d-ing-s. |
| 1 | Precedence. |
| 2 | Precedent-s. |
| 3 | Precipice-s. |
| 4 | Precipitate-d-ing-tion. |
| 5 | Precipitous. |
| 6 | Precise-ly-ness. |
| 7 | Precision. |
| 8 | Preconcert-ed-ing. |
| 9 | Predecessor-s. |
| 5700 | Predetermine-d-ing. |
| 1 | Predetermination-s. |
| 2 | Predicament. |
| 3 | An awkward predicam'nt. |
| 4 | Predict-ed-ing-s. |
| 5 | Prediction-s. |
| 6 | Predispose-d-ing-s. |
| 7 | Predominate-d-ing-s. |
| 8 | Preëminent-ly. |
| 9 | Preëngage-d-ing-ment-s. |
| 5710 | Prefer-red-ring-s. |
| 1 | Which do you prefer? |
| 2 | Would prefer. |
| 3 | Preferable-y. |
| 5714 | Is preferable to. |

| Nos. | PRE |
|---|---|
| 5715 | Prejudice-d-ing-s. |
| 6 | Prejudicial-ly. |
| 7 | Preliminary-ies-ily. |
| 8 | Premature-ly. |
| 9 | Premeditate-d-ing-s. |
| 5720 | Premeditation. |
| 1 | Premium-s. |
| 2 | Prepare-d-ing-s. |
| 3 | Prepare buoys for buoying the channel-s. |
| 4 | Preparation-s. |
| 5 | Preparations are making for. |
| 6 | Preponderance. |
| 7 | Prerogative-s. |
| 8 | Prescribe-d-ing-ption-s. |
| 9 | Prescriptive right-s. |
| 5730 | Present-ed-ing. |
| 1 | At present. |
| 2 | Not at present. |
| 3 | Presence. |
| 4 | Your presence is necessary. |
| 5 | Your presence is desired. |
| 6 | Preserve-d-ing. |
| 7 | Preservation. |
| 8 | Preside-d-ing-s. |
| 9 | Presiding officer. |
| 5740 | President. |
| 1 | President of the court. |
| 2 | President of the United States. |
| 3 | Press-ed-ing-es. |
| 4 | Pressure-s. |
| 5 | Presume-d-ing-s. |
| 6 | Presumption-s. |
| 7 | Presumptive. |
| 8 | Presumptuous. |
| 9 | Pretend-ed-ing-s. |
| 5750 | Pretence-sion-s. |
| 1 | Prevail-ed-ing-s. |
| 2 | Could you prevail upon? |
| 3 | Could not prevail upon. |
| 4 | Cannot prevail upon. |
| 5 | Did you prevail upon? |
| 6 | Has, or have prevailed upon. |
| 7 | Prevailing weather. |
| 8 | Prevailing winds. |
| 9 | Prevailing currents. |
| 5760 | Prevalence-t. |
| 1 | Prevent-ed-ing-s. |
| 5762 | Cannot prevent. |

| Nos. | PRE |
|---|---|
| 5763 | Could not prevent. |
| 4 | Must prevent. |
| 5 | Preventer brace-s. |
| 6 | Previous-ly. |
| 7 | Prey. |
| 8 | Price-s. |
| 9 | Pride-d-ing. |
| 5770 | Primary-ily. |
| 1 | Primer-s. |
| 2 | Priming. |
| 3 | Prince-ss. |
| 4 | Principal-ly. |
| 5 | Principle-s. |
| 6 | Print-ed-ing. |
| 7 | Printing press-es. |
| 8 | Printing materials. |
| 9 | Printer-s. |
| 5780 | Prior-ity. |
| 1 | Prison-s. |
| 2 | Prisoner-s. |
| 3 | Have you any prisoners? |
| 4 | I have no prisoners. |
| 5 | I have prisoners. |
| 6 | Is a prisoner. |
| 7 | Is not a prisoner. |
| 8 | Land all prisoners to. |
| 9 | Look out for the prisoners. |
| 5790 | Put all prisoners in confinement. |
| 1 | Release all prisoners. |
| 2 | Receive the prisoners. |
| 3 | See that the prisoners do not escape. |
| 4 | Private. |
| 5 | Private signal, make your. |
| 6 | Privates. |
| 7 | Privacy-tely. |
| 8 | Privateer-s. |
| 9 | Is a privateer, or are privateers. |
| 5800 | Enemy's privateer-s. |
| 1 | Privilege-d-s. |
| 2 | Privity. |
| 3 | Prize-s. |
| 4 | Bring the prize to me. |
| 5 | Is a prize to the. |
| 6 | Send the prize to. |
| 7 | The prize-s. |
| 8 | Probable-y-ility-ies. |
| 9 | It is probable. |
| 5810 | It is not probable. |
| 5811 | Proceed-ed-ing-s. |

| Nos. | PRO |
|---|---|
| 5812 | Am not ready to proceed. |
| 3 | Are you ready to proceed on the service ordered? |
| 4 | Has, or have proceeded. |
| 5 | Has, or have not proce'ded. |
| 6 | I am ready to proceed. |
| 7 | I must proceed immediately. |
| 8 | Proceed immediately to. |
| 9 | Proceed when ready to. |
| 5820 | Proceed into port and return without unnecessary delay with all the provisions you can carry. |
| 1 | Proceed with flag of truce and communicate with the enemy; deliver the dispatches, and return with answers. |
| 2 | Proceed into port for supplies. |
| 3 | When will you be ready to proceed on the service ordered? |
| 4 | You will proceed to. |
| 5 | You will proceed immediately to. |
| 6 | Proclaim-ed-ing-s. |
| 7 | Proclamation-s. |
| 8 | Procure-d-ing-s. |
| 9 | Can procure. |
| 5830 | Cannot procure. |
| 1 | Will procure. |
| 2 | Produce-d-ing-s. |
| 3 | Profess-ed-ing-s. |
| 4 | Profit-s-able-y. |
| 5 | Progress-es. |
| 6 | Prohibit-ed-ing-s. |
| 7 | Project-s. |
| 8 | Prolong-ed-ing-s. |
| 9 | Prominent-ly. |
| 5840 | Promise-d-ing-s. |
| 1 | Promontory-ies. |
| 2 | Promote-d-ing-s. |
| 3 | Promotion-s. |
| 4 | Prompt-ed-ing-s. |
| 5 | Promptness-itude. |
| 6 | With promptitude. |
| 7 | Promulgate-d-ing-s. |
| 8 | Propel-led-ling-s. |
| 9 | Propeller-s. |
| 5850 | Proper-ly. |

| Nos. | PRO |
|---|---|
| 5851 | Propriety-ies. |
| 2 | Propitious-ly. |
| 3 | Proportion-s. |
| 4 | Propose-d-ing. |
| 5 | It is, or has been proposed. |
| 6 | Proscribe-d-ing-s. |
| 7 | Prosecute-d-ing-s. |
| 8 | Prosecution-s. |
| 9 | Prospect-s-ive-ly. |
| 5860 | Protect-ed-ing-s. |
| 1 | Protect the unarmed vessels or boats. |
| 2 | Protection-s. |
| 3 | Protest-ed-ing-s. |
| 4 | Protract-ed-ing-s. |
| 5 | Proud-ly. |
| 6 | Prove-d-s. Proof-s. |
| 7 | Provide-d-ing-s. |
| 8 | Provisions. |
| 9 | Can you spare me provisions? |
| 5870 | Bring off provisions. |
| 1 | Endeavor to obtain provisions. |
| 2 | Are the provisions cook'd? |
| 3 | Shall I cook provisions? |
| 4 | Provisions, cook, for the number of days and number of men indicated by signal. |
| 5 | Short of provisions. |
| 6 | Want provisions landed. |
| 7 | Provoke-d-ing-s. |
| 8 | Provocation-s. |
| 9 | Provost Martial-s. |
| 5880 | Prudent-ly. |
| 1 | Prudence. |
| 2 | Pry-ed-ing-ies. |
| 3 | Public-ly. |
| 4 | Publicity. |
| 5 | Pull-ing-s. |
| 6 | Pump-s. |
| 7 | Deck pumps. |
| 8 | Hand pump-s. |
| 9 | Steam pumps. |
| 5890 | Punctual-ly. |
| 1 | Punctuality. |
| 2 | Punish-ed-ing-ment-s. |
| 3 | Purchase-d-ing-s. |
| 4 | Pure-ly. |
| 5 | Purify-ied-ies. |
| 5896 | Purport-s. |

| Nos. | RAI |
|---|---|
| 5897 | Purpose-s. |
| 8 | Pursuant-ce. |
| 9 | Pursue-d-ing-s-it. |
| 5900 | In pursuit of. |
| 1 | Push-ed-ing-es. |
| 2 | Pusillanimous. |
| 3 | Put. |
| 4 | Putrid. |
| 5 | Putrify-ied-ing-ies. |
| 6 | Puzzle-d-ing-s. |
| 7 | Quadrant-s. |
| 8 | Qualify-ied-ies. |
| 9 | Quality-ies. |
| 5910 | Of a bad quality. |
| 1 | Of a good quality. |
| 2 | Quantity-ies. |
| 3 | A considerable quantity. |
| 4 | A small quantity. |
| 5 | What quantity? |
| 6 | Quarantine-d-ing-s. |
| 7 | Quarantine ground-s. |
| 8 | Quarrel-ed-ing-s-some. |
| 9 | Quart-s. |
| 5920 | Quarter. |
| 1 | In what quarter? |
| 2 | On the port quarter. |
| 3 | On the starboard quarter. |
| 4 | Quarters. |
| 5 | At general quarters. |
| 6 | At night quarters. |
| 7 | Quarter deck. |
| 8 | Quarter master-s. |
| 9 | Quarter watch-es. |
| 5930 | Quell-ed-ing-s. |
| 1 | Query-ies. |
| 2 | Question-ed-ing-s. |
| 3 | Quibble-d-ing-s. |
| 4 | Quick-ly. |
| 5 | As quickly as possible. |
| 6 | Quicksand-s. |
| 7 | Quicksilver. |
| 8 | Quick-match-es. |
| 9 | Quitting. |
| 5940 | Quite. |
| 1 | Quoin-s. |
| 2 | Quote-d-ing-s. |
| 3 | Quotation-s. |
| 4 | Race-d-ing-s. |
| 5 | Propeller races badly. |
| 6 | Rage-d-ing-s. |
| 7 | Rail-s. |
| 5948 | Railroad-s. |

| Nos. | RAI |
|---|---|
| 5949 | Railroad cars. |
| 5950 | Railroad iron. |
| 1 | Railroad track-s. |
| 2 | Railroad is destroyed. |
| 3 | Railroad is in our possession. |
| 4 | Railroad is in possession of the enemy. |
| 5 | Rain-ed-ing-y-s. |
| 6 | Raise-d-ing-s. |
| 7 | Raisins. |
| 8 | Rake-d-ing-s. |
| 9 | Rakish-ly. |
| 5960 | Rally-ies-ing-ied. |
| 1 | Ram-s. |
| 2 | Ram the enemy's principal vessel. |
| 3 | Ram whenever you can. |
| 4 | Rammer-s. |
| 5 | Rammers and spongers. |
| 6 | Rampart-s. |
| 7 | Rancid. |
| 8 | Random. |
| 9 | At random. |
| 5970 | Random firing. |
| 1 | Random shots. |
| 2 | Range-s. |
| 3 | Within range. |
| 4 | Not within range. |
| 5 | Are you within range? |
| 6 | What is the range? |
| 7 | Range-ing. |
| 8 | Range alongside. |
| 9 | Ranging alongside. |
| 5980 | Rank-s. |
| 1 | Is of superior rank. |
| 2 | Is of inferior rank. |
| 3 | Rank and file. |
| 4 | What is his rank? |
| 5 | Rapid-ly. |
| 6 | Rapidity. |
| 7 | Rapture-s-ous-ly. |
| 8 | Rare-ly. |
| 9 | Rash-ly-ness. |
| 5990 | Rats. |
| 1 | Rate-d-ing-s. |
| 2 | At a great rate. |
| 3 | What rate is she? |
| 4 | Rate of sailing, try. |
| 5 | Rate of steaming, try. |
| 6 | Rather. |
| 5997 | Ratify-ied-ing-ies. |

| Nos. | REC |
|---|---|
| 5998 | Ratification-s. |
| 9 | Rations. |
| 6000 | Rations of bread. |
| 1 | Rations of meat. |
| 2 | Half rations. |
| 3 | Whole rations. |
| 4 | Two-thirds rations. |
| 5 | Send rations to the. |
| 6 | Send rations for the. |
| 7 | Send the number of rations indicated by numeral signal. |
| 8 | Rational-ly. |
| 9 | Rattle-d-ing-s. |
| 6010 | Rattle down rigging. |
| 1 | Ravage-d-ing-s. |
| 2 | Raw. |
| 3 | Raw hide-s. |
| 4 | Reach-ed-ing-es. |
| 5 | Can you reach? |
| 6 | I can reach. |
| 7 | Reaction-ary. |
| 8 | Read-ing-s. |
| 9 | Have you read? |
| 6020 | I have read. |
| 1 | I have not read. |
| 2 | Ready-iness. |
| 3 | I am ready. |
| 4 | I am not ready. |
| 5 | Can be ready very soon. |
| 6 | When will you be ready? |
| 7 | Hold yourself in readiness. |
| 8 | Readily. |
| 9 | Real-ly-ity-ities. |
| 6030 | Reap-ed-ing. |
| 1 | Rear. |
| 2 | From the rear. |
| 3 | In the rear. |
| 4 | To the rear. |
| 5 | Rear guard. |
| 6 | Rear Admiral. |
| 7 | Rear Admiral's flag. |
| 8 | Reason. |
| 9 | Do not know the reason. |
| 6040 | What is the reason? |
| 1 | Reassemble-d-ing-age. |
| 2 | Rebuild-ing-s. |
| 3 | Recall-ed-ing-s. |
| 4 | A general recall. |
| 5 | Hoist the general recall. |
| 6 | Recall of boats. |
| 6047 | Recall all chasing vessels. |

| Nos. | REC |
|---|---|
| 6048 | Recapture-d-ing-s. |
| 9 | Is a recapture. |
| 6050 | Has been recaptured. |
| 1 | Recede-ing-s. |
| 2 | Receive-d-ing-s. |
| 3 | Receipt-s. |
| 4 | Recent-ly. |
| 5 | Recess-es. |
| 6 | Reciprocity-ies. |
| 7 | Reckon-ed-ing-s. |
| 8 | Dead reckoning. |
| 9 | Reclaim-ed-ing-s. |
| 6060 | Recognize-d-ing-s. |
| 1 | Recoil-ed-ing-s. |
| 2 | Recollect-ed-ing-s. |
| 3 | Recommence-d-ing-ment. |
| 4 | Recommences. |
| 5 | Recommend-ed-ing-s. |
| 6 | Can recommend. |
| 7 | Cannot recommend. |
| 8 | Would not recommend. |
| 9 | Recommendation-s. |
| 6070 | Recompense-d-ing-s. |
| 1 | Reconcile-d-ing-s. |
| 2 | Reconciliation-s. |
| 3 | Is, or are, reconciled. |
| 4 | Is, or are, not reconciled. |
| 5 | Reconnoiter-ed-ing-s. |
| 6 | I have reconnoitered the enemy. |
| 7 | Reconnoiter the enemy's position. |
| 8 | Reconnoitering party-ies, send. |
| 9 | Record-s. |
| 6080 | Recorder-s. |
| 1 | Recourse. |
| 2 | Recover-ed-ing-s. |
| 3 | Quite recovered. |
| 4 | Have recovered the. |
| 5 | Have not been able to recover the. |
| 6 | Recreation-s. |
| 7 | Recruit-ed-ing-s. |
| 8 | Recruiting party-ies. |
| 9 | Rectify-ied-ing-ies. |
| 6090 | Recur-red-ring-s. |
| 1 | Red. |
| 2 | Reddish color. |
| 3 | Redeem-ed-ing-s. |
| 4 | Redoubt-s. |
| 6095 | Redress-ed-ing-es. |

| Nos. | REF |
|---|---|
| 6096 | Reduce-d-ing-s. |
| 7 | Reduction-s. |
| 8 | Reef-s. |
| 9 | A dangerous reef. |
| 6100 | A reef of rocks. |
| 1 | Look out for reefs. |
| 2 | Has run upon a reef. |
| 3 | Reef-ed ing-s. |
| 4 | Close reef your sails. |
| 5 | Take in one reef. |
| 6 | Take in two reefs. |
| 7 | Take in three reefs. |
| 8 | Take one reef in foresail. |
| 9 | Take one reef in mainsail. |
| 6110 | Shake out one reef. |
| 1 | Shake out two reefs. |
| 2 | Shake out all reefs. |
| 3 | Reëstablish-ed-ing-es. |
| 4 | Reëstablish the force in its position. |
| 5 | Reëstablished, I am, or we are. |
| 6 | Reeve-rove-ing-s. |
| 7 | Reeve running rigging. |
| 8 | Refer-red-ring-s. |
| 9 | Refit-ted-ting-s. |
| 6120 | In want of refitting-s. |
| 1 | Refit as soon as possible. |
| 2 | Reform-ed-ing-s. |
| 3 | Reform the line. |
| 4 | Reform the order. |
| 5 | Refract-ed-ing-ion-s. |
| 6 | Refrain-ed ing-s. |
| 7 | Refresh-ed-ing. |
| 8 | Refreshment-s. |
| 9 | Proceed to the place indicated for refreshments for the people. |
| 6130 | Permission is given to send for refreshments for the crews. |
| 1 | The vessel designated has refreshments on board. |
| 2 | Refuge. |
| 3 | Take refuge. |
| 4 | Harbor of refuge. |
| 5 | Seek a harbor of refuge. |
| 6 | Refugee-s. |
| 7 | Refuse-d-ing-s. |
| 8 | Has, or have, refused. |
| 9 | Refusal-s. |
| 6140 | Refute-d-ing-ation-s. |

| Nos. | REG |
|---|---|
| 6141 | Regain-ed-ing-s. |
| 2 | Can you regain your position? |
| 3 | I can regain my position. |
| 4 | Regain, if possible, your position. |
| 5 | Regard-ed-ing-s. |
| 6 | Regardless. |
| 7 | Regiment-s. |
| 8 | Regret-ed-ing-s. |
| 9 | Is, or are, greatly regretted. |
| 6150 | Very much regret. |
| 1 | Regular-ly-ity. |
| 2 | By no means regular. |
| 3 | The greatest regularity. |
| 4 | Regular-s. |
| 5 | Regulate-d-ing-s. |
| 6 | Regulation-s. |
| 7 | Not well regulated. |
| 8 | Very well regulated. |
| 9 | Reinforce-d-ing-ments. |
| 6160 | Has, or have, been reinforced. |
| 1 | In want of reinforcements. |
| 2 | Reinforce the. |
| 3 | Reinforcements are expected. |
| 4 | Reinforcements have arrived. |
| 5 | You will be reinforced. |
| 6 | Reign-ing-s. |
| 7 | Reigning sovereign-s. |
| 8 | Reinstate-d-ing. |
| 9 | Reject-ed-ing-s. |
| 6170 | Rejoice-d-ing-s. |
| 1 | Rejoin-ed-ing-s. |
| 2 | Rejoin me as soon as possible. |
| 3 | Has, or have, rejoined. |
| 4 | You will rejoin. |
| 5 | Relapse-d-ing-s. |
| 6 | Has had a relapse. |
| 7 | Relate-d-ing-s. |
| 8 | Relax-ed-ing-es. |
| 9 | Very much relaxed. |
| 6180 | Relaxation-s. |
| 1 | Release-d-ing-s. |
| 2 | Relent-ed-ing-s. |
| 3 | Relentless. |
| 4 | Has relented. |
| 5 | Relieve-d-ing-lief-s. |
| 6186 | A great relief. |

| Nos. | REN |
|---|---|
| 6187 | Am greatly relieved. |
| 8 | Cannot relieve. |
| 9 | Is, or are, relieved. |
| 6190 | To be relieved. |
| 1 | You will relieve. |
| 2 | Religious-ly. |
| 3 | Relinquish-ed-ing-es. |
| 4 | Must relinquish. |
| 5 | Reluctant-ly. |
| 6 | Reluctance. |
| 7 | Rely-ied-ing-s. |
| 8 | Do not rely upon. |
| 9 | Must rely upon. |
| 6200 | Remain-ed-ing-s. |
| 1 | Am I to remain? |
| 2 | Do you remain? |
| 3 | Do not remain. |
| 4 | You, or they, are to remain. |
| 5 | You, or they, are not to remain. |
| 6 | Remark-ed-ing-s. |
| 7 | Remedy-ied-ing-ies. |
| 8 | Provide remedy-ies. |
| 9 | Remember-ed-ing-s. |
| 6210 | Do, or does, not remember. |
| 1 | Do you remember? |
| 2 | Will you remember? |
| 3 | Remember me, or us. |
| 4 | Remind-ed-ing-s. |
| 5 | Remiss-ness. |
| 6 | Remit-ted-ting-s. |
| 7 | Remittance-s. |
| 8 | Remission. |
| 9 | Remnant-s. |
| 6220 | Remonstrate-d-ing-s. |
| 1 | Remote-ly. |
| 2 | Remove-d-ing-s. |
| 3 | Remunerate-d-ing-s. |
| 4 | Rendezvous. |
| 5 | Is, or are, to rendezvous at. |
| 6 | To th' rendezvous, proceed. |
| 7 | Where does he, or, do they, rendezvous? |
| 8 | Rendezvous No. 1. |
| 9 | Rendezvous No. 2. |
| 6230 | Rendezvous No. 3. |
| 1 | Renew-ed-ing-s. |
| 2 | Renew, I intend to, the engagement. |
| 6233 | Prepare to renew the engagement. |

| Nos. | REN |
|---|---|
| 6234 | Renew the engagement without unnecessary loss of time. |
| 5 | Repair-ed-ing. |
| 6 | Repair on board of this, or the vessel designated. |
| 7 | Repair-s. |
| 8 | Cannot be repaired here. |
| 9 | Has, or have, been repair'd. |
| 6240 | In want of repairs badly. |
| 1 | Repass-ed-ing-es. |
| 2 | Repass the fort-s. |
| 3 | Repass the obstruction-s. |
| 4 | Repeat-ed-ing-s. |
| 5 | Repeat the message-s. |
| 6 | Repeat what follows. |
| 7 | Repel-led-ling-s. |
| 8 | Replace-d-ing-s. |
| 9 | Replenish-ed-ing-es. |
| 6250 | Reply-ied-ing-ies. |
| 1 | In reply to. |
| 2 | Made no reply to. |
| 3 | Report-ed-ing. |
| 4 | Has, or have, reported. |
| 5 | Is, or was, reported. |
| 6 | Will you report me? |
| 7 | Reports. |
| 8 | Reprehend-ed-ing-s. |
| 9 | Reprehensible-ly. |
| 6260 | Represent-ed-ing-s. |
| 1 | Has, or have, represented. |
| 2 | Must be represented. |
| 3 | Will represent the. |
| 4 | Repress-ed-ing-ion-es. |
| 5 | Reprieve-d-s. |
| 6 | Reprimand-ed-ing-s. |
| 7 | Reprisal-s. |
| 8 | Reproach-ed-ing-es. |
| 9 | Reproachful. |
| 6270 | Reprobate-d-ing-s. |
| 1 | Reprobation. |
| 2 | Reprove-d-ing-s-reproof-s. |
| 3 | Repugnant-ance. |
| 4 | Repulse-d-s. |
| 5 | Has, or have, been repulsed. |
| 6 | Repute-d. |
| 7 | Reputation-s. |
| 8 | Request-ed-ing-s. |
| 6279 | Request can be complied with. |

| Nos. | RES |
|---|---|
| 6280 | Request cannot be complied with. |
| 1 | You will request that. |
| 2 | Require-d-ing-s. |
| 3 | Requirement-s. |
| 4 | Requisite-s. |
| 5 | Requisition-s. |
| 6 | Rescue-d-ing. |
| 7 | Hasten to the rescue of the. |
| 8 | Rescue the wrecked people if it be possible to do so. |
| 9 | Resent-ed-ing-s. |
| 6290 | Resentment-s. |
| 1 | Resume-d-s. |
| 2 | Advance the reserve-s. |
| 3 | Bring forwa'd the reserve-s. |
| 4 | Reserve will attack in front. |
| 5 | Reserve will attack the lee column. |
| 6 | Reserve will attack the weather column. |
| 7 | Reside-d-ing-s. |
| 8 | Residence-s. |
| 9 | Resign-ed-ing-s. |
| 6300 | Resignation-s. |
| 1 | Resist-ed-ing-s. |
| 2 | Resistance. |
| 3 | Made considerable resistance. |
| 4 | Made but little resistance. |
| 5 | Made no resistance. |
| 6 | Resolute-ly. |
| 7 | Resolution-s. |
| 8 | Resolve-d-ing-s. |
| 9 | Resort-ed-ing-s. |
| 6310 | Resource-s. |
| 1 | Respect-ed-s. |
| 2 | In respect to the. |
| 3 | Respectable-y. |
| 4 | Respective-ly. |
| 5 | Respite-d-s. |
| 6 | Responsible-ility-ies. |
| 7 | Rest-ed-ing-s. |
| 8 | Restore-d-ing-s. |
| 9 | Restore the order of battle. |
| 6320 | Restore the order, or formation. |
| 1 | Restrain-ed-ing-s. |
| 2 | Restraint-s. |
| 3 | Restrict-ed-ing-s. |
| 4 | Restriction-s. |
| 6325 | Result-ed-ing. |

| Nos. | RES |
|---|---|
| 6326 | Results. |
| 7 | Resume-d-ing-s. |
| 8 | Resume your station-s. |
| 9 | Has, or have, resumed station-s. |
| 6330 | Retain-ed-ing-s. |
| 1 | Retake-n-s. |
| 2 | Retaliate-d-ing-s. |
| 3 | Retard-ed-ing-s. |
| 4 | Retire-d-ing-s. |
| 5 | Retract-ed-ing-s. |
| 6 | Retreat-ed-ing-s. |
| 7 | Has, or have, retreated. |
| 8 | Is, or are, retreating. |
| 9 | Prepare to retreat in order. |
| 6340 | Retrench-ment. |
| 1 | Retrieve-d-ing-s. |
| 2 | Return-ed-ing-s. |
| 3 | Do not return. |
| 4 | Return as soon as possible. |
| 5 | When did you return? |
| 6 | When will you, or can you, return? |
| 7 | Return-s. |
| 8 | Am waiting for returns. |
| 9 | Send your returns. |
| 6350 | Reverse-d-ing-s. |
| 1 | Met a reverse. |
| 2 | Review-ed-ing-s. |
| 3 | Revise-d-ing-s. |
| 4 | Revision-s. |
| 5 | Revive-d-ing-s. |
| 6 | Revoke-d-ing-s. |
| 7 | Revocation-s. |
| 8 | Revolt-ed-ing-s. |
| 9 | Revolution-s. |
| 6360 | Revolutionary. |
| 1 | Reward-ed-ing. |
| 2 | Reward-s. |
| 3 | Rheumatism-ic. |
| 4 | Rice. |
| 5 | Ride-ing-s. |
| 6 | Ride out the gale at anch'r. |
| 7 | Rifle-s. |
| 8 | Rifle cannon. |
| 9 | Rifle muskets. |
| 6370 | Send rifle cannon. |
| 1 | Rifleman-men. |
| 2 | Rig-ged. |
| 3 | Full rigged. |
| 4 | Not rigged. |
| 6375 | Rigging. |

| Nos. | ROU |
|---|---|
| 6376 | Running rigging. |
| 7 | Standing rigging. |
| 8 | Right. |
| 9 | You are right. |
| 6380 | Rigid. |
| 1 | Rigid discipline enforce. |
| 2 | Rigor-ous-ly-s. |
| 3 | Ring-s. |
| 4 | Ring bolt-s. |
| 5 | Ringleader-s. |
| 6 | Riot-s-ous-ly. |
| 7 | Ripple-s. |
| 8 | Rise-n-s-rose. |
| 9 | Risk-s-y. |
| 6390 | Do not run any risk. |
| 1 | There is great risk. |
| 2 | Without any risk. |
| 3 | River-s. |
| 4 | Rivet-s. |
| 5 | Road-s. |
| 6 | A bad road. |
| 7 | A good road. |
| 8 | Roadstead-s. |
| 9 | A bad roadstead. |
| 6400 | A good roadstead. |
| 1 | Rob-bed-bing. |
| 2 | Robber-s. |
| 3 | Robbery-ies. |
| 4 | Rock-s-y. |
| 5 | Are there any rocks? |
| 6 | Near the rocks. |
| 7 | On the rocks. |
| 8 | There is a rock, or are rocks. |
| 9 | Very rocky. |
| 6410 | Rocket-s. |
| 1 | In need of rockets. |
| 2 | Send rockets. |
| 3 | Roll-er-s. |
| 4 | Roller hand spike-s. |
| 5 | Room-s-y. |
| 6 | Rope-s. |
| 7 | Rosin. |
| 8 | Rot-ten-ness. |
| 9 | Rotary. |
| 6420 | Rotation-s. |
| 1 | Rough-ly. |
| 2 | Rough weather. |
| 3 | Rough sea-s. |
| 4 | Round-ed-ing. |
| 5 | Coming round. |
| 6 | Going round. |
| 6427 | Rout-ed. |

| Nos. | ROU | Nos. | SAP |
|---|---|---|---|
| 6428 | Routine. | 6476 | Form in three columns of sailing. |
| 9 | Row-ed-ing. | 7 | Form in line ahead. |
| 6430 | Row boat-s. | 8 | Form in line abreast. |
| 1 | Row guard during the nig't. | 9 | Form in two lines abreast. |
| 2 | Rub-bed-bing-s. | 6480 | Form in three lines abreast. |
| 3 | Rubber. | 1 | Form line ahead, as most convenient, without regard to numbers or seniority. |
| 4 | Rudder-s. | 2 | Form line abreast, as most convenient, without regard to numbers or seniority. |
| 5 | Rudder is disabled. | 3 | Sails. |
| 6 | Have you a spare rudder piece? | 4 | Furl sails. |
| 7 | In want of a spare rudder. | 5 | Loose sails. |
| 8 | I have a spare rudder piece. | 6 | Loose sails to a bowline. |
| 9 | Can make a spare rudder. | 7 | Reef your sails. |
| 6440 | Make a jury rudder. | 8 | Bend sails. |
| 1 | Ruin-ed-ous. | 9 | Mend sails. |
| 2 | Ruins. | 6490 | Sailmaker-s. |
| 3 | Rumor-s. | 1 | Need sailmaker-s. |
| 4 | Run-ning-s. | 2 | Sally port-s. |
| 5 | Rupture-d-s. | 3 | Salt. |
| 6 | Rust-ed-ing-s-y. | 4 | Salt beef. |
| 7 | Sacrifice-d-ing-s. | 5 | Salt pork. |
| 8 | At a great sacrifice. | 6 | Salutary. |
| 9 | At any sacrifice. | 7 | Salute-d-ing-s. |
| 6450 | Sad-ly-ness. | 8 | May I salute? |
| 1 | Sad affair. | 9 | Need not salute. |
| 2 | Safe-ly-ty. | 6500 | Shall I salute? |
| 3 | For the safety of the. | 1 | Will not salute. |
| 4 | For your, or their, safety. | 2 | Same. |
| 5 | It is not safe to go on shore. | 3 | The same kind. |
| 6 | The bar is not safe. | 4 | The same way. |
| 7 | Would it be safe. | 5 | Sanction-ed-ing-s. |
| 8 | Safer-est. | 6 | Is, or are, sanctioned. |
| 9 | Sail-ed-ing-s. | 7 | Will not, or would not, sanction the. |
| 6460 | All sail set. | 8 | Sand-s-y. |
| 1 | Am over pressed with sail. | 9 | Sand bank-s. |
| 2 | Boats ahead shorten sail. | 6510 | Sandy bottom. |
| 3 | Boats astern make more sail. | 1 | Sandy beach. |
| 4 | How many sail? | 2 | Have you any sand? |
| 5 | Make sail. | 3 | Send for sand. |
| 6 | Shorten sail. | 4 | In want of sand. |
| 7 | Take in all sail and out oars. | 5 | Sand bags. |
| 8 | You are carrying too much sail. | 6 | Sanguine-ly. |
| 9 | You want more sail. | 7 | Sanguinary. |
| 6470 | Try rate of sailing. | 8 | Sardinia-n. |
| 1 | Form the 1st order of sail'g. | 6519 | Sap-s. |
| 2 | Form the 2d order of sail'g. | | |
| 3 | Form the 3d order of sail'g. | | |
| 4 | Form the 5th ord'r of sail'g. | | |
| 6475 | Form in two columns of sailing. | | |

| Nos. | SAP | Nos. | SEA |
|---|---|---|---|
| 6520 | Sapped-ping. | 6570 | Ride with a long scope. |
| 1 | Sappers. | 1 | Ride with a short scope. |
| 2 | Sappers and miners. | 2 | Scour-ed-ing-s. |
| 3 | Satisfy-ied-ing-ies. | 3 | Scour the coast-s. |
| 4 | Am, is, or are, satisfied. | 4 | Scout-s. |
| 5 | Am, is, or are not, satisfied. | 5 | Send out scouts. |
| 6 | Satisfaction. | 6 | Scrape-ed-ing-s. |
| 7 | Is, or are, satisfactory. | 7 | Scraper-s. |
| 8 | Is, or are not, satisfactory. | 8 | Screen-s. |
| 9 | No satisfaction. | 9 | Screw-ed-ing. |
| 6530 | Saturate-d-ing-s. | 6580 | Screws. |
| 1 | Saturation. | 1 | Scrub-bed-bing. |
| 2 | Saturday-s. | 2 | Scrub clothes. |
| 3 | Saturday evening-s. | 3 | Scrub hammocks. |
| 4 | Saturday morning-s. | 4 | Scrub and wash clothes and hammocks. |
| 5 | Saturday noon. | | |
| 6 | Saturday night-s. | 5 | Scruple-d-ing-s. |
| 7 | Savage-s. | 6 | Scrupulous-ly. |
| 8 | Save-d-ing-s. | 7 | Scrutiny-ies. |
| 9 | Is, or are, saved. | 8 | Scrutinize-d-ing-s. |
| 6540 | Is, or are not, saved. | 9 | Scud. |
| 1 | Was, or were, saved. | 6590 | Scud-ded-ding. |
| 2 | Was, or were not, saved. | 1 | Scupper-s. |
| 3 | Saw-see-seen. | 2 | Scurvy. |
| 4 | Saw-ed-ing. | 3 | Scuttle-d-ing-s. |
| 5 | Hand saw-s. | 4 | Skulk-ed-ing-s. |
| 6 | Sawyer-s. | 5 | Skulker-s. |
| 7 | Say-ing-said-s. | 6 | Sea. |
| 8 | It is said that. | 7 | Rough sea. |
| 9 | Scotland-s. | 8 | Smooth sea. |
| 6550 | Scaffold-ed-ing-s. | 9 | A very heavy sea. |
| 1 | Scale-d-ing-s. | 6600 | Has, or have, just came in from sea. |
| 2 | Scaling ladders. | | |
| 3 | Scandal-s. | 1 | Not much sea. |
| 4 | Scandalous-ly. | 2 | Prepare for sea. |
| 5 | Scandalous conduct. | 3 | Put to sea. |
| 6 | Scandalize-d-ing-s. | 4 | When will you be ready for sea? |
| 7 | Scantling-s. | | |
| 8 | Scarce-ly-ness. | 5 | When she has gone to sea. |
| 9 | Is, or are, very scarce. | 6 | When we get to sea. |
| 6560 | Not very scarce. | 7 | Seaman-men. |
| 1 | Scarcity. | 8 | In need of seamen. |
| 2 | Scarf-ed-ing-s. | 9 | Have seamen. |
| 3 | Schooner-s. | 6610 | Have no seamen. |
| 4 | Schooner rigged. | 1 | Sea room. |
| 5 | Scope-s. | 2 | Sea side. |
| 6 | Give a good scope of cable. | 3 | Sea shore-s. |
| 7 | Has, or have, too much scope. | 4 | Search-ed-ing. |
| | | 5 | Did not search. |
| 8 | Has, or have not, enough scope. | 6 | Have you searched? |
| | | 7 | Have searched. |
| 6569 | Let her have more scope. | 6618 | Have not searched. |

| Nos. | SEA | Nos. | SET |
|---|---|---|---|
| 6619 | Let her, them, be search'd. | 6671 | Send immediately. |
| 6620 | Season-s. | 2 | Send on board for. |
| 1 | Seasonable-y. | 3 | Send on shore for. |
| 2 | Second-ed-ing-s. | 4 | Send an officer to. |
| 3 | Secret-ed-ing-s. | 5 | Will you send? |
| 4 | Is a secret. | 6 | You are to send. |
| 5 | To be kept secret. | 7 | Senior-s. |
| 6 | Secret dispatch-es. | 8 | Senior officer commanding boats or vessels repair on board of the commander in-chief's vessel. |
| 7 | Secret key to signals. | 9 | The senior officer wishes. |
| 8 | Secret sign'l key, No. 1, use. | 6680 | The senior officer directs that. |
| 9 | Secret sign'l key, No. 2, use. | 1 | The senior officer is absent. |
| 6630 | Secret sign'l key, No. 3, use. | 2 | Senior officer-s. |
| 1 | Secret sign'l key, No. 4, use. | 3 | Sense-ible-y. |
| 2 | Secret sign'l key, No. 5, use. | 4 | Sensation-s. |
| 3 | Secretary-ies. | 5 | Sensitive-ly. |
| 4 | Secretary to flag officer. | 6 | Sentence-d-ing-s. |
| 5 | Secretary to the legation. | 7 | Sentence of the court-martial. |
| 6 | Section-s. | 8 | Sentence communicated to the. |
| 7 | Sectional-ly. | 9 | Sentence executed at the time designated. |
| 8 | Sectional dock-s. | 6690 | Sentence is commuted. |
| 9 | Secure-d-ing-s. | 1 | Sentence of court is disapproved. |
| 6640 | Securely. | 2 | Sentinel-s-sentry-ies. |
| 1 | See-seen-ing-saw. | 3 | Sentry-box-es. |
| 2 | Can you see? | 4 | Separate-d-ing. |
| 3 | Could not see. | 5 | Are, or have, separated. |
| 4 | Did you see? | 6 | Was, or were, separated. |
| 5 | Did not see. | 7 | When did you, or they, separate? |
| 6 | Have you seen? | 8 | We separated on the day shown by numeral sign'l. |
| 7 | Have not seen. | 9 | September. |
| 8 | Should you see. | 6700 | September gale-s. |
| 9 | Should you not see. | 1 | Series. |
| 6650 | Was, or were, seen. | 2 | Serious-ly-ness. |
| 1 | Was, or were not, seen. | 3 | Sergeant-s. |
| 2 | When did you see? | 4 | Sergeant's guard. |
| 3 | When last seen. | 5 | Orderly sergeant. |
| 4 | Where were they seen? | 6 | Serve-d-ing-s. |
| 5 | Seek-ing-sought-s. | 7 | Servant-s. |
| 6 | Seem-ed-ing-s. | 8 | Service-able-s. |
| 7 | Seine-s. | 9 | Set-sitting-sat. |
| 8 | Fishing seine-s needed. | 6710 | Has set in. |
| 9 | Send me your fishing seine. | 1 | Will set in. |
| 6660 | Go fishing with seines. | 6712 | Settle-d-ing-s. |
| 1 | Seize-d-ing-s. | | |
| 2 | Seizings. | | |
| 3 | Seldom. | | |
| 4 | Select-ed-ing-s. | | |
| 5 | Selection-s. | | |
| 6 | Send-ing-s-t. | | |
| 7 | Can you send? | | |
| 8 | Cannot send. | | |
| 9 | Do not send. | | |
| 6670 | Have you sent? | | |

| Nos. | SET |
|---|---|
| 6713 | Is settling fast. |
| 4 | Is settling by the head. |
| 5 | Is settling by the stern. |
| 6 | Is not settling very fast. |
| 7 | Seven-th. |
| 8 | Seventeen-th. |
| 9 | Seventy-ieth. |
| 6720 | Several-ly. |
| 1 | Severe-ly. |
| 2 | Severity-ies. |
| 3 | Not severe-ly. |
| 4 | Not too severely. |
| 5 | Great severity. |
| 6 | Sextant-s. |
| 7 | Light sextant-s. |
| 8 | Surer sextant-s. |
| 9 | Want a sextant. |
| 6730 | Send a sextant to. |
| 1 | Shabby-ily-ness. |
| 2 | Shackle-s. |
| 3 | Shackle pins. |
| 4 | Spare shackles. |
| 5 | Shade-d-ing-s. |
| 6 | Shadow-s. |
| 7 | Shaft-s. |
| 8 | Propeller shaft-s. |
| 9 | Main shaft-s. |
| 6740 | Shaft alley-s. |
| 1 | Rock shaft-s. |
| 2 | Shake-n-s-shook. |
| 3 | Shall. |
| 4 | Shall I? |
| 5 | Shall he? |
| 6 | Shall you? |
| 7 | Shall we? |
| 8 | Shall they? |
| 9 | Shallow-s. |
| 6750 | Shallowest. |
| 1 | Shame-d-ful. |
| 2 | Shank painter-s. |
| 3 | Shape-d-ing-s. |
| 4 | Shape course-s. |
| 5 | Share-d-ing-s. |
| 6 | Sharp-ly. |
| 7 | Shatter-ed-ing-s. |
| 8 | She. |
| 9 | She is. |
| 6760 | She is not. |
| 1 | Shell-s. |
| 2 | Shell guns. |
| 3 | Commence with shells. |
| 6764 | Discontinue firing shells. |

| Nos. | SHO |
|---|---|
| 6765 | In need of shrapnel shells. |
| 6 | Want shells for 24-pdr. howitzers. |
| 7 | Want shells for 12-pdr. howitzers. |
| 8 | Want shells for 10-inch mortars. |
| 9 | Want shells for 13-inch mortars. |
| 6770 | Want shells of the calibres indicated by numeral signal-s. |
| 1 | Shelter-ed-ing-s. |
| 2 | There is good shelter to the. |
| 3 | There is good shelter at, or, in the. |
| 4 | There is no shelter. |
| 5 | Well sheltered. |
| 6 | Seek for shelter. |
| 7 | Shift-ed-ing-s. |
| 8 | Shift berth. |
| 9 | Shift of wind. |
| 6780 | Do not shift berth. |
| 1 | May I shift berth? |
| 2 | Shingle beach-es. |
| 3 | Ship-s-ping. |
| 4 | Tack ship. |
| 5 | Wear ship. |
| 6 | Moor ship. |
| 7 | The ship-s in the. |
| 8 | To what ship? |
| 9 | Can the ship-s? |
| 6790 | What ship-s? |
| 1 | Ship's company. |
| 2 | For the ship's company. |
| 3 | To the ship's company. |
| 4 | With the ship's company. |
| 5 | Your ship's company. |
| 6 | Shipwreck-ed-s. |
| 7 | Shipwrecked people. |
| 8 | Shipwright-s. |
| 9 | Shirt s. |
| 6800 | Blue shirts. |
| 1 | White shirts. |
| 2 | Shoal-ed-ing. |
| 3 | Shoals. |
| 4 | Can weather the shoal-s. |
| 5 | Cannot weather the shoal-s. |
| 6 | Has struck on a shoal. |
| 7 | Has weathered the shoal. |
| 6808 | It is shoal water. |

| Nos. | SHO |
|---|---|
| 6809 | Is the shoal, or, are the shoals buoyed? |
| 6810 | Place a buoy on the shoals. |
| 1 | The shoal-s buoyed. |
| 2 | Shock-ed-s. |
| 3 | Shoe-d-ing-s-shod. |
| 4 | Short-ing-s. |
| 5 | Shore-d-ing-s. |
| 6 | Shore up your decks. |
| 7 | Get out shores to keep the vessel upright. |
| 8 | Has been on shore. |
| 9 | Going on shore. |
| 6820 | Lookout for a line from the shore. |
| 1 | Send a line ashore by a cask. |
| 2 | Will you go on shore? |
| 3 | Shall be glad to meet you on shore. |
| 4 | Do not communicate with the shore. |
| 5 | You may com'unicate with the shore. |
| 6 | Close to the shore. |
| 7 | Haul off the shore. |
| 8 | Is on shore. |
| 9 | Is not on shore. |
| 6830 | On shore. |
| 1 | Off shore. |
| 2 | Shore is bold. |
| 3 | Shore is dangerous. |
| 4 | Water is very deep close to the shore. |
| 5 | Shot-ted-ting-s. |
| 6 | Canister shot. |
| 7 | Eighteen pound shot. |
| 8 | Grape shot. |
| 9 | Forty-two pound shot. |
| 6840 | Musket shot. |
| 1 | Thirty-two pound shot. |
| 2 | Twenty-four pound shot. |
| 3 | Twelve pound shot. |
| 4 | Six pound shot. |
| 5 | Round shot. |
| 6 | Rifle shot. |
| 7 | Conical shot. |
| 8 | Shot your guns. |
| 9 | Shot plugs. |
| 6850 | Short-en-ed-ing-s. |
| 1 | Short of. |
| 6852 | Shorten in cable. |

| Nos. | SIG |
|---|---|
| 6853 | Shorten sail. |
| 4 | Should. |
| 5 | Shoulder-s. |
| 6 | Shovel-s. |
| 7 | Show-n-ing-s. |
| 8 | Show your colors. |
| 9 | Show your number. |
| 6860 | Show your private signal. |
| 1 | Shrapnel. |
| 2 | Shrapnel shell required. |
| 3 | Shrapnel, have a full supply of. |
| 4 | Use shrapnel against the enemy. |
| 5 | Shrink-s-shrunk. |
| 6 | Shroud-s. |
| 7 | Fore shrouds. |
| 8 | Main shrouds. |
| 9 | Mizzen shrouds. |
| 6870 | Shun-ned-ning-s. |
| 1 | Shut-ting-s. |
| 2 | Sick-ly. |
| 3 | Send sick and wounded to the vessel, or place designated. |
| 4 | Are the sick properly cared for? |
| 5 | Are the sick doing well? |
| 6 | Have but few sick. |
| 7 | Have a large sick list. |
| 8 | How many are sick? |
| 9 | Land the sick. |
| 6880 | The place is sickly. |
| 1 | The place is not sickly. |
| 2 | Side-s. |
| 3 | Side lights. |
| 4 | On both sides. |
| 5 | On the other side. |
| 6 | On this side. |
| 7 | On which side? |
| 8 | On the port side. |
| 9 | On the starboard side. |
| 6890 | On the north side. |
| 1 | On the east side. |
| 2 | On the south side. |
| 3 | On the west side. |
| 4 | Siege-s. |
| 5 | Laid siege. |
| 6 | Raised the siege. |
| 7 | Sight-ed-ing-s. |
| 8 | Can keep in sight of the. |
| 6899 | Cannot keep in sight of the. |

| Nos. | SIG |
|---|---|
| 6900 | Can you keep in sight of the? |
| 1 | Keep in sight of the. |
| 2 | Lost sight of the. |
| 3 | Nothing in sight. |
| 4 | Out of sight. |
| 5 | Land is in sight. |
| 6 | Sign-ed-ing-s. |
| 7 | Signature-s. |
| 8 | Signal-s. |
| 9 | Answer signal-s. |
| 6910 | Comply with the signal. |
| 1 | Destroy your signals. |
| 2 | Do not understand your signals. |
| 3 | Discontinue repeating signals. |
| 4 | Do you understand the signals? |
| 5 | Enforce signal-s. |
| 6 | Flags cannot be distinguished where now exhibited. |
| 7 | Fire a gun to attract attention to signals. |
| 8 | Repeat all signals until further orders. |
| 9 | Repeat the last signal. |
| 6920 | Repeat senior officers' signals. |
| 1 | Make the signal for. |
| 2 | Have made signal for. |
| 3 | Pay more attention to signals. |
| 4 | Signal for boats to return. |
| 5 | Signal to boats to advance. |
| 6 | Signal boats to attack. |
| 7 | Signal boats to retreat. |
| 8 | When the signal is made to. |
| 9 | Signal book-s. |
| 6930 | Destroy signal books. |
| 1 | Send signal book-s to the flag ship. |
| 2 | Signaled-ing. |
| 3 | Signify-ied-ing-ies. |
| 4 | Significant-ly. |
| 5 | Significance. |
| 6 | Silent-ly. |
| 7 | Silence. |
| 8 | Silk-en. |
| 9 | Silver-ed-ing. |
| 6940 | Similar-ly. |

| Nos. | SLI |
|---|---|
| 6941 | Simple-y. |
| 2 | Simplify-ied-ing-ies. |
| 3 | Simultaneous-ly. |
| 4 | Since. |
| 5 | Since when? |
| 6 | How long since? |
| 7 | Sincere-ly. |
| 8 | Sincerity. |
| 9 | Single-d-ing. |
| 6950 | Single out. |
| 1 | Sink-ing, sunk-s. |
| 2 | Is sinking. |
| 3 | In a sinking condition. |
| 4 | Sir. |
| 5 | Sit-ting-s-sat. |
| 6 | Sit down in the boats. |
| 7 | Situate-d-ion. |
| 8 | Six-th. |
| 9 | Sixteen-th. |
| 6960 | Sixty-ieth. |
| 1 | Size-s. |
| 2 | Large size-s. |
| 3 | Larger-est size-s. |
| 4 | Medium size-s. |
| 5 | Small size-s. |
| 6 | Smaller-est size-s. |
| 7 | Various sizes. |
| 8 | What size do you want? |
| 9 | What size is the? |
| 6970 | Skill-ed. |
| 1 | Skillful-ly. |
| 2 | Skirmish-ed-ing-es. |
| 3 | Skirmishers. |
| 4 | Call in skirmishers. |
| 5 | Send out skirmishers. |
| 6 | Slack-s. |
| 7 | Slack water. |
| 8 | Very slack. |
| 9 | Slacken-ing-s. |
| 6980 | Slacken speed. |
| 1 | Slant-ing-s. |
| 2 | A slant of wind. |
| 3 | A good slant. |
| 4 | Sleep-ing-slept-s. |
| 5 | Slide-s. |
| 6 | Slight-ly. |
| 7 | Sling-s. |
| 8 | Bale slings. |
| 9 | Butt slings. |
| 6990 | Slip-s. |
| 1 | Cut or slip. |
| 6992 | I am going to slip. |

| Nos. | SLI | Nos. | SPE |
|---|---|---|---|
| 6993 | Go into the slip. | 7040 | Solidity. |
| 4 | Sloop-s. | 1 | Solve-d-ing-s. |
| 5 | Dispatch the sloop to. | 2 | Solution-s. |
| 6 | I wish to speak the sloop. | 3 | Solvent-s. |
| 7 | The stranger is a sloop-of-war. | 4 | Some. |
| | | 5 | Somebody-one. |
| 8 | Overhaul the sloop. | 6 | Sometime-s. |
| 9 | Slop clothing. | 7 | Soon. |
| 7000 | Slow-er-s. | 8 | As soon as. |
| 1 | Slow down. | 9 | How soon? |
| 2 | Go slower. | 7050 | Not so soon as. |
| 3 | Slowly. | 1 | Sooner-est. |
| 4 | Is approaching slowly. | 2 | Sorrow-s-ful-ly. |
| 5 | Gains slowly. | 3 | Sorry. |
| 6 | Smack. | 4 | Sort-s. |
| 7 | Fishing smack-s. | 5 | Sortie-s. |
| 8 | Small-er-est. | 6 | The enemy is about to make a sortie. |
| 9 | Small pox. | | |
| 7010 | Shall I send men to the small-pox hospital? | 7 | Repel the sortie. |
| | | 8 | The sortie has been driven back. |
| 1 | Small pox is very bad. | | |
| 2 | Small pox is of a mild type. | 9 | Sound-ed-ing-s. |
| 3 | Small pox, guard against. | 7060 | Go ahead, sound, and report in fathoms. |
| 4 | Send all small-pox patients to the hospital. | | |
| | | 1 | Go ahead, sound, and report in feet. |
| 5 | Smart-ly. | | |
| 6 | Smartest. | 2 | Have you had soundings? |
| 7 | Smith-s-ery-ies. Blacksmith-s. | 3 | Have got bottom. |
| 8 | Smoke-ing-s. | 4 | No soundings yet. |
| 9 | Smoke of a steamer seen in the direction indicated by compass signal. | 5 | Soundings are regular. |
| | | 6 | Soundings are not regular. |
| | | 7 | Report soundings in feet. |
| 7020 | Smooth-ly-ness. | 8 | Report soundings in fathoms. |
| 1 | Smooth water. | | |
| 2 | Smooth-er-est. | 9 | Soup. |
| 3 | Snatch-block-s. | 7070 | Source-s. |
| 4 | Snow-ed-ing-s. | 1 | Space-s. |
| 5 | Snug-ly. | 2 | Spain-iard-s-ish. |
| 6 | Get everything snug. | 3 | Spar-s. |
| 7 | So. | 4 | Spare. |
| 8 | Soap. | 5 | Can you spare? |
| 9 | We want soap. | 6 | Can spare. |
| 7030 | Sober-ly. | 7 | Cannot spare. |
| 1 | Soft. | 8 | Speak-ing-s-spoke-n. |
| 2 | Soft bottom. | 9 | Did he, or they, speak? |
| 3 | Soft bread. | 7080 | Did you speak? |
| 4 | Solder. | 1 | Did not speak. |
| 5 | Soldier-s-ly. | 2 | Speak the boat, or vessel, seen. |
| 6 | Solicit-ed-ing-s. | | |
| 7 | Solicitation-s. | 3 | Wish to speak. |
| 8 | Solicitous. | 4 | Spear-s. |
| 7039 | Solid-ly. | 7085 | Special-ly. |

| Nos. | SPE | Nos. | STE |
|---|---|---|---|
| 7086 | Specie-s. | 7133 | Square-d-ing-s. |
| 7 | Specify-ied-ing-ies. | 4 | Squall-s-y. |
| 8 | Specification-s. | 5 | Stab-bed-bing. |
| 9 | Specimen-s. | 6 | Staff officer-s. |
| 7090 | Speculate-d. | 7 | Stage-s-ing. |
| 1 | Speculation-s. | 8 | Stagnant water. |
| 2 | Speed-y-ily. | 9 | Stake-d-ing-s. |
| 3 | With the greatest speed. | 7140 | Stake out the channel. |
| 4 | Spell-ing. | 1 | Stand-ing-stood-s. |
| 5 | Spend-spent. | 2 | Stand in towards the. |
| 6 | Sphere-ical-ly. | 3 | Stand off. |
| 7 | Spike-s. | 4 | Stand out. |
| 8 | In need of spikes. | 5 | Stand off and on. |
| 9 | Spike guns. | 6 | Was, or were, standing. |
| 7100 | Guns are spiked. | 7 | Starboard. |
| 1 | Spindle-s. | 8 | Beam. |
| 2 | Spirit-ous-s. | 9 | Bow. |
| 3 | Spiritous liquors. | 7150 | Quarter. |
| 4 | Splendid-ly. | 1 | Side. |
| 5 | Splendor-s. | 2 | Tack. |
| 6 | Splice-d-ing-s. | 3 | Guns. |
| 7 | Splinter-ed-ing-s. | 4 | Broadside. |
| 8 | Splinter nettings. | 5 | Haul your wind, to starboard tack. |
| 9 | Split-ting-s. | 6 | Heave to, on the starboard tack. |
| 7110 | Spoil-ed-ing-s-spoilt. | 7 | Start-ed-ing-s. |
| 1 | Spot-s. | 8 | Starve-d-ing-s. |
| 2 | Spread-ing-s. | 9 | Starvation-s. |
| 3 | Spread out more to the left. | 7160 | State-s. |
| 4 | Spread out more to the right. | 1 | Statement-s. |
| 5 | Spring-s-sprung. | 2 | Statesman-men. |
| 6 | Get springs on your cables. | 3 | Station-s. |
| 7 | Spring your broadside. | 4 | Are you at your station? |
| 8 | Spring water. | 5 | Is, or are, stationed. |
| 9 | Spy-ies-ing. | 6 | What station is? |
| 7120 | Squadron-s. | 7 | Where are you stationed? |
| 1 | A large squadron. | 8 | Quit your station-s. |
| 2 | A small squadron. | 9 | Return to your station-s. |
| 3 | A squadron of cavalry. | 7170 | Remain at present station-s until it moderates. |
| 4 | Enemy's squadron. | 1 | Stave-stove. |
| 5 | Our squadron. | 2 | Stay-ing. |
| 6 | Reserve squadron. | 3 | Stays. |
| 7 | Squadron will close up. | 4 | Staysail-s. |
| 8 | Squadron will spread out. | 5 | Steady-ily-iness. |
| 9 | Squadron will prepare to anchor in the present order. | 6 | Steal-s-stole-n. |
| 7130 | Squadron will anchor. | 7 | Steam-ed-ing-s. |
| 1 | Squadron will get under way. | 8 | Steamer-s. |
| 7132 | Squadron will tack or go about. | 9 | Blow off steam. |
| | | 7180 | Get up steam. |
| | | 7181 | Steam chest. |

| Nos. | STE |
|---|---|
| 7182 | Steam drum. |
| 3 | Steam pipe-s. |
| 4 | Steel. |
| 5 | Steep. |
| 6 | Steep bank. |
| 7 | Steep to. |
| 8 | Steer-ed-ing-s. |
| 9 | How is she, or are they, steering? |
| 7190 | How was she, or were they, steering? |
| 1 | Intend to steer for. |
| 2 | Steer after me. |
| 3 | Steer more to port. |
| 4 | Steer more to starboard. |
| 5 | Steer as per compass sign'l. |
| 6 | Stem-med-ming-s. |
| 7 | Can stem the tide. |
| 8 | Cannot stem the tide. |
| 9 | Step-ped-ping-s. |
| 7200 | Step masts and make sail. |
| 1 | Stern-s. |
| 2 | Steward-s. |
| 3 | Stick-ing-s-stuck. |
| 4 | Sticky bottom. |
| 5 | Stiff-ly-ness. |
| 6 | Still-ness. |
| 7 | Stimulate-ed-ing-s. |
| 8 | Stipulate-d-ing-s. |
| 9 | Stipulation-s. |
| 7210 | Stir-red-ring-s. |
| 1 | Stirring up the mud. |
| 2 | Stock-s. |
| 3 | A good stock. |
| 4 | On the stocks. |
| 5 | Stone-s. |
| 6 | Stop-ped-ping-s. |
| 7 | Store-s. |
| 8 | Store-house-s. |
| 9 | Store-ship-s. |
| 7220 | Store-room-s. |
| 1 | Boatswain's stores. |
| 2 | Carpenter's stores. |
| 3 | Gunner's stores. |
| 4 | Naval stores. |
| 5 | Navigator's stores. |
| 6 | Ordnance stores. |
| 7 | In store. |
| 8 | Not in store. |
| 9 | Send for stores. |
| 7230 | Send requisitions for stores. |
| 7231 | Storm-ed-ing-y-s. |

| Nos. | SUB |
|---|---|
| 7232 | Stout-ly. |
| 3 | Stouter-est. |
| 4 | Stove-s. |
| 5 | Stow-ed-ing. |
| 6 | Stowage. |
| 7 | Straggle-d-ing-s. |
| 8 | Straggler-s. |
| 9 | Have picked up stragglers. |
| 7240 | Stragglers have been captured by the enemy. |
| 1 | Strain-ed-ing-s. |
| 2 | Strait-en-ing. |
| 3 | Strand-ed-ing. |
| 4 | Strands. |
| 5 | Strange-ly. |
| 6 | Stranger-s. |
| 7 | Stratagem-s. |
| 8 | Streak-ed-s. |
| 9 | Stream-s. |
| 7250 | Street-s. |
| 1 | Strength-en-ed. |
| 2 | Stress. |
| 3 | By stress of weather. |
| 4 | Stretch-ed-ing-s. |
| 5 | Strict-ly. |
| 6 | Strict-er-est. |
| 7 | Strictness. |
| 8 | Strike-ing-s-struck. |
| 9 | String-strung. |
| 7260 | Strip-ped-ping. |
| 1 | Strive-en-s-strove. |
| 2 | Strong-er-est. |
| 3 | Struggle-d-ing-s. |
| 4 | Stubborn-ness. |
| 5 | Studding sail-s. |
| 6 | Study-ied-ing-ies. |
| 7 | Stuff-ed-ing. |
| 8 | Stuffing box-es. |
| 9 | Stump-s. |
| 7270 | Stun-ned-ning. |
| 1 | Stupid-ity. |
| 2 | Style-s. |
| 3 | Subaltern-s. |
| 4 | Subdivide-d-sion-s. |
| 5 | Subdue-d-ing-s. |
| 6 | Subject-ed-ing-s. |
| 7 | Subjection. |
| 8 | Submit-ted-ting-s. |
| 9 | Submission-s. |
| 7280 | Submissive-ly. |
| 1 | Subordinate-d-s. |
| 7282 | Subordination. |

| Nos. | SUB |
|---|---|
| 7283 | Subsequent-ly. |
| 4 | Subside-d-ing. |
| 5 | Subsidy-ies. |
| 6 | Subsist-ed-ing-s. |
| 7 | Subsistence. |
| 8 | Substance-s. |
| 9 | Substantial-ly. |
| 7290 | Substitute-d-ing-s. |
| 1 | Suburbs. |
| 2 | Subvert-ed-ing-s. |
| 3 | Submissive. |
| 4 | Succeed-ed-ing-s. |
| 5 | Success-es. |
| 6 | Successor-s. |
| 7 | Succor-ed-ing-s. |
| 8 | Such. |
| 9 | Sudden-ly-ness. |
| 7300 | Suffer-ed-ing-s. |
| 1 | Have you suffered? |
| 2 | Have not suffered. |
| 3 | Sufficient-ly. |
| 4 | Have you sufficient? |
| 5 | Has, or have, sufficient. |
| 6 | Has, or have not, sufficient. |
| 7 | Is, or are, sufficient. |
| 8 | Is, or are not, sufficient. |
| 9 | Will be sufficient. |
| 7310 | Will not be sufficient. |
| 1 | Suffocate-d-ing-ion-s. |
| 2 | Sugar. |
| 3 | In want of sugar. |
| 4 | Suggest-ed-ing-s. |
| 5 | Suggestion-s. |
| 6 | Suit-ed-ing-s. |
| 7 | Suitable-y. |
| 8 | Suite-s. |
| 9 | Sulphur. |
| 7320 | Sum-s. |
| 1 | Summer-s. |
| 2 | Summit-s. |
| 3 | Summon-ed-ing-s. |
| 4 | Sun. |
| 5 | At sunrise. |
| 6 | At sunset. |
| 7 | Sunday-s. |
| 8 | Evening. |
| 9 | Morning. |
| 7330 | Night. |
| 1 | Noon. |
| 2 | Sundry. |
| 3 | Sundries. |
| 7334 | Supper-s. |

| Nos. | SUR |
|---|---|
| 7335 | Superintend-ed-ing-s. |
| 6 | Superintendence. |
| 7 | Superior-s. |
| 8 | Superiority. |
| 9 | Supernumerary-ies. |
| 7340 | Supersede-d-ing-s. |
| 1 | Supply-ied-ing-ies. |
| 2 | Can you supply? |
| 3 | Cannot supply. |
| 4 | Has, or have, been suppl'd. |
| 5 | May be supplied. |
| 6 | Will be supplied. |
| 7 | You will supply. |
| 8 | Support-ed-ing-s. |
| 9 | Keep in support'g distance. |
| 7350 | Will you support? |
| 1 | You shall be supported. |
| 2 | You will support me. |
| 3 | Suppose-d-ing-s. |
| 4 | If it be supposed. |
| 5 | Supposed to be. |
| 6 | Suppress-ed-ing-es. |
| 7 | Supreme-ly. |
| 8 | Supremacy. |
| 9 | Sure-ly. |
| 7360 | Surf. |
| 1 | A heavy surf. |
| 2 | How is the surf now? |
| 3 | Is there too much surf? |
| 4 | Not much surf. |
| 5 | Surf boat-s. |
| 6 | Damaged. |
| 7 | Required. |
| 8 | Send. |
| 9 | Surface-s. |
| 7370 | Condenser-s. |
| 1 | Surgeon-s. |
| 2 | Surgical-ly. |
| 3 | Surmount-ed-ing-s. |
| 4 | Surpass-ed-ing-es. |
| 5 | Surplus. |
| 6 | Surprise-d-ing-s. |
| 7 | Beware of surprise. |
| 8 | Endeavor to surprise. |
| 9 | Surrender-ed-ing-s. |
| 7380 | Surround-ed-ing-s. |
| 1 | Survey-ed-ing-ies. |
| 2 | A survey will be held upon. |
| 3 | Hold a survey upon. |
| 4 | Survive-d-ing-s. |
| 7385 | Survivor-s. |

| Nos. | SUS |
|---|---|
| 7386 | Suspect-ed-ing-s. |
| 7 | Suspicious-ly. |
| 8 | Is or are suspicious. |
| 9 | Nothing suspicious. |
| 7390 | Suspend-ed-ing-s. |
| 1 | Suspension-s. |
| 2 | Sustain-ed-ing-s. |
| 3 | Swamp-ed-ing-s. |
| 4 | Swamps-y. |
| 5 | Too swampy for infantry. |
| 6 | Too swampy for transporting ordnance. |
| 7 | Sway-ed-ing-s. |
| 8 | Swear-s-swore-n. |
| 9 | Swearing. |
| 7400 | Swede-n-ish-s. |
| 1 | Sweep-ing-s-swept. |
| 2 | Sweeps. |
| 3 | Cannot use sweeps. |
| 4 | Get out your sweeps. |
| 5 | Have you any sweeps? |
| 6 | Using sweeps. |
| 7 | Swell-s. |
| 8 | A heavy swell. |
| 9 | There is too much swell on. |
| 7410 | There is very little swell on. |
| 1 | Swim-s-ming-swum-swam. |
| 2 | Swing-ing-s. |
| 3 | Swinging boom. |
| 4 | Swivel-s. |
| 5 | Armed with swivels. |
| 6 | Sword-s. |
| 7 | Symbol-s. |
| 8 | Symptoms. |
| 9 | Syphon. |
| 7420 | System-s. |
| 1 | Systematic-al-ly. |
| 2 | Table-s. |
| 3 | Tack-ed-ing-s. |
| 4 | Tack ship. |
| 5 | Tack in succession. |
| 6 | Tack together. |
| 7 | Tack or wear, as most convenient. |
| 8 | Tackle-s. |
| 9 | Gun tackle. |
| 7430 | Tactics. |
| 1 | Tailor-s. |
| 2 | Taint-ed-s. |
| 3 | Take-ing-en-s-took. |
| 7434 | Talk-s. |

| Nos. | TEL |
|---|---|
| 7435 | Tall-er-est. |
| 6 | Tallow. |
| 7 | Tally-ied-ies. |
| 8 | Tank-s. |
| 9 | Bring off the tank-s. |
| 7440 | Can you spare the water tank? |
| 1 | Have finished with the tank. |
| 2 | Have not finished with the tank. |
| 3 | Tar-red-ring. |
| 4 | Coal tar. |
| 5 | Stockholm tar. |
| 6 | Tardy-ily-iness. |
| 7 | Target-s. |
| 8 | Prepare to lay out a target in the direction given by compass signal, and at the distance in yards shown by numeral sig'l. |
| 9 | Place the target more to port. |
| 7450 | Place the target more to starboard. |
| 1 | Pick up target. |
| 2 | Take the target further off. |
| 3 | Too far off, the target is. |
| 4 | Tarpaulin-s. |
| 5 | Hatch tarpaulins. |
| 6 | Taste-d-ing-s. |
| 7 | Tax-es. |
| 8 | Tea-s. |
| 9 | Teach-es-ing-taught. |
| 7460 | Teacher-s. |
| 1 | Teak. |
| 2 | Tear-tore-torn. |
| 3 | Tedious-ness. |
| 4 | Telegraph-ic-s. |
| 5 | Destroy the telegraph, if possible to do so. |
| 6 | The telegraph has been destroyed. |
| 7 | We could not destroy the telegraph. |
| 8 | Communicate by telegraph. |
| 9 | Telegraphic Dictionary. |
| 7470 | Use. |
| 1 | Telescope-s. |
| 2 | Tell-ing-s-told. |
| 3 | Tell him, or them to. |
| 7474 | He told. |

| Nos. | TEL | Nos. | THI |
|---|---|---|---|
| 7475 | They told. | 7527 | It. |
| 6 | Who told? | 8 | It has. |
| 7 | You told. | 9 | It has not. |
| 8 | Temper-ed-ing-s. | 7530 | It has not been. |
| 9 | Temperate-ly. | 1 | It will. |
| 7480 | Temperature-s. | 2 | It will not. |
| 1 | Tempest-s. | 3 | It may. |
| 2 | Tempestuous-ly. | 4 | It may not. |
| 3 | Temporary. | 5 | The. |
| 4 | Temporize-d-ing-s. | 6 | Them. |
| 5 | Tempt-ed-ing-s. | 7 | Themselves. |
| 6 | Temptation-s. | 8 | Thence. |
| 7 | Ten-th. | 9 | Their-s. |
| 8 | Tenacious-ly-ness. | 7540 | Thereabouts. |
| 9 | Tenacity. | 1 | Thereby. |
| 7490 | Tend-ed-ing-s. | 2 | Therefore. |
| 1 | Tendency-ies. | 3 | Is, or are, there. |
| 2 | Tender-ly-ness. | 4 | There is, or are. |
| 3 | Tension. | 5 | There is, or are, not. |
| 4 | Tent-s. | 6 | There can be. |
| 5 | In need of tents. | 7 | There cannot be. |
| 6 | Pitch your tents. | 8 | There may be. |
| 7 | Send tents on shore. | 9 | There may not be. |
| 8 | Strike your tents. | 7550 | There should be. |
| 9 | Terms. | 1 | There should not be. |
| 7500 | Terminate-d-ing-s. | 2 | There was. |
| 1 | Termination-s. | 3 | There was not. |
| 2 | Terrible-y. | 4 | There will be. |
| 3 | Terrify-ied-ing-ies. | 5 | There will not be. |
| 4 | Terrific. | 6 | Therein. |
| 5 | Terror-s. | 7 | Thermometer-s. |
| 6 | Testify-ied-ing-ies. | 8 | These-those. |
| 7 | Than. | 9 | They. |
| 8 | Thank-ed-ing-s. | 7560 | Can. |
| 9 | Thankful-ly-ness. | 1 | Cannot. |
| 7510 | Thank you. | 2 | Did. |
| 1 | Thank them, or him. | 3 | Did not. |
| 2 | That. | 4 | Do. |
| 3 | I. | 5 | Do not. |
| 4 | I am. | 6 | Had. |
| 5 | I have. | 7 | Had not. |
| 6 | I was. | 8 | Have. |
| 7 | You, or your. | 9 | Have not. |
| 8 | He, or his. | 7570 | May. |
| 9 | He is. | 1 | May not. |
| 7520 | He has. | 2 | Shall. |
| 1 | He has not. | 3 | Shall not. |
| 2 | We, or our. | 4 | Will not. |
| 3 | They, or their. | 5 | Will. |
| 4 | The. | 6 | Were not. |
| 5 | With. | 7 | Were. |
| 7526 | Which. | 7578 | Thick-en. |

| Nos. | THI |
|---|---|
| 7579 | Thicker-est. |
| 7580 | Thickly. |
| 1 | Thickness. |
| 2 | Thief-ves. |
| 3 | Thieving-theft. |
| 4 | Thigh-s. |
| 5 | Thigh bone-s. |
| 6 | Thimble-s. |
| 7 | Thin-ly-ness. |
| 8 | Thing-s. |
| 9 | Think-ing-s-thought. |
| 7590 | Do you think? |
| 1 | Do not think. |
| 2 | Thirteen-th. |
| 3 | Thirty-ieth. |
| 4 | This. |
| 5 | Is. |
| 6 | Is not. |
| 7 | Has. |
| 8 | Has not. |
| 9 | Was. |
| 7600 | Was not. |
| 1 | Will. |
| 2 | Will not. |
| 3 | Thorough-ly. |
| 4 | Though. |
| 5 | Thought-ful-ly. |
| 6 | Thoughtfulness. |
| 7 | Thoughtlessness. |
| 8 | Thousand-s. |
| 9 | Threaten-ed-ing. |
| 7610 | Threat-s. |
| 1 | Three. |
| 2 | Through. |
| 3 | Through and through. |
| 4 | Throw-n-threw. |
| 5 | Throw-ed-ing. |
| 6 | Throw a sail, and place it over the leak. |
| 7 | Thrust-s. |
| 8 | Thrust bearing-s. |
| 9 | Thunder-ed ing. |
| 7620 | Thunder storm-s. |
| 1 | Thursday. |
| 2 | Evening. |
| 3 | Morning. |
| 4 | Noon. |
| 5 | Night. |
| 6 | Thus. |
| 7 | Thwart-ed-ing. |
| 8 | Thwarts. |
| 7629 | Thwartships. |

| Nos. | TIN |
|---|---|
| 7630 | Ticket-s. |
| 1 | Tide-s. |
| 2 | Ebb tide. |
| 3 | Eddy tide-s in shore. |
| 4 | Every tide. |
| 5 | Flood tide. |
| 6 | Keep in the tide. |
| 7 | Keep out of the tide. |
| 8 | Lee tide. |
| 9 | Neap tide-s. |
| 7640 | Spring tide-s. |
| 1 | Weather tide. |
| 2 | What is the strength of the tide? |
| 3 | When the tide. |
| 4 | Tide rises and falls the number of feet indicated by numeral signal. |
| 5 | What is the rise and fall of the tide? |
| 6 | Tie-d-ing-s. |
| 7 | Tie-s. |
| 8 | Tier-s. |
| 9 | Cable tiers. |
| 7650 | Tierce-s. |
| 1 | Tight-ly-ness. |
| 2 | Tight-en. |
| 3 | Tighter-est. |
| 4 | Tiller-s. |
| 5 | Tiller ropes. |
| 6 | Timber-s. |
| 7 | Time-ly. |
| 8 | At any time. |
| 9 | Every time. |
| 7660 | First time. |
| 1 | Lost time. |
| 2 | Long time. |
| 3 | Will not have time. |
| 4 | Will have time. |
| 5 | What time? |
| 6 | Short time. |
| 7 | Times. |
| 8 | Several times. |
| 9 | Many times. |
| 7670 | Hard times. |
| 1 | Timid-ly. |
| 2 | Timidity. |
| 3 | Tin-s. |
| 4 | Cans. |
| 5 | Cups. |
| 6 | Pans. |
| 7677 | Sheets. |

| Nos. | TIR |
|---|---|
| 7678 | Tire-d-ing-s. |
| 9 | Tiresome. |
| 7680 | To. |
| 1 | Tobacco. |
| 2 | Together. |
| 3 | Proceed together. |
| 4 | Pull together. |
| 5 | Start together. |
| 6 | Return together. |
| 7 | Make and shorten sail together. |
| 8 | Tack together. |
| 9 | Wear together. |
| 7690 | Work together. |
| 1 | Tolerable-y. |
| 2 | To-morrow. |
| 3 | Evening. |
| 4 | Morning. |
| 5 | Night. |
| 6 | Noon. |
| 7 | Ton-s. |
| 8 | Coal. |
| 9 | Tonnage. |
| 7700 | Tongue-s. |
| 1 | Too. |
| 2 | Few. |
| 3 | Little. |
| 4 | Many. |
| 5 | Much. |
| 6 | Strong. |
| 7 | Stormy. |
| 8 | Tools. |
| 9 | Engineer's tools. |
| 7710 | Carpenter's tools. |
| 1 | Sailmaker's tools. |
| 2 | Top-s. |
| 3 | Top-gallant. |
| 4 | Topmast-s. |
| 5 | Topsail-s. |
| 6 | Top hamper. |
| 7 | Torrent-s. |
| 8 | Torture-s. |
| 9 | Torture d-ing. |
| 7720 | Total-s. |
| 1 | Amount. |
| 2 | Loss. |
| 3 | Number. |
| 4 | Touch-ed-ing-es. |
| 5 | Tough-ly-ness. |
| 6 | Tourniquet-s. |
| 7 | In need of tourniquets. |
| 7728 | Spare tourniquets ? |

| Nos. | TRA |
|---|---|
| 7729 | Take tourniquets with you. |
| 7730 | Tow-ed-ing-s. |
| 1 | Cast off the tow. |
| 2 | Cannot take the vessel in tow. |
| 3 | Take the vessel-s or boat-s in tow. |
| 4 | Towline-s. |
| 5 | Take towline-s. |
| 6 | Cut, or cast off, towline-s. |
| 7 | Pay out more towline. |
| 8 | Shorten in towline-s. |
| 9 | Send for towline-s. |
| 7740 | Towards. |
| 1 | Tower-s. |
| 2 | Can you see the light-house tower ? |
| 3 | The light-house tower is in sight. |
| 4 | The light-house tower is not in sight. |
| 5 | Destroy the light-house tower. |
| 6 | Town-s. |
| 7 | Do not fire into the town. |
| 8 | Fire into the town. |
| 9 | Shall I fire into the town ? |
| 7750 | Throw shells into the town. |
| 1 | Thr'w shells over the town. |
| 2 | Set fire to the town and retreat. |
| 3 | Hold the town as long as you can. |
| 4 | Trace-d-ing-s. |
| 5 | Tracing linen. |
| 6 | Tracing paper. |
| 7 | Track-ed-ing-s. |
| 8 | Trade. |
| 9 | Prohibit trade. |
| 7760 | Permit trade. |
| 1 | Train-ed-ing-s. |
| 2 | Do not fire the train. |
| 3 | Fire the train. |
| 4 | Lay a train. |
| 5 | Train your guns on the enemy. |
| 6 | Train your guns more to the left. |
| 7 | Train your guns more to the right. |
| 7768 | Train your guns upon the compass point shown. |

| Nos. | TRA |
|---|---|
| 7769 | Traitor-s. |
| 7770 | Traitorous-ly. |
| 1 | Tranquil-ly. |
| 2 | Transact-ed-ing-s. |
| 3 | Transaction-s. |
| 4 | Transfer-red-ring-s. |
| 5 | Transfer the prisoners. |
| 6 | Transfer the crew-s. |
| 7 | Transfer the recruits. |
| 8 | Transfer your flag to the. |
| 9 | Transfer accounts, send. |
| 7780 | Transfer prisoners to. |
| 1 | Transfers. |
| 2 | Make. |
| 3 | Translate-d-ing-s. |
| 4 | The communication. |
| 5 | Transmit-ted-ting-s. |
| 6 | Transmission. |
| 7 | Transpire-d-ing-s. |
| 8 | It has transpired. |
| 9 | It has not transpired. |
| 7790 | Transport-s. |
| 1 | Empty transports. |
| 2 | Prepare transports for the reception of. |
| 3 | Coming from. |
| 4 | Going to. |
| 5 | Expected with reinforcements. |
| 6 | Transported-ing. |
| 7 | Men. |
| 8 | Provisions. |
| 9 | Guns. |
| 7800 | Ammunition. |
| 1 | Traverse-d-ing. |
| 2 | Traverses. |
| 3 | Erect traverses. |
| 4 | Treachery-ies. |
| 5 | Treacherous-ly. |
| 6 | Treason-s. |
| 7 | Treasonable-y. |
| 8 | Treasurer-s. |
| 9 | Treat-ed-ing-s. |
| 7810 | Treasury Department. |
| 1 | Secretary of the Treasury. |
| 2 | Treasury notes. |
| 3 | Treasury Department instructions. |
| 4 | Treasury circular-s. |
| 5 | Treasure-s. |
| 7816 | Have treasure on board. |

| Nos. | TRO |
|---|---|
| 7817 | Receive the treasure on board. |
| 8 | Look out for the treasure. |
| 9 | Guard the treasure well. |
| 7820 | Treaty-ies. |
| 1 | Treaty of alliance. |
| 2 | Treaty of peace. |
| 3 | Treble. |
| 4 | Tree-s. |
| 5 | Chess tree-s. |
| 6 | Tremble-d-ing-s. |
| 7 | Tremulous-ly-ness. |
| 8 | Tremendous-ly. |
| 9 | Trench-es. |
| 7830 | Triangle-s. |
| 1 | Triangular-ly. |
| 2 | Triangulate-d-ing. |
| 3 | Triangulation-s. |
| 4 | Tributory-ies. |
| 5 | Trick-s. |
| 6 | Tricky. |
| 7 | Trickster-s. |
| 8 | Trifle-d-ing-s. |
| 9 | Trifler-s. |
| 7840 | Trim-med-ming-s. |
| 1 | Trim ship. |
| 2 | Triumph-ed-ing-s. |
| 3 | Triumphant-ly. |
| 4 | Troop-s. |
| 5 | Embark troops. |
| 6 | For troops. |
| 7 | Full of troops. |
| 8 | Has, or have, troops. |
| 9 | Land troops. |
| 7850 | Landed-ing troops. |
| 1 | Prepare to receive troops. |
| 2 | Prepare to land the troops. |
| 3 | Troop ship-s. |
| 4 | Troops are ready. |
| 5 | Troops will be ready. |
| 6 | Troops are expected. |
| 7 | Troops have arrived at. |
| 8 | Trophy-ies. |
| 9 | Trouble-d-ing-s. |
| 7860 | Troublesome. |
| 1 | Troublesome business. |
| 2 | Trowsers. |
| 3 | Blue trowsers. |
| 4 | Blue frocks and trowsers. |
| 5 | Blue frocks and white trowsers. |
| 7866 | White trowsers. |

| Nos. | TRO |
|---|---|
| 7867 | White frocks and trowsers. |
| 8 | White frocks and blue trowsers. |
| 9 | Truce-s. |
| 7870 | Flag of truce. |
| 1 | Do not receive the flag of truce. |
| 2 | Receive the flag of truce. |
| 3 | Send a flag of truce. |
| 4 | Truce is at an end. |
| 5 | Truce will not be recognized any longer. |
| 6 | Truce has been broken. |
| 7 | Truce may be renewed if requested. |
| 8 | Truck-s. |
| 9 | True-ly. |
| 7880 | Truth-ful-ly-ness. |
| 1 | Trumpet-s. |
| 2 | Trumpeter-s. |
| 3 | Trust-ed-ing. |
| 4 | Trustworthy. |
| 5 | Try-ied-ing-ies. |
| 6 | Have you tried? |
| 7 | Have tried. |
| 8 | Have not tried. |
| 9 | Will try. |
| 7890 | Tub-s. |
| 1 | Fire tubs. |
| 2 | Tube-s. |
| 3 | Boiler tubes. |
| 4 | Plug tubes. |
| 5 | Leaky tubes. |
| 6 | Tuesday-s. |
| 7 | Evening. |
| 8 | Morning. |
| 9 | Night. |
| 7900 | Noon. |
| 1 | Tumult-s. |
| 2 | Tumultuous-ly. |
| 3 | Tun-s, ton-s. |
| 4 | Turbulent-ly. |
| 5 | Turbulence. |
| 6 | Turn-ed-ing-s. |
| 7 | Turn about. |
| 8 | Turn away the stranger. |
| 9 | Turtle. |
| 7910 | Twelve-th. |
| 1 | Twenty-ieth. |
| 2 | Twine. |
| 3 | Twist-ed-ing-s. |
| 7914 | Twice. |

| Nos. | UND |
|---|---|
| 7915 | Two. |
| 6 | Tyranny-ies. |
| 7 | Tyranical-ly. |
| 8 | Tyranize-d-ing-s. |
| 9 | Tyrant-s. |
| 7920 | Ulcer-s. |
| 1 | Ultimate-ly. |
| 2 | Unable. |
| 3 | I am, to. |
| 4 | They are, to. |
| 5 | We are, to. |
| 6 | Unaccountable-y. |
| 7 | Unaccustomed. |
| 8 | Unacknowledged. |
| 9 | Unacquainted. |
| 7930 | Unanswerable. |
| 1 | Unarmed. |
| 2 | Vessels protect the. |
| 3 | Vessels convoy. |
| 4 | Unattended. |
| 5 | Unauthorized. |
| 6 | Unavoidable-y. |
| 7 | Unaware-s. |
| 8 | Unbecoming. |
| 9 | Unbend-ing-unbent. |
| 7940 | Unbend sails. |
| 1 | Unbend cables. |
| 2 | Unbit-ted. |
| 3 | Unbounded. |
| 4 | Uncertain. |
| 5 | Uncertainty-ies. |
| 6 | Unchangeable-y. |
| 7 | Uncivil-ly. |
| 8 | Uncivilized. |
| 9 | Uncomfortable. |
| 7950 | Uncommon-ly. |
| 1 | Unconcern-ed-ly. |
| 2 | Unconditional-ly. |
| 3 | Unconquerable-y. |
| 4 | Unconscious-ly. |
| 5 | Uncover-ed-ing. |
| 6 | Undeceive-d-ing. |
| 7 | Undecided. |
| 8 | Underrate-d-ing. |
| 9 | Undergo-ing-s. |
| 7960 | Undergone. |
| 1 | Underhand. |
| 2 | Underhanded. |
| 3 | Undermine-d-ing-s. |
| 4 | Understand-ing-s-understood. |
| 5 | Do you understand? |
| 7966 | Do not understand. |

| Nos. | UND | Nos. | UNS |
|---|---|---|---|
| 7967 | Does he understand. | 8019 | Unintentional-ly. |
| 8 | Is it understood. | 8020 | Unite-d-ing. |
| 9 | It is perfectly understood. | 1 | United States flag. |
| 7970 | Undertake-n-s-undertook. | 2 | United States man-of-war. |
| 1 | Hazardous undertaking. | 3 | United States of Colombia. |
| 2 | He, or they, undertook to. | 4 | Union. |
| 3 | Undertaking-s. | 5 | Union flag. |
| 4 | Underweigh-way. | 6 | Universal-ly. |
| 5 | I am. | 7 | Unjust-ly. |
| 6 | Get. | 8 | Unjustifiable-y. |
| 7 | Shall I get? | 9 | Unknown. |
| 8 | Do not get. | 8030 | Unlawful-ly-ness. |
| 9 | Squadron will get. | 1 | Unless. |
| 7980 | The flotilla will get. | 2 | Unlicensed. |
| 1 | The boats will get. | 3 | Unlike-ly. |
| 2 | Undeserve-d-ing. | 4 | Unload-ed-ing. |
| 3 | Undetermine-d. | 5 | Unlucky-ily. |
| 4 | Undisciplined. | 6 | Unmanageable. |
| 5 | Undiscovered. | 7 | Unman-ned. |
| 6 | Undo-undid. | 8 | Unmanly. |
| 7 | Undoubted-ly. | 9 | Unmerciful-ly. |
| 8 | Undress-ed-ing. | 8040 | Unmolested-ing. |
| 9 | Ship. | 1 | Unmoor-ed-ing. |
| 7990 | Uneasy-ily. | 2 | Ship-s. |
| 1 | Uneasiness. | 3 | Not ready to unmoor. |
| 2 | Unequal-ly. | 4 | Ready to unmoor. |
| 3 | Unequaled. | 5 | When will you be ready to unmoor? |
| 4 | Unexecuted. | 6 | Prepare to unmoor. |
| 5 | Unexpected-ly. | 7 | Unmoved. |
| 6 | Unfair-ness. | 8 | Unnecessary-ily. |
| 7 | Unfairly. | 9 | Unobserved. |
| 8 | Unfaithful-ness. | 8050 | Unoccupied. |
| 9 | Unfathomed-able. | 1 | Unpardonable-ly. |
| 8000 | Unfavorable-y. | 2 | Unpleasant-ly-ness. |
| 1 | Unfeeling. | 3 | Unpopular. |
| 2 | Unfinished. | 4 | Unprecedented. |
| 3 | Unfit-ness. | 5 | Unprepared. |
| 4 | Unforseen. | 6 | Unprotected. |
| 5 | Unfortified. | 7 | Appear to be unprotected. |
| 6 | Place. | 8 | Unprovoked. |
| 7 | Unfortunate-ly. | 9 | Attack. |
| 8 | Unfriendly. | 8060 | Assault. |
| 9 | Unfrequented. | 1 | Unqualified. |
| 8010 | Unguarded-ly. | 2 | Unreasonable-y. |
| 1 | Unhappy-ily. | 3 | Unreeve-rove. |
| 2 | Unhealthy-iness. | 4 | Unrewarded. |
| 3 | Unhurt. | 5 | Unrig-ged-ging. |
| 4 | Uniform-s. | 6 | Unruly. |
| 5 | Uniformly-ity. | 7 | Unsafe-ly. |
| 6 | Uniformed. | 8 | Unserviceable. |
| 7 | Uninhabited. | | |
| 8018 | Unintelligible. | 8069 | Unsettled. |

| Nos. | UNS | Nos. | VES |
|---|---|---|---|
| 8070 | Unship-ped. | 8118 | Valiant-ly. |
| 1 | Unsuccessful-ly. | 9 | Valid-ity. |
| 2 | Unsupportable-y. | 8120 | Valley-s. |
| 3 | Untenable. | 1 | Value-d-ing. |
| 4 | Unthankful. | 2 | Valuable. |
| 5 | Until. | 3 | Valve s. |
| 6 | Unto. | 4 | Safety valve-s. |
| 7 | Untouched. | 5 | Valve gear. |
| 8 | Untoward. | 6 | Van. |
| 9 | Unusual. | 7 | Form the van. |
| 8080 | Is very unusual. | 8 | In the van. |
| 1 | Unwarrantable-y. | 9 | The van will. |
| 2 | Unwelcome. | 8130 | The squadron. |
| 3 | Unwholesome-ness. | 1 | Vane-s. |
| 4 | Unwilling-ly-ness. | 2 | Vanish-ed-ing. |
| 5 | Unworthy-ily-iness. | 3 | Vanity-ies. |
| 6 | Up. | 4 | Variance. |
| 7 | Upward. | 5 | Vary-ed-ing. |
| 8 | Upon. | 6 | Variable-y. |
| 9 | Upper. | 7 | Variation-s. |
| 8090 | Uppermost. | 8 | What is the variation here? |
| 1 | Upright-ly-ness. | 9 | Veal. |
| 2 | Upset-ting-s. | 8140 | Veer-ed-ing. |
| 3 | Urge-d-ing-s. | 1 | Vegetables. |
| 4 | Urgent. | 2 | Get as many vegetables as you can. |
| 5 | Us. | 3 | Send for fresh vegetables for the crew. |
| 6 | Use-d-ing-s. | 4 | Vegetables can't be found. |
| 7 | Useful-ly. | 5 | Velocity-ies. |
| 8 | Usefulness. | 6 | Vent-s. |
| 9 | Useless-ly. | 7 | Vent bit-s. |
| 8100 | Usual-ly. | 8 | Vent piece-s. |
| 1 | Usurp-ed-ing. | 9 | Ventilate-d-ing. |
| 2 | Usurpation-s. | 8150 | Ventilation. |
| 3 | Utensil-s. | 1 | Ventilator-s. |
| 4 | Cooking utensils. | 2 | Venture-d-ing. |
| 5 | Utility. | 3 | Will not venture. |
| 6 | Utmost. | 4 | Do not venture. |
| 7 | Vacant. | 5 | Veracity. |
| 8 | Vacancy-ies. | 6 | Verbal-ly. |
| 9 | Vaccine. | 7 | Verbatim. |
| 8110 | Vaccinate-ed-ing. | 8 | Verdict-s. |
| 1 | Have you any vaccine matter on board? | 9 | Verify-ied-ies. |
| 2 | I have vaccine matter. | 8160 | Verifying. |
| 3 | My crew has been vaccinated. | 1 | Vertical-ly. |
| 4 | My crew has not been vaccinated. | 2 | Very. |
|  |  | 3 | Fast. |
| 5 | Send me vaccine if it can be spared. | 4 | Slow. |
|  |  | 5 | Vessel-s. |
| 6 | Vaccinate your crew. | 8166 | Count the vessels and report the number. |
| 8117 | Vain-ly. |  |  |

| Nos. | VES |
|---|---|
| 8167 | Do not quit the vessel in your boats, as life boats are going to you. |
| 8 | Does the vessel, or do the vessels? |
| 9 | Vessel-s look-s like. |
| 8170 | Your only chance safety is in sticking by your vessel. |
| 1 | Veteran-s. |
| 2 | Vex-ed-ing-es. |
| 3 | Vexation-ous. |
| 4 | Vibrate-d-ing. |
| 5 | Vice-s. |
| 6 | Vicious-ly-ness. |
| 7 | Vicinity. |
| 8 | Victory-ies. |
| 9 | A great victory has been won. |
| 8180 | Victor-s. |
| 1 | Victorious-ly. |
| 2 | Victuals. |
| 3 | Victualled-ing. |
| 4 | View-ed-ing. |
| 5 | Vigilant-ly. |
| 6 | Vigilance. |
| 7 | The greatest vigilance. |
| 8 | Vigor. |
| 9 | Vigorous-ly. |
| 8190 | Village-s. |
| 1 | Villain-ous-ly. |
| 2 | Vindicate-d-ing. |
| 3 | Vindication. |
| 4 | Vinegar. |
| 5 | Violate-ed-ing-s. |
| 6 | Violation. |
| 7 | Violence. |
| 8 | Violent-ly. |
| 9 | Virtue-al-ly. |
| 8200 | Virtuous-ly. |
| 1 | Visible-ly. |
| 2 | Vision-s. |
| 3 | Visit-ed-ing-s. |
| 4 | Visits. |
| 5 | Visitor-s. |
| 6 | Vital-ly. |
| 7 | Vitality. |
| 8 | Vocabulary-ies. |
| 9 | French. |
| 8210 | German. |
| 1 | Italian. |
| 8212 | Portuguese. |

| Nos. | WAR |
|---|---|
| 8213 | Russian. |
| 4 | Spanish. |
| 5 | Voice-s. |
| 6 | Volley-s. |
| 7 | Volume-s. |
| 8 | Voluminous. |
| 9 | Volunteer-ed-ing. |
| 8220 | Volunteers. |
| 1 | Voluntarily. |
| 2 | Vouch-ed-ing. |
| 3 | Voucher-s. |
| 4 | Send vouchers for. |
| 5 | Voyage-s. |
| 6 | Vulnerable. |
| 7 | Wad-s. |
| 8 | Wadding. |
| 9 | Wade-ing-s. |
| 8230 | Wage-d-ing-s. |
| 1 | War. |
| 2 | Wages. |
| 3 | Wagon-s. |
| 4 | Wait-ed-ing-s. |
| 5 | Am I to wait? |
| 6 | Is he to wait? |
| 7 | Wait until further orders. |
| 8 | Wait until the weather moderates. |
| 9 | Wake-s. |
| 8240 | In my wake. |
| 1 | In your wake. |
| 2 | Keep more in the wake of your second ahead. |
| 3 | Keep more in the wake of each other. |
| 4 | Want-ed-ing-s. |
| 5 | Want-s. |
| 6 | In want of coal. |
| 7 | In want of fuel. |
| 8 | In want of immediate assistance. |
| 9 | In want of medical aid. |
| 8250 | In want of medicines. |
| 1 | In want of provisions. |
| 2 | In want of water. |
| 3 | In want of an anchor. |
| 4 | In want of an anchor and cable. |
| 5 | Are you in want of assistance? |
| 6 | What are your wants? |
| 7 | War-s. |
| 8258 | Warlike. |

| Nos. | WAR | Nos. | WEA |
|---|---|---|---|
| 8259 | War has been declared between. | 8307 | Water is shoaling. |
| 8260 | The movements appear to be warlike. | 8 | Waterways. |
| 1 | Wardroom-s. | 9 | Ware-s. |
| 2 | Warm-ly. | 8310 | Way-s. |
| 3 | Warm-ed-ing. | 1 | A different way. |
| 4 | Warn off the stranger. | 2 | By the way of. |
| 5 | Warp-ed-ing-s. | 3 | The same way. |
| 6 | Warp in or out. | 4 | Which way was she going? |
| 7 | Warping lines, send | 5 | Which way are you going? |
| 8 | Warrant-s. | 6 | We. |
| 9 | Warrant officer-s. | 7 | Are. |
| 8270 | Was. | 8 | Are not. |
| 1 | It. | 9 | Can. |
| 2 | He. | 8320 | Cannot. |
| 3 | My. | 1 | Did. |
| 4 | Not. | 2 | Did not. |
| 5 | She. | 3 | Do. |
| 6 | The. | 4 | Do not. |
| 7 | There. | 5 | Could. |
| 8 | Washington-s. | 6 | Could not. |
| 9 | Birthday. | 7 | Have. |
| 8280 | City. | 8 | Have not. |
| 1 | From Washington City. | 9 | May. |
| 2 | Have you any news from Washington City? | 8330 | May not. |
| 3 | To Washington City. | 1 | Weak-ly. |
| 4 | Send to Washington City. | 2 | Is very weak. |
| 5 | Wash-ed-ing-es. | 3 | Weaken-ed-ing-s. |
| 6 | Clothes. | 4 | Wear-wore-worn. |
| 7 | Day-s. | 5 | Wear ship immediately. |
| 8 | Waste-d-ing-s. | 6 | Wear ship together. |
| 9 | Cotton-waste. | 7 | Wear ship in succession. |
| 8290 | Hemp-waste. | 8 | Wear as convenient. |
| 1 | Wasteful-ly. | 9 | Wear, the sternmost vessels first. |
| 2 | Watch-ed-ing-es. | 8340 | Weather. |
| 3 | Watchful-ly-ness. | 1 | Bad weather. |
| 4 | Watch-es. | 2 | Better weather. |
| 5 | Regular watch-es. | 3 | Fine weather. |
| 6 | The officer-s of the watch. | 4 | Pleasant weather. |
| 7 | Watch officer-s. | 5 | Rainy weather. |
| 8 | Watch the movements of the. | 6 | Thick weather. |
| 9 | Water. | 7 | Should the weather. |
| 8300 | Fathoms water. | 8 | Weather has been. |
| 1 | Gallons water. | 9 | Weather may be. |
| 2 | Fresh water. | 8350 | Weather is very uncertain. |
| 3 | Good water. | 1 | When the weath'r changes. |
| 4 | Water is bad. | 2 | Weather-ly. |
| 5 | Water is brackish. | 3 | Can weather. |
| 8306 | Water ship from shore. | 4 | Cannot weather. |
| | | 5 | Has, or have, weathered. |
| | | 8356 | Try to weather the. |

| Nos. | WEA |
|---|---|
| 8357 | Is very weatherly. |
| 8 | Is not weatherly. |
| 9 | Wedge-s. |
| 8360 | Wednesday-s. |
| 1 | Evening. |
| 2 | Morning. |
| 3 | Night. |
| 4 | Noon. |
| 5 | Weed. |
| 6 | Grief weed. |
| 7 | Sea weed. |
| 8 | Week-ly. |
| 9 | Last week. |
| 8370 | Next week. |
| 1 | Several weeks. |
| 2 | Weekly accounts. |
| 3 | Weekly reports. |
| 4 | Weigh-ed-ing-s. |
| 5 | Anchor. |
| 6 | Do not weigh. |
| 7 | Cannot weigh. |
| 8 | Weigh, outermost vessels first. |
| 9 | Welcome. |
| 8380 | Weld-ed-ing-s. |
| 1 | Well. |
| 2 | All is well. |
| 3 | All are well on board. |
| 4 | As well as. |
| 5 | I hope you are quite well. |
| 6 | Not as well as. |
| 7 | Not very well. |
| 8 | Very well. |
| 9 | Very well I thank you. |
| 8390 | Went. |
| 1 | Were. |
| 2 | They? |
| 3 | They not? |
| 4 | You? |
| 5 | You not? |
| 6 | You ever? |
| 7 | We? |
| 8 | We not? |
| 9 | When were? |
| 8400 | When were you? |
| 1 | When were they? |
| 2 | Wet-ting. |
| 3 | Wet clothes, pipe up to dry. |
| 4 | Whale-s. |
| 5 | Whale boat-s. |
| 8406 | Can you land safely in a whale boat? |

| Nos. | WHY |
|---|---|
| 8407 | Is your whale boat in good order? |
| 8 | Have you a whale boat? |
| 9 | Send your whale boat. |
| 8410 | Wharf-s. |
| 1 | Wharfage. |
| 2 | What? |
| 3 | What number of men and what materials do you require? |
| 4 | Wheat-en. |
| 5 | Wheel-ed-ing. |
| 6 | Wheel into line. |
| 7 | Wheel to the left. |
| 8 | Wheel to the right. |
| 9 | Wheels. |
| 8420 | When-ever. |
| 1 | I. |
| 2 | I am. |
| 3 | I can. |
| 4 | He. |
| 5 | It. |
| 6 | We. |
| 7 | They. |
| 8 | They are. |
| 9 | We are. |
| 8430 | You. |
| 1 | You are. |
| 2 | Will. |
| 3 | Where. |
| 4 | Are you bound to? |
| 5 | Are you from? |
| 6 | I am. |
| 7 | You are. |
| 8 | Was, or were. |
| 9 | They are. |
| 8440 | We are. |
| 1 | We were. |
| 2 | Whether. |
| 3 | Which. |
| 4 | Whilst. |
| 5 | Whirlpool-s. |
| 6 | Whirlwind-s. |
| 7 | White. |
| 8 | Whiting. |
| 9 | Who. |
| 8450 | Whom. |
| 1 | Whose. |
| 2 | Whole-ly. |
| 3 | Wholesome. |
| 4 | Why. |
| 8455 | Why not? |

| Nos. | WHY |
|---|---|
| 8456 | Why should? |
| 7 | Wide. |
| 8 | How wide is the? |
| 9 | It is wide. |
| 8460 | It is not wide. |
| 1 | Widen-ed-ing. |
| 2 | Width-s. |
| 3 | Wife-ves. |
| 4 | Wild-ly. |
| 5 | Wildest. |
| 6 | Wilful-ly-ness. |
| 7 | Will. |
| 8 | Be. |
| 9 | Not. |
| 8470 | Not be. |
| 1 | Willing-ly-ness. |
| 2 | I am willing. |
| 3 | I am not willing. |
| 4 | They are willing. |
| 5 | They are not willing. |
| 6 | They were willing. |
| 7 | They were not willing. |
| 8 | Win-won. |
| 9 | Winch-es. |
| 8480 | Wind-s. |
| 1 | Keep close to the wind. |
| 2 | Keep by the wind. |
| 3 | A fair wind. |
| 4 | A head wind. |
| 5 | By the wind. |
| 6 | Off the wind. |
| 7 | How was the wind? |
| 8 | The wind was. |
| 9 | Windward-ly. |
| 8490 | Beat-ing to windward. |
| 1 | Keep well to windward. |
| 2 | Pull to windward. |
| 3 | Stand to windward and keep a sharp lookout for sails. |
| 4 | The stranger is dead to windward. |
| 5 | How is the vessel to windward standing? |
| 6 | How does the vessel to windward bear? |
| 7 | Windlass-es. |
| 8 | Window-s. |
| 9 | Wing-s. |
| 8500 | Wing and wing. |
| 1 | Winter-y. |
| 8502 | In the winter. |

| Nos. | WOR |
|---|---|
| 8503 | Winter clothing. |
| 4 | Winter quarters. |
| 5 | Winter weather. |
| 6 | Wire-s. |
| 7 | Priming wire-s. |
| 8 | Wise-ly. |
| 9 | Wisdom. |
| 8510 | Wish-ed-ing. |
| 1 | Wishes. |
| 2 | To. |
| 3 | It is my wish that. |
| 4 | Does not wish. |
| 5 | Is it your wish? |
| 6 | If you wish. |
| 7 | It is the wish of. |
| 8 | With. |
| 9 | Him. |
| 8520 | Me. |
| 1 | Them. |
| 2 | You. |
| 3 | Withdraw-drew-ing. |
| 4 | From action. |
| 5 | Do not withdraw. |
| 6 | Enemy is withdrawing. |
| 7 | Within. |
| 8 | Without. |
| 9 | Withstand-s. |
| 8530 | Withstood. |
| 1 | Witness-es. |
| 2 | Woman-men. |
| 3 | Wonder-ful-ly. |
| 4 | Wood-en. |
| 5 | Cannot procure wood. |
| 6 | Cut wood. |
| 7 | Procure wood. |
| 8 | Wooding. |
| 9 | Party-ies. |
| 8540 | Wool-en-s. |
| 1 | Woolen clothing. |
| 2 | Word-ed-ing. |
| 3 | Words. |
| 4 | Work. |
| 5 | Working. |
| 6 | Party-ies. |
| 7 | Send for working party-ies. |
| 8 | Send working party-ies. |
| 9 | Workman-men. |
| 8550 | Worm-s. |
| 1 | Worm eaten. |
| 2 | Worm holes. |
| 8553 | Worry-ied-ing. |

| Nos. | WOR |
|---|---|
| 8554 | Worse-t. |
| 5 | Much worse. |
| 6 | No worse. |
| 7 | Could not be worse. |
| 8 | Worth. |
| 9 | Worthy-ily. |
| 8560 | Worthless-ness. |
| 1 | Would. |
| 2 | It? |
| 3 | Not? |
| 4 | You? |
| 5 | They? |
| 6 | We? |
| 7 | Wound-ed. |
| 8 | Badly wounded. |
| 9 | Many wounded. |
| 8570 | No one wounded. |
| 1 | Slightly wounded. |
| 2 | Seriously wounded. |
| 3 | The wounded are. |
| 4 | The wounded are not. |
| 5 | The wounded are doing well. |
| 6 | Wreck-ed-s. |
| 7 | Bring off all you can from the wreck. |
| 8 | Can you reach the wreck? |
| 9 | Cannot get alongside of the wreck. |
| 8580 | Cannot save the wreck. |
| 1 | Destroy the wreck. |
| 2 | Enemy is in possession of the wreck. |
| 3 | Enemy has attacked the wreck. |
| 4 | Wrench-ed-ing. |
| 5 | Wrenches. |
| 6 | Monkey wrench-es. |
| 7 | Screw wrench-es. |
| 8 | Wretch-ed-ness. |
| 9 | Wretchedly. |
| 8590 | Write-wrote. |
| 1 | Writer-s. |
| 2 | Written. |
| 3 | Have written. |
| 4 | Have not written. |
| 5 | Have you written? |
| 6 | Wrong-s. |
| 7 | Very wrong. |
| 8 | Wrongful-ly. |
| 9 | Wrought iron. |
| 8600 | Yard-s. |

| Nos. | ZEA |
|---|---|
| 8601 | Yarn-s. |
| 2 | Spun yarn. |
| 3 | Yaw-s-ing. |
| 4 | Yawing about. |
| 5 | Year-s-ly. |
| 6 | Last year. |
| 7 | This year. |
| 8 | Next year. |
| 9 | Every year. |
| 8610 | How many years? |
| 1 | Several years. |
| 2 | Yellow. |
| 3 | Bunting. |
| 4 | Fever. |
| 5 | Yeoman-men. |
| 6 | Yes-affirmative-consent. |
| 7 | Yesterday. |
| 8 | Evening. |
| 9 | Morning. |
| 8620 | Noon. |
| 1 | Yet. |
| 2 | Not yet. |
| 3 | Yield-ed-ing-s. |
| 4 | Yonder. |
| 5 | You. |
| 6 | Are. |
| 7 | Are not. |
| 8 | Did. |
| 9 | Did not. |
| 8630 | Do. |
| 1 | Do not. |
| 2 | Have. |
| 3 | Have not. |
| 4 | May. |
| 5 | May not. |
| 6 | Must. |
| 7 | Must not. |
| 8 | I should. |
| 9 | Should. |
| 8640 | Were. |
| 1 | Were not. |
| 2 | Would. |
| 3 | Would not. |
| 4 | Your-self-selves. |
| 5 | Your orders will be sent. |
| 6 | Young-er. |
| 7 | Youngest. |
| 8 | Youth-ful-ly. |
| 9 | Zeal. |
| 8650 | With zeal and energy we must succeed. |

| Nos. | ZEA | Nos. | ZIN |
|---|---|---|---|
| 8651 | Your zeal has been particularly noticed. | 8654 | A zealous coöperation is expected. |
| 2 | Without zeal and energy we cannot expect to be successful. | 5 | Zinc. |
| | | 6 | Paint-s. |
| | | 8657 | Sheet-s. |
| 8653 | Zealous-ly. | | |

# BOAT, SQUADRON, AND FLOTILLA SIGNALS.

## GEOGRAPHICAL PART.

[*Geographical Pendant hoisted or separately.*]

| | A. |
|---|---|
| 1 | Accomac Co., Va. |
| 2 | Abaco. |
| 3 | Abaco Isles. |
| 4 | Abacou. |
| 5 | Abbeville. |
| 6 | Abrigo Island. |
| 7 | Abrolhos. |
| 8 | Absecom Inlet, N. J. |
| 9 | Absecom Light-house. |
| 10 | Acapulco. |
| 1 | Accotink. |
| 2 | Acklin Island, W. I. |
| 3 | Admiral's Cove. |
| 4 | Adriatic. |
| 5 | Africa. |
| 6 | Agamenticus Hill, Me. |
| 7 | Aggermore Rock. |
| 8 | Agnes Island. |
| 9 | Aguada Bay. |
| 20 | Aguadilla Bay. |
| 1 | Agua del Key. |
| 2 | Agugas Point. |
| 3 | Ajon Reef. |
| 4 | Ajuero. |
| 5 | Alacran-s. |
| 6 | Albany, N. Y. |
| 7 | Albemarle Sound, N. C. |
| 8 | Albion Bank. |
| 9 | Alcatrases Shoals, Cuba. |
| 30 | Alcatrazes, Brazil. |
| 1 | Alcoutra. |
| 2 | Alcoy Island. |
| 3 | Alexandria, Va. |
| 4 | Algatroba Point. |
| 5 | Algiers. |
| 6 | Allanis Hole. |
| 7 | Alligator Pond Key. |
| 8 | Alligator Reef. |
| 39 | All Saints, W. I. |
| 40 | All Saint's Bay, Brazil. |
| 1 | Almirante Bay. |
| 2 | Alright Cape. |
| 3 | Altowaba. |
| 4 | Altovelo. |
| 5 | Alvarado. |
| 6 | Amufades, Brazil. |
| 7 | Amazon River. |
| 8 | Ambergris Key, W. I. |
| 9 | Amelia Island Light-house. |
| 50 | Amelia Island. |
| 1 | Amelia River. |
| 2 | Amelia Sound, Ga. |
| 3 | America, North. |
| 4 | America, South. |
| 5 | American Shoal. |
| 6 | Amet Island. |
| 7 | Amherst Harbor. |
| 8 | Amsterdam. |
| 9 | Anasco Bay. |
| 60 | Anastasia Island. |
| 1 | Anchora Islands. |
| 2 | Anchor Islands, Fla. |
| 3 | Andrews, St. |
| 4 | Anegada. |
| 5 | Angerstein's Rocks. |
| 6 | Angostura. |
| 7 | Anguilla, W. I. |
| 8 | Anguilleta Islands. |
| 9 | Anhatomirim Island. |
| 70 | Annandale. |
| 1 | Annapolis, Md. |
| 2 | Annapolis. |
| 3 | Ann, Cape, Mass. |
| 4 | Ann Channel. |
| 5 | Annisquam, Mass. |
| 6 | Anotta Bay. |
| 7 | Anse a Chouchou Bay. |
| 8 | Anse a Claire. |
| 9 | Anse a Galet. |
| 80 | Anses a Pitres. |

81 Anticosti Island.
2 Antigonish.
3 Antigua, W. I.
4 Antonio, Cape.
5 Anton Lizardo.
6 Ants, W. I.
7 Antwerp.
8 Apalachicola Bay, Fla.
9 Ape's Hole Creek.
90 Apple River.
1 Apronague River.
2 Aqua de la Estancia.
3 Aquadores River.
4 Aqua Fort Harbor.
5 Aqueduct, Georgetown, D. C.
6 Aquia Creek, Potomac River.
7 Aquin Bay.
8 Aracary River.
9 Aracati Town.
100 Arachat Harbor.
1 Aransas Pass, Texas.
2 Aransas Light-house.
3 Araya.
4 Arcadins.
5 Arcas.
6 Archimedes Bank.
7 Arena Gorda.
8 Arenas Key.
9 Arenas Point.
110 Arenas Point.
1 Argyle Island, Ga.
2 Armedinos Shoal.
3 Arrecibo.
4 Arichat Harbor.
5 Arsenal Point, Potomac River.
6 Arundel, Ann, county, Md.
7 Artibonite River.
8 Arvoredo Island.
9 Ashapee Harbor.
120 Aspinwall.
1 Aspotogon Harbor.
2 Assateague Island.
3 Assateague Inlet.
4 Assateague Light-house.
5 Atchafalaya.
6 Atchafalaya Bay, La.
7 Atlantic Coast.
8 Atlantic, North.
9 Atlantic, South.
130 Atrato River.
1 Atwood's Key.
2 Audierne Island.
3 Augusta, Ga.
4 Augusta River.
5 Augustine, St., Fla.
136 Austria.
137 Aux Cayes.
8 Aves Islands.
9 Azores.
140 Azua.

B.

141 Babaro.
2 Baburuco.
3 Bacalar.
4 Bacalou Island.
5 Backalieu Island.
6 Back Harbor.
7 Back River, Mass.
8 Back River, Va.
9 Back River Light-house.
150 Back Bone Rock.
1 Baffin's Bay.
2 Bahama Banks.
3 Bahama Islands.
4 Bahama, Cuba.
5 Bahia Alejandro.
6 Bahia, Brazil.
7 Bahia Cabello.
8 Bahia Honda, Fla.
9 Bahia Honda Harbor.
160 Bahia Harbor, Cuba.
1 Bahia Falsa, Brazil.
2 Baie du Mesle.
3 Bajo de Eumedio.
4 Baitiqueri, Cuba.
5 Baie de Ferret.
6 Baie de Flammands.
7 Bajo Navida.
8 Bajo Seco.
9 Baker's Island, Me.
170 Baker's Island Light-house.
1 Baker's Island, Mass.
2 Balair Bay.
3 Balandra Bay.
4 Bald Head, N. C.
5 Balize Rock.
6 Baleine Rock.
7 Baline Cove.
8 Balize.
9 Balize, Miss.
180 Ball's Creek.
1 Balona Shoals, Cuba.
2 Baltimore, Md.
3 Baltic.
4 Bande de l'Arier Bay.
5 Bane Harbor.
6 Banes Port, Cuba.
7 Bangor, Me.
8 Banks of Fla.
189 Bannister Road.

190 Baradaires Bay.
1 Barahona.
2 Barancas, Fla.
3 Barawally Bay, W. I.
4 Barbaioas Bay.
5 Barbuda, W. I.
6 Barbadoes, W. I.
7 Barburet Islands.
8 Barbour's River.
9 Barcelona.
200 Bare Bush Key.
1 Bariay Harbor, Cuba.
2 Barilla River.
3 Barnegat, N. J.
4 Barnegat Light-house.
5 Barn Island Harbor.
6 Barn Islands, Col.
7 Barnett's Harbor.
8 Barnstable Bay, Mass.
9 Barra de St. Vincent, Brazil.
210 Barne's Point.
1 Barrataria.
2 Barra Ciega, Mexico.
3 Barren Bay.
4 Barren Island, Md.
5 Barren Inlet.
6 Barrow Harbor.
7 Barrington.
8 Barrington Bay.
9 Barrister Bay.
220 Barrysway Bay.
1 Bartlett's Reef.
2 Bartlett's Creek.
3 Basin Bark.
4 Basque Harbor.
5 Basse-terre, W. I.
6 Basse, St. Philipe, Caycos, W. I.
7 Bass Harbor, Me.
8 Bass Harbor Light-house.
9 Bass River.
230 Bass Rip.
1 Bastimento Harbor, Col.
2 Bath, Me.
3 Bathurst, Town.
4 Baxo del Comboy.
5 Baxo Nicolao Shoal, Cuba.
6 Baxo Nuevo.
7 Baxo Negro.
8 Baxo de Gallardo.
9 Bayanhibe Harbor.
240 Bayanette.
1 Bayaha Harbor.
2 Bay de l'Eau.
3 Bay de Portage.
244 Bay l'Argent.
245 Bay of Acul.
6 Bay of All Saints.
7 Bay of Biscay.
8 Bay of Bulls.
9 Bay, Bull's, S. C.
250 Bay of Cortez, Cuba.
1 Bay of Cutteau.
2 Bay of Despair.
3 Bay of Fair and False.
4 Bay of Funday.
5 Bay of Ilha Grande.
6 Bay of Islands. N. F.
7 Bay of Islands.
8 Bay of Juliana.
9 Bay of Lort.
260 Bay of Neyba.
1 Bay of Ocoa, Cuba.
2 Bay of Perlas.
3 Bay of Rencontre.
4 Bay of Rotte.
5 Bay of San Christoval.
6 Bay of St. Anthony.
7 Bay of St. Barbe.
8 Bay of St. Genevieve.
9 Bay of St. John.
270 Bay of St. Joseph.
1 Bay of St. Louis.
2 Bay of Thurin.
3 Bay of Truxillo.
4 Bay Roberts.
5 Bay Verte.
6 Bay New Brunswick.
7 Bay d'Omar.
8 Bay of Rocks.
9 Bay of St. Louis.
280 Bayou St. John's, La.
1 Bayou St. John's Light-house.
2 Beach of Destretto.
3 Beach Channel, Fla.
4 Beach of Pernambuco.
5 Beach of Yorres.
6 Beacon.
7 Beacon Inlet.
8 Beagle Island.
9 Beak Point.
290 Bear Bay.
1 Bear Reef Head.
2 Bear Island, Me.
3 Bear Island Light-house.
4 Bear Inlet.
5 Bears' Cove.
6 Beata Island, W. I.
7 Beaufort, N. C.
8 Beaufort, S. C.
9 Beaver Harbor.
300 Beauchene Island.

301 Beaver Tail Light-house, R. I.
2 Bedeque Bay.
3 Bedford, New, Mass.
4 Bedford Reef, L. I. S.
5 Belem City.
6 Belfast, Me.
7 Belgium.
8 Belize.
9 Bell Mountain.
310 Bell Point.
1 Bellaca Rock.
2 Belle Harbor.
3 Belle Islands.
4 Belle Isle.
5 Belle Isle, Straits of.
6 Bell's Run.
7 Beminis.
8 Ben Davis Point.
9 Benedict.
320 Benevento.
1 Bennet's Creek.
2 Bequia Granadines.
3 Berbice.
4 Bergen.
5 Berkly Sound.
6 Bermija Island.
7 Bergantin Bay.
8 Bermudas.
9 Bernal Chico Islands.
330 Berry Islands.
1 Berwick Bay, La.
2 Bescie River.
3 Beverly.
4 Bickerton Harbor.
5 Big Annemessix.
6 Big Pelican Island.
7 Billy Rook.
8 Billingsgate Island.
9 Biloxi.
340 Biloxi Light-house.
1 Bird's Ferry.
2 Bird Island.
3 Bird Rocks.
4 Bird Key, Morant Keys.
5 Bird Rock, W. I.
6 Bird Islands.
7 Birch Island.
8 Bishops.
9 Bishops and Clerk's.
350 Bishop's Head.
1 Bishop's Lagoon.
2 Black Bay.
3 Blackbeard Island.
4 Black Head Bay.
355 Blackstone's Isl'd, Potomac.
356 Blackstone's Island Light-house.
7 Black Point.
8 Black River.
9 Black River, Mosquito Coast.
360 Black Rock.
1 Black Rock Harbor.
2 Black Rock, Mass.
3 Black Rock Point.
4 Black Sea.
5 Black Walnut Cove.
6 Bladensburg.
7 Blanca Island.
8 Blancherotte.
9 Blanquilla Island.
370 Blanquilla Shoal.
1 Blas San.
2 Blind Bay.
3 Block Island, R. I.
4 Block Island Light-house.
5 Bloody Bay.
6 Bloodsworth Island.
7 Blowing Rock.
8 Bluefield's Bay.
9 Bluefield's Lagoon.
380 Blue Hill Bay, Me.
1 Blue Pinion Harbor.
2 Bluff Cape.
3 Bluff Point.
4 Blythe Island.
5 Boat Harbor.
6 Boca Chica.
7 Boca de Cumaysa.
8 Boca de Romana.
9 Boca de Majello.
390 Boca de Nixao.
1 Boca de Quiabou.
2 Boca de Za.
3 Boca de Nigua.
4 Boca Yuma.
5 Boca Tigre.
6 Boca del Toro.
7 Boca Grande.
8 Boca Grande.
9 Boca Grande, Harbor, Fla.
400 Boca Grande Key, Fla.
1 Boca Huevo.
2 Boca Mona.
3 Boca Navios.
4 Boca Valliente.
5 Bocas Islands, W. I.
6 Body's Island, N. C.
7 Body's Island Light-house.
8 Bodkin Swash, Md.
409 Bodkin Point.

410 Bogue Banks.
1 Bogue Inlet.
2 Bohemia River.
3 Bolanderos Islands.
4 Boliver Point, Texas.
5 Boliver Point Light-house.
6 Bom Abrigo.
7 Bombay Hook.
8 Bombay Hook Light-house.
9 Bonacca Islands.
420 Bonaventura Isles.
1 Bonaventure Port.
2 Bonavista Bay.
3 Bonavista Port.
4 Bonne Bay.
5 Bonetta Cove.
6 Bon Fouca Light-house, La.
7 Bonqueron.
8 Booby Island.
9 Boom Rock.
430 Boon Island, Me.
1 Boon Island Light-house.
2 Bootes Rock.
3 Boquerones Point.
4 Borracha Island.
5 Borracha Key.
6 Boss Spit.
7 Boston, Mass.
8 Boston Light-house.
9 Bottomless Bay.
440 Boucan Point.
1 Bowbear Harbor, Me.
2 Bowditch's Ledge, Mass.
3 Bowler's Rock, Rappahannock.
4 Bowles Bank.
5 Boxey Harbor.
6 Brace's Cove, Mass.
7 Braganza Bank.
8 Braha Harbor.
9 Brador Bay.
450 Brackman Bluff.
1 Bram's Point.
2 Brandywine Shoal Light-house.
3 Brangman's Bluff.
4 Brant Island.
5 Brant Island Light Vessel.
6 Brant Point.
7 Branford Reef.
8 Brandywine.
9 Bras d'Or.
460 Brazil Coast.
1 Brazil Rock.
2 Brazos River.
463 Breakneck Passage.
464 Breakwater.
5 Breakwater Light-house.
6 Brenton's Bay.
7 Brenton's Reef.
8 Brenton's Reef Light Vessel.
9 Brent's Point.
470 Brentsville.
1 Breton Bay.
2 Breton Cape.
3 Breton Islands.
4 Briar's Point.
5 Bridgeton.
6 Bridgeport, Conn.
7 Bridgeport Light-house.
8 Bridgeport Harbor.
9 Brier's Island.
480 Brigadier's Island, Me.
1 Brigantine Bay.
2 Brigus Bay.
3 Brigus Harbor.
4 Bristol, Rhode Island.
5 British Guyana.
6 Briton Harbor.
7 Broa Bay, Cuba.
8 Broad Bay.
9 Broad Road.
490 Broad Sound.
1 Brockelsby River.
2 Brodie Rocks.
3 Brono Neck.
4 Brothers, Bahamas.
5 Brothers Islands.
6 Broughton Islands.
7 Brown's Head.
8 Brown's Head Light-house.
9 Brown's Inlet.
500 Brown's Shoal, W. I.
1 Brownsville, Texas.
2 Brune Bank, Jamaica.
3 Brunet Island.
4 Brule Shoals.
5 Brunswick, Ga.
6 Bryan Island.
7 Bryantown.
8 Buck's Harbor, Maine.
9 Buck Island, W. I.
510 Bucksport, Maine.
1 Buenavista Point, Cuba.
2 Buen Ayre Island, W. I.
3 Buenos Ayres.
4 Buey Inlet.
5 Bujio del Gato.
6 Bull's Bay and Harbor, S. C.
7 Bull's Bay Light-house.
8 Bull Point.
519 Bull's Rock.

520 Bumbo Island.
1 Bunker's Ledge, Maine.
2 Burgado.
3 Burgeo Islands.
4 Burin Bay.
5 Burnt Island Light-house.
6 Burin Inlet.
7 Butler's Inlet.
8 Brush Key.
9 Butler's Hole, Mass.
530 Buzzard's Bay, Mass,
1 Buzzard Roost Island.

C.

2 Cabagan River, Cuba.
3 Cabollones Channel, Cuba.
4 Caballos, Port.
5 Cabane Bay.
6 Cabello Porto.
7 Cabbage Island.
8 Cabeza de Toro.
9 Cabezo.
540 Cabo Falso.
1 Cabonico Harbor, Cuba.
2 Cabra Island, W. I.
3 Cabrera.
4 Cæsar's Creek.
5 Cadiz.
6 Cagio River, Cuba.
7 Cahil Rock.
8 Caicos Islands.
9 Caicos Passage.
550 Calavina Harbor.
1 Calvada Island, Brazil.
2 Calcazieu River, La.
3 Calcasieu.
4 Caleton, St. Domingo.
5 Caledonia Bay.
6 Calliagua Bay.
7 Calvert County, Md.
8 Cambridge, Mass.
9 Cambridge, Md.
560 Camden Harbor, Me.
1 Camel's Islands Harbor.
2 Campbell Island.
3 Campbell Town.
4 Campêche.
5 Campo Bello Island, Maine.
6 Canada, Lower.
7 Canada, Upper.
8 Canada Bay.
9 Canal de la Hacha, Cuba.
570 Cananova, Cuba.
1 Canaries.
572 Cancun Island.
573 Candelaria Bay.
4 Canje Creek.
5 Canoe Cove, W. I.
6 Canso Cape.
7 Canso Harbor.
8 Canton.
9 Cape Alwright.
580 Cape Anguille.
1 Cape Ann, Mass.
2 Cape Ann Harbor, Mass.
3 Cape Antonio, Cuba.
4 Cape Argos.
5 Cape Bainet.
6 Cape Bear.
7 Cape Blanco.
8 Cape Bluff Harbor.
9 Cape Bonavista.
590 Cape Breaker.
1 Cape Broyle Harbor.
2 Cape Bueno, Cuba.
3 Cape Busios.
4 Cape Cassepour.
5 Cape Canaveral, Fla.
6 Cape Cameron.
7 Cape Canso.
8 Cape Capstan.
9 Cape Carysfort.
600 Cape Castlereagh.
1 Cape Catoche.
2 Cape Charles, Labrador.
3 Cape Charles Harbor.
4 Cape Charles, Virginia.
5 Cape Chattè.
6 Cape Chignecto.
7 Cape Cod, Mass.
8 Cape Cod Light-house.
9 Cape Comete, W. I.
610 Cape Corrientes, Cuba.
1 Cape Cruz, Cuba.
2 Cape Dama Maria.
3 Cape Deceit.
4 Cape Deseado.
5 Cape Desolation.
6 Cape Despair.
7 Cape D'Or.
8 Cape East.
9 Cape Elizabeth, Maine.
620 Cape Elizabeth Light-house.
1 Cape Engano.
2 Cape Enragé.
3 Cape Espiritu Santo.
4 Cape English.
5 Cape Egmont.
6 Cape Fairweather.
7 Cape Fear, N. C.
628 Cape Fear River, N. C.

| | |
|---|---|
| 629 | Cape Florida, Fla. |
| 630 | Cape Florida Light-house. |
| 1 | Cape Fourchu. |
| 2 | Cape Freels. |
| 3 | Cape Frio, Brazil. |
| 4 | Cape Garupi, Brazil. |
| 5 | Cape Gaspé. |
| 6 | Cape George. |
| 7 | Cape St. George. |
| 8 | Cape Gloucester. |
| 9 | Cape Good Success. |
| 640 | Cape Gracios a Dios. |
| 1 | Cape Haldiman. |
| 2 | Cape Hatteras, N. C. |
| 3 | Cape Haytien Harbor. |
| 4 | Cape Henlopen. |
| 5 | Cape Henry. |
| 6 | Cape Horn. |
| 7 | Cape Hogan. |
| 8 | Cape Inman. |
| 9 | Cape Jack Shoal. |
| 650 | Cape Jellison Harbor, Me. |
| 1 | Cape John. |
| 2 | Cape Jude. |
| 3 | Cape La Hume. |
| 4 | Cape La Vela. |
| 5 | Cape Lookout. |
| 6 | Cape May. |
| 7 | Cape Maize. |
| 8 | Cape Melville. |
| 9 | Cape Maysi. |
| 660 | Cape Neddick. |
| 1 | Cape Neddock, Me. |
| 2 | Cape Negro. |
| 3 | Cape Negro Harbor. |
| 4 | Cape Nicholas. |
| 5 | Cape Norman. |
| 6 | Cape North. |
| 7 | Cape Observation. |
| 8 | Cape Orange. |
| 9 | Cape Penas. |
| 670 | Cape Pillar. |
| 1 | Cape Pine. |
| 2 | Cape Poge, Mass. |
| 3 | Cape Porcupine. |
| 4 | Cape Porpoise, Me. |
| 5 | Cape Porpoise Harbor. |
| 6 | Cape Powles. |
| 7 | Cape Quebra. |
| 8 | Cape Race. |
| 9 | Cape Race Rocks. |
| 680 | Cape Raphael. |
| 1 | Cape Ray. |
| 2 | Cape Red. |
| 3 | Cape Roger Harbor. |
| 684 | Cape Roman, S. C. |
| 685 | Cape Romano, Fla. |
| 6 | Cape Rosier. |
| 7 | Cape Rouge Harbor. |
| 8 | Cape Roxo. |
| 9 | Cape Roxo, Porto Rico. |
| 690 | Cape Round. |
| 1 | Cape Sable, Fla. |
| 2 | Cape Sable, N. S. |
| 3 | Cape St. Antonio. |
| 4 | Cape St. Blas, Fla. |
| 5 | Cape St. Francis. |
| 6 | Cape St. George, N. F. |
| 7 | Cape St. George, Fla. |
| 8 | Cape St. George, St. Domingo. |
| 9 | Cape St. Gregory, N. F. |
| 700 | Cape St. John, N. F. |
| 1 | Cape St. Lewis. |
| 2 | Cape St. Martha Grande. |
| 3 | Cape St. Mary, N. F. |
| 4 | Cape St. Mary. |
| 5 | Cape St. Michael. |
| 6 | Cape St. Nicholas. |
| 7 | Cape St. Pablo. |
| 8 | Cape St. Roman. |
| 9 | Cape St. Roque. |
| 710 | Cape St. Sebastian. |
| 1 | Cape Santa Ines Medio. |
| 2 | Cape Schelky. |
| 3 | Cape Spear. |
| 4 | Cape Split Harbor, Me. |
| 5 | Cape Sunday. |
| 6 | Cape Tate. |
| 7 | Cape Thomas. |
| 8 | Cape Three Points. |
| 9 | Cape Tiburon, Col. |
| 720 | Cape Tiburon. |
| 1 | Cape Tryon. |
| 2 | Cape Turner. |
| 3 | Cape Virgins. |
| 4 | Cape Whittle. |
| 5 | Cape York. |
| 6 | Caper's Island. |
| 7 | Capodiette Bay. |
| 8 | Caplin Bay. |
| 9 | Caplin Bay, N. F. |
| 730 | Capstan Rocks. |
| 1 | Captain's Island. |
| 2 | Caracas. |
| 3 | Caracoles. |
| 4 | Carboniere Island. |
| 5 | Cardenas. |
| 6 | Cardigan Shoal. |
| 7 | Careenage Harbor. |
| 8 | Careenage. |
| 9 | Carenera Chico. |
| 740 | Caribana Port. |

741 Caribou Channel.
2 Caribou Harbor.
3 Caribou Reef.
4 Cariacou Grenadines.
5 Carlet Island.
6 Carlisle Bay.
7 Carleton Road.
8 Carleton Mountain.
9 Carlos Bay, Fla.
750 Carmen Island.
1 Carmen Town.
2 Carmichael Pond.
3 Carva Grande Shoals.
4 Caroline Bay.
5 Carolina City.
6 Carreto Harbor.
7 Carriage Harbor.
8 Carribe Islands.
9 Cartago Lagoon.
760 Carthagena.
1 Carysfort Reef, Fla.
2 Carysfort Reef Light-house.
3 Cartwright's Harbor.
4 Casa de Muertos Islands.
5 Casas River.
6 Cascapedia Bay.
7 Cascajal Isles.
8 Cascumpregue Harbor.
9 Casco Bay.
770 Cashe's Ledge, Me.
1 Casilda Port.
2 Casique Hill.
3 Casta Bay.
4 Castana Bay.
5 Castillo Island.
6 Castine Harbor.
7 Castle Harbor.
8 Castle Island.
9 Castle Pinckney.
780 Castle of San Juan de Ulloa.
1 Catalina Harbor.
2 Catalinita.
3 Catalinia.
4 Catharine Point.
5 Catherine's, St.
6 Cat Arms.
7 Catfish Point.
8 Catch Harbor.
9 Cat Cove.
790 Cat Island, Miss.
1 Cat Island, Mass.
2 Catt Island, W. I.
3 Cavallos Port.
4 Cavaillon Bay.
5 Cavanas.
796 Cayaguaneque Port.
797 Cayamas Port.
8 Caycos Islands.
9 Caycos Passage.
800 Cayenne.
1 Cayes.
2 Cayman Brack.
3 Caymans.
4 Cayman, Grand.
5 Cayman, Little.
6 Caymites.
7 Cayo Bivoras, Fla.
8 Cayo Diana.
9 Cayo Holandes, Fla.
810 Cayo Marquese, Fla.
1 Cayo, La.
2 Cayo Piedras.
3 Cayo Grande Roques.
4 Cayo Moa.
5 Cayo Lavantados.
6 Cayes St. Louis.
7 Caye a Raimiers.
8 Cayos de Vacas, Fla.
9 Cayte River.
820 Cebellos Harbor.
1 Cedar Hummock.
2 Cedar Inlet.
3 Cedar Island.
4 Cedar Islands.
5 Cedar Keys, Fla.
6 Cedar Point, Md.
7 Cedar Point, Upper.
8 Cedar Point, Mass.
9 Centreville.
830 Cerberus Rock.
1 Cerberus Shoal.
2 Chabou.
3 Chacalacas River.
4 Chacha-Chachare Island.
5 Chagauramus Bay.
6 Chagles.
7 Chagres.
8 Chaleur Bay.
9 Chamalacon River.
840 Champlain Lake.
1 Chance Harbor.
2 Chandeleur Islands, La.
3 Chandeleur Isl'd Light-house.
4 Chandler's Reach.
5 Chandler's River, Me.
6 Change Island Tickle.
7 Chapman's Point.
8 Chaptico.
9 Charles's Island.
850 Charleston.
1 Charleston, S. C.
852 Charlotte.

853 Charlotte Harbor, Fla.
4 Charlotte Harbor, Labrador.
5 Charlotte Town.
6 Charlotte Port.
7 Chateaudin Road.
8 Chatham, Mass.
9 Chatteaux Bay.
860 Chatte Cape.
1 Cheraw River, S. C.
2 Chedabucto Bay.
3 Cheesemans.
4 Chelsea.
5 Cherokee River.
6 Cherry Point.
7 Cherrystone Inlet.
8 Chesapeake Bay.
9 Chester.
870 Chester River, Md.
1 Chester Town.
2 Chesconessix River.
3 Chichibicoa Cape.
4 Chichiriviche Harbor.
5 Chickaseen.
6 Chico Bank.
7 Chignecto Bay.
8 Chili.
9 Chiloe Island.
880 Chira.
1 Chiltepec River.
2 Chimanas Islands.
3 Chincoteague.
4 Chincoteague Shoals.
5 Chiriqui Lagoon.
6 Choco.
7 Choctaw Point.
8 Chopowansic.
9 Choptank.
890 Chotank.
1 Chouchou Bay.
2 Christianstaed.
3 Christiana.
4 Christopher's, St.
5 Christmas Sound.
6 Chub Cut.
7 Chuburna.
8 Chupara River.
9 Church Creek.
900 Chuspa.
1 Cienfuegos.
2 Cinque Isles Bay.
3 Cispata Harbor.
4 City of Cape Haytien.
5 City of St. John.
6 Clark's Point.
7 Clatiste Harbor.
908 Clay Island.
909 Clearbottom Bay.
910 Clopper's Bar, Texas.
1 Clove Sound.
2 Club Heads.
3 Clyde River.
4 Coaster's Harbor.
5 Coast, Castle Cape.
6 Cob Point.
7 Coca Key, Cuba.
8 Coche Island.
9 Cochinos Bay.
920 Cochinos Island.
1 Cockburn Harbor.
2 Cockpit Point.
3 Cockspur Island.
4 Cockle's Creek.
5 Coco Point.
6 Cocos Bay.
7 Cod, Cape.
8 Cod Harbor.
9 Cod Roy Road.
930 Coddle's Harbor.
1 Codera, Cape.
2 Coffin Island.
3 Coffin's Patches, Fla.
4 Coffin Island, S. C.
5 Cofre de Perote.
6 Cohansey, N. J.
7 Cohasset Rocks.
8 Colares Island.
9 Cold Spring.
940 Cole's Care, S. C.
1 Colindiba River.
2 Colinet Bay.
3 Collier's Bay.
4 Collerton River.
5 Colombia.
6 Colonia.
7 Colonel's Island.
8 Coloras Islands.
9 Colorado Reef.
950 Colorado River.
1 Columbia, D. C.
2 Columbiano.
3 Columbier Island.
4 Columbine Shoals.
5 Colville Bay.
6 Commodore's Island.
7 Comowine River.
8 Cone River, Va.
9 Conch Harbor.
960 Conch Reef.
1 Conceicao.
2 Conception Bay.
3 Conception Island.
964 Connaigre Bay.

|  |  |
|---|---|
| 965 | Connecticut. |
| 6 | Connanticut Island. |
| 7 | Connecticut River. |
| 8 | Conney Bay. |
| 9 | Connire Bay. |
| 970 | Constantinople. |
| 1 | Contoy Island. |
| 2 | Cook Bay. |
| 3 | Cook Port. |
| 4 | Cook's Harbor. |
| 5 | Cooper's Island. |
| 6 | Coosa River. |
| 7 | Copename River. |
| 8 | Copenhagen. |
| 9 | Core Sound, N. C. |
| 980 | Coral Island. |
| 1 | Corbin Bay. |
| 2 | Corbin Harbor. |
| 3 | Corentine River. |
| 4 | Corientes Cape. |
| 5 | Cormorant Point. |
| 6 | Cormorant's Cape. |
| 7 | Cornfield Harbor. |
| 8 | Corn Island. |
| 9 | Cornwallis. |
| 990 | Coro River. |
| 1 | Coosaw River, S. C. |
| 2 | Country Harbor. |
| 3 | Courtland Bay. |
| 4 | Cotterals Key. |
| 5 | Cove, Dyer's. |
| 6 | Cove Point, Md. |
| 7 | Cove Bay. |
| 8 | Cow Head. |
| 9 | Cow Keys. |
| 1000 | Cozumel Island. |
| 1 | Crab Island. |
| 2 | Crab Island. |
| 3 | Craddock Creek. |
| 4 | Cranberry Island. |
| 5 | Crane Island. |
| 6 | Craney Island. |
| 7 | Crany Islands Flats. |
| 8 | Crany Island Light-house. |
| 9 | Crapeaud Road. |
| 1010 | Crawfish Key. |
| 1 | Creighton Shoal. |
| 2 | Cremalire Cove. |
| 3 | Croatan Sound, N. C. |
| 4 | Crocker's Reef. |
| 5 | Crockett's Bay. |
| 6 | Crocodile Point. |
| 7 | Cromwell's Ledge. |
| 8 | Crooked Islands. |
| 9 | Crooked Islands Passage. |
| 1020 | Croque Harbor. |
| 1021 | Cross Rip, Mass. |
| 2 | Crow Harbor. |
| 3 | Crow Harbor, Ga. |
| 4 | Crow Inlet. |
| 5 | Crow Isles. |
| 6 | Cruz Harbor. |
| 7 | Cruz, Santa. |
| 8 | Cuagua Islands. |
| 9 | Cuckold Creek. |
| 1030 | Cuba. |
| 1 | Cubagua Island. |
| 2 | Cuidado Reef. |
| 3 | Cuidadella. |
| 4 | Culebra Island. |
| 5 | Cumana. |
| 6 | Cumarebo Bay. |
| 7 | Cumbahee Bank. |
| 8 | Cumbahee River. |
| 9 | Cumberland Arm. |
| 1040 | Cumberland Harbor. |
| 1 | Cumberland Sound. |
| 2 | Curacao Island. |
| 3 | Curlew Harbor. |
| 4 | Curnau. |
| 5 | Curtis Point. |
| 6 | Cutter Harbor. |
| 7 | Cutterhunk Island. |
| 8 | Cutwell Harbor. |
| | **D.** |
| 9 | Damariscotta River, Me. |
| 1050 | Damnable Harbor. |
| 1 | Dames Point, Fla. |
| 2 | Dantzic Coves. |
| 3 | Darien, Ga. |
| 4 | Darien, Gulf of. |
| 5 | Dartmouth Bay. |
| 6 | Dartmouth. |
| 7 | Das Bocas. |
| 8 | Dauphin Island. |
| 9 | Davis Bank. |
| 1060 | Davis Cove. |
| 1 | Davis Straits. |
| 2 | Dead Islands Harbor. |
| 3 | Deadman Islet. |
| 4 | Deadman's Chest. |
| 5 | Deadman's Harbor. |
| 6 | Deane Harbor. |
| 7 | Dean Cape. |
| 8 | Debardacaire. |
| 9 | Decrow's Point. |
| 1070 | Deep Bay. |
| 1 | Deep Creek, Va. |
| 2 | Deep Harbor. |
| 1073 | Deep Water Shoals, Va. |

1074 Deep Water Sound.
5 Deep Water Creek.
6 Deer Harbor.
7 Deer Island, Me.
8 Deer Island.
9 De Gras Cove.
1080 Dehert's Bay.
1 Delaware Bay.
2 Delaware Breakwater.
3 Delaware City.
4 Delaware Heads.
5 Delaware River.
6 Demerara.
7 Denbigh Island.
8 Denmark.
9 Deseada.
1090 Desecheo Island.
1 Desirade.
2 Desire Port.
3 Desolate Bay.
4 Despair Cape.
5 Destretto.
6 Devil's Bay.
7 Delesdernier's Point.
8 Del Boqueron.
9 De Lobos Island.
1100 Del Rincon Bay.
1 Delute Harbor.
2 Devil's Island.
3 Dewees Point.
4 Diagon Bay.
5 Diamond Shoal, N. C.
6 Diamond Reef.
7 Diana Bank.
8 Dice's Head.
9 Diego Ramirez Island.
1110 Diego's Islands.
1 Dildo Harbor.
2 Dios Keys.
3 Dislocation Harbor.
4 Discourse Shoal.
5 Dividing Creek.
6 Dixie.
7 Dixon Rock.
8 Doboy Inlet.
9 Doctor's Island.
1120 Dog Island, Fla.
1 Dog Island, Miss.
2 Dog Island, W. I.
3 Dog River.
4 Dog Rock.
5 Do Meyo.
6 Dom Rodrigo.
7 Dominica.
8 Domingo, St.
129 Dorchester.

1130 Doris Cove.
1 Double Headed Shot Keys.
2 Douglas Passage.
3 Douglas Town.
4 Dover Bay.
5 Dover Port.
6 Doyle Reef.
7 Dragon Bay.
8 Dragon's Mouth.
9 Drake's Island.
1140 Drum Flat.
1 Drum Point.
2 Drunken Man's Key.
3 Dry Bank Light-house.
4 Dry Harbor.
5 Dry Tortugas.
6 Dry Tortugas, Fort.
7 Duarte Islands.
8 Dublin.
9 Duck Key.
1150 Duck Island.
1 Duck Harbor.
2 Dumfries, Va.
3 Dumpling Rocks.
4 Dumpling, North.
5 Dungeness Point.
6 Dunkirk.
7 Durel's Ledge.
8 Dutch.
9 Dutch Island.
1160 Dutch Key.
1 Dyer's Bay.
2 Dyer's Cove.

## E.

3 Eagle Cove.
4 Eagle Harbor.
5 Eagle Island.
6 East Bay.
7 East Cape.
8 East Caycos.
9 Eastern Bay.
1170 Eastern Passage.
1 Eastern Entrance.
2 Eastern Harbor.
3 Eastern Point.
4 Eastern Sandbore.
5 East Greenwich.
6 East Lake.
7 East Southeast Keys.
8 Eastville.
9 Eaton Neck.
1180 Ebenicook Harbor.
1 Edenton, N. C.
1182 Eddy Cove.

| | |
|---|---|
| 1183 | Eddy Point. |
| 4 | Eddystone Rock. |
| 5 | Edgartown, Mass. |
| 6 | Edisto, North. |
| 7 | Edisto, South. |
| 8 | Edgemoggin. |
| 9 | Eel Island. |
| 1190 | Egg Harbor, N. J. |
| 1 | Egg Island. |
| 2 | Egg Island, Bocas. |
| 3 | Egg Passage. |
| 4 | Egmont Bay. |
| 5 | Egmont Harbor. |
| 6 | Egmont Key. |
| 7 | Elba Island. |
| 8 | Egypt. |
| 9 | Elbow Reef. |
| 1200 | El Chincho Shoals. |
| 1 | El Coche Island. |
| 2 | Eleuthera. |
| 3 | Elizabeth City, N. C. |
| 4 | Elizabeth Cape. |
| 5 | Elizabeth River, Va. |
| 6 | Elk River, Md. |
| 7 | Ellis Bay. |
| 8 | Elliot's Key. |
| 9 | Elliot's Reef. |
| 1210 | El Portete. |
| 1 | El Rincon. |
| 2 | El Roque. |
| 3 | Elsinborough, N. J. |
| 4 | Enceado de Brito. |
| 5 | Endymion Reef. |
| 6 | England. |
| 7 | Englée Harbor. |
| 8 | English Bank. |
| 9 | English Harbor. |
| 1220 | English Key. |
| 1 | Englishman's Bay. |
| 2 | Enragé Cape. |
| 3 | Ensenada de la Roda. |
| 4 | Ensenada de Majana. |
| 5 | Entry Island. |
| 6 | Ephram Banks. |
| 7 | Epinotte River. |
| 8 | Escocesa Bay. |
| 9 | Escondido Harbor. |
| 1230 | Escondido Port. |
| 1 | Escosivas. |
| 2 | Escribanos Harbor. |
| 3 | Escrido Island. |
| 4 | Escumanac Point. |
| 5 | Esmeralda Bay. |
| 6 | Espanola Point. |
| 7 | Espiritu Santo. |
| 1238 | Esquimaux Bay. |
| 1239 | Essequibo. |
| 1240 | Estancia Colorada. |
| 1 | Etang Harbor. |
| 2 | Europe. |
| 3 | Eustatius, St. |
| 4 | Eustou Bay. |
| 5 | Evansport. |
| 6 | Evount's Isles. |
| 7 | Execution Rocks. |
| 8 | Exuma. |

## F.

| | |
|---|---|
| 9 | Facheux. |
| 1250 | Fairfax Court-House. |
| 1 | Fair and False Bay. |
| 2 | Fairweather Cape. |
| 3 | Fairweather Island. |
| 4 | Falkland Islands. |
| 5 | Falkner's Island. |
| 6 | Fallen City. |
| 7 | Falmouth. |
| 8 | Falmouth, Va. |
| 9 | Falmouth, Jamaica. |
| 1260 | Falmouth, N. S. |
| 1 | False Bank. |
| 2 | False Bay. |
| 3 | False Cape. |
| 4 | False Cape Horn. |
| 5 | False Hook, N. J. |
| 6 | Farewell Cape. |
| 7 | Favorite Cove. |
| 8 | Fear, Cape. |
| 9 | Federal Point. |
| 1270 | Fell's Point. |
| 1 | Fenwick's Island. |
| 2 | Fermose Harbor. |
| 3 | Fernandina. |
| 4 | Fernando Noronha. |
| 5 | Ferrolle Point. |
| 6 | Ferryland Harbor. |
| 7 | Ferryland Head. |
| 8 | Ferry Reef. |
| 9 | Fiddle Shoal. |
| 1280 | Fifteen Point Church. |
| 1 | Figo Island. |
| 2 | Figuera Island. |
| 3 | Fincham Island. |
| 4 | Finisterre Cape. |
| 5 | Fire Island. |
| 6 | Fire Island Inlet. |
| 7 | Fisga Point. |
| 8 | Fisherman's Bank. |
| 9 | Fisherman's Harbor. |
| 1290 | Fisherman's Point. |
| 1291 | Fisher's Island, Conn. |

1292 Fishing Rip.
3 Fishing Ship Harbor.
4 Fish Shoal.
5 Fitzroy Rock.
6 Five Fathom Bank.
7 Five Islands Harbor.
8 Flag Hill.
9 Flamingo Bay.
1300 Flat Bay.
1 Flat River.
2 Flemish Cape.
3 Flemish Bank.
4 Fleur de Lis Harbor.
5 Flinder's Bay.
6 Flores Island.
7 Florida.
8 Florida Coast.
9 Florida Cape.
1310 Florida Reefs.
1 Flushing Bay.
2 Flynn's Knoll.
3 Fogo Islands.
4 Folger Shoal.
5 Folly Island, Me.
6 Fond la Grange Bay.
7 Fool's Rock.
8 Forked Cape.
9 Forked Harbor.
1320 Forlorn Hope.
1 Formigas.
2 Fort Amherst.
3 Fort Amsterdam.
4 Fort Calhoun, Va.
5 Fort Cameron.
6 Fort Capron, Fla.
7 Fort Carroll, Md.
8 Fort Caswell, N. C.
9 Fort Corcoran.
1330 Fort Diamond.
1 Fort Ellsworth.
2 Forteau Bay.
3 Fort George.
4 Fort Jefferson, Tortugas.
5 Fort Lafayette.
6 Fort Lauderdale.
7 Fort Livingston.
8 Fort Madison.
9 Fort Mifflin.
.340 Fortress Monroe.
1 Fort Norfolk.
2 Fort Pierce, Fla.
3 Fort Point Cove.
4 Fort Royal.
5 Fort St. Lewis.
6 Fort Taylor, Key West.
347 Fort Macon, Ga.
1348 Fortune Bay.
9 Fortune Harbor.
1350 Fortune Island.
1 Fortune River.
2 Fouchee Harbor.
3 Foul Hole.
4 Fourchu Cape.
5 Fowey Rocks, Fla.
6 Fowling Point.
7 Fox Harbor.
8 Fox Island.
9 Fox Island Harbor.
1360 Fox Island Passage.
1 Fox Point.
2 France.
3 Francois Bay.
4 Francois Cape.
5 Frankfort.
6 Franklin Island.
7 Franklin Point.
8 Franklin Sound.
9 Frank's Island, La.
1370 Frayles.
1 Frederickstadt.
2 Freeman's Bay.
3 Freestone Point.
4 Freels, Cape.
5 French Cove.
6 French Keys.
7 French Reef.
8 Friar's Head.
9 Friars.
1380 Friar's Point.
1 Frio, Cape, Brazil.
2 Frio Island.
3 Frisbee's Ledge.
4 Frying Pan.
5 Frying Pan Shoals, N. C.
6 Fundy, Bay.
7 Funk Island.
8 Fuerta Isle.
9 Fury Harbor.

G.

1390 Gabarus Bay.
1 Gabia Grande.
2 Gabion Shoal.
3 Gadsden's Point.
4 Galafre River.
5 Galera Point.
6 Galet Cove.
7 Galina Point.
8 Galleguilla.
9 Galloping Andrews.
1400 Gallows Point.

1401 Gally Boy's Harbor.
2 Galtaus Harbor.
3 Galveston.
4 Gambier Harbor.
5 Gannet Rock.
6 Gannets.
7 Garden Key.
8 Gardner's Bay.
9 Gardner's Point.
1410 Garia Bay.
1 Gagathey Inlet.
2 Garrotte Harbor.
3 Gaskin Bank.
4 Gaspa Grande Island.
5 Gasparilla Island.
6 Gaspe Bay, Cape.
7 Gaudaloupe.
8 Gay Head, Mass.
9 Gay's Cove, Me.
1420 Gedney's Channel.
1 Geeseberry Point.
2 Genoa.
3 George, Fort, Island.
4 George Harbor.
5 George Island, Fla.
6 George's Banks and Shoals.
7 George's River.
8 George's, St.
9 Georgetown.
1430 Georgetown, D. C.
1 Georgetown, S. C.
2 Georgia.
3 Georgi Greco.
4 German Anchorage.
5 Germany.
6 Gibara Harbor.
7 Gilbert's Bar, Fla.
8 Gilbert's Passage.
9 Gilbert's River.
1440 Gilkey Harbor.
1 Gingerbread.
2 Glasgow.
3 Glasgow Harbor.
4 Giego Inlet.
5 Gloucester, Mass.
6 Gloucester, Va.
7 Glover's Reef.
8 Glymont.
9 Goat Island.
1450 Goat Island, R. I.
1 Goatzacoalcos River.
2 Goff's Key.
3 Goillon Reef.
4 Gold Coast.
5 Goldsborough Harbor.
1456 Gonaives.

1457 Gonave Island.
8 Good Hope, Cape.
9 Good Success Bay.
1460 Goose Bay.
1 Goose Cove.
2 Goree Road.
3 Gosport, Va.
4 Gorgona Island.
5 Gott's Cove.
6 Governor's Island.
7 Governor's Town.
8 Gracios a Dios.
9 Grafton Island.
1470 Graham Ledge.
1 Grammer's Rocks.
2 Grampuses, Colombia.
3 Granada.
4 Granadillos.
5 Granby Island.
6 Granchora.
7 Grande, Rio, Texas.
8 Grand Bank.
9 Grand Bay.
1480 Grand Bruit Harbor.
1 Grand Cayman.
2 Grand Cul de Sac.
3 Grand del Oro.
4 Grandedigue Road.
5 Grandentry Harbor.
6 Grandfather's Cove.
7 Grand Gonave Bay.
8 Grand Harbor.
9 Grand Key, Fla.
1490 Grand Key, W. I.
1 Grand le Pierre.
2 Grand Para.
3 Grand Passage.
4 Grand Point.
5 Grand River.
6 Grandsway Harbor.
7 Grand Seche Shoal.
8 Grand Terre.
9 Grand Turk's Island.
1500 Grange.
1 Grassy Island.
2 Grassy Point.
3 Gravel Channel, Mass.
4 Grave's Island.
5 Graves, Mass.
6 Great Adventure Cove.
7 Great Bahama.
8 Great Bank.
9 Great Barrysway Point.
1510 Great Bay de l'Eau.
1 Great Bay, W. I.
1512 Great Bay, Virgin Gorda.

1513 Great Burin Harbor.
4 Great Cat Arms.
5 Great Chance Harbor.
6 Great Choptank River, Md.
7 Great Colinet Island.
8 Great Coney Arm.
9 Great Constable.
1520 Great Corn Island.
1 Great Duck Island.
2 Great Egg Harbor.
3 Great Exuma.
4 Great Fox River.
5 Great Gallows Harbor.
6 Great Guano Key.
7 Great Gull Bank.
8 Great Harbor.
9 Great Harbor Deep.
1530 Great Harbor.
1 Great Heneagua.
2 Great Isaac.
3 Great Inagua.
4 Great Jarvis Harbor.
5 Great Matchipongo Inlet.
6 Great Miquelon Island.
7 Great Paradise Harbor.
8 Great Paredon.
9 Great Passage Island.
1540 Great Picuda.
1 Great Point.
2 Great Pond Harbor.
3 Great Quirpon Harbor.
4 Great Racoon Key.
5 Great Rip, Mass.
6 Great River.
7 Great Roads.
8 Great Round Harbor.
9 Great Round Shoal, Mass.
1550 Great Rustico Harbor.
1 Great Salmon River.
2 Great Sandy Harbor.
3 Great Satilla River.
4 Great South Harbor.
5 Great St. Julien Harbor.
6 Great St. Lawrence Harbor.
7 Great Tancook.
8 Great Virgin Island.
9 Great Wicomico.
1560 Greece.
1 Grecian Shoal.
2 Green Bay.
3 Greenbury Point.
4 Green Bay, Colombia.
5 Green Harbor.
6 Green Harbor, N. S.
7 Green Island.
1568 Green Island, G. of M.
1569 Green Island, Me.
1570 Green Island, N. S.
1 Green Island, N. F.
2 Green Island Harbor.
3 Greenland.
4 Green Port.
5 Green River Inlet.
6 Greenspond.
7 Greenville Bay.
8 Greenville.
9 Greenwich.
1580 Grenada.
1 Greytown.
2 Gibraltar.
3 Griffin Cove.
4 Griguet Bay.
5 Grime Rock.
6 Grindstone Island.
7 Gryson's Island.
8 Groais Island.
9 Gros Islet Bay.
1590 Guadaloupe.
1 Guagmico River.
2 Guajaba Island.
3 Guanaja Island.
4 Guanamau River.
5 Guana Point.
6 Guanashani.
7 Guanayara River.
8 Guanico Harbor.
9 Guanta Bay.
1600 Guanima Keys.
1 Guantananco Harbor.
2 Guaraceo Island.
3 Guaraguao.
4 Guarapari River.
5 Guaratiba Point.
6 Guaratuba.
7 Guaurabo River.
8 Guaya, Trinidad.
9 Guayabo River.
1610 Guayacanes.
1 Guayamo Bay.
2 Guiana.
3 Guilford Creek.
4 Guincha Key.
5 Guinea, Coast of.
6 Guines River.
7 Gulf of Darien.
8 Gulf of Honduras.
9 Gulf of Mexico.
1620 Gulf of Morrisquillo.
1 Gulf of Paria.
2 Gulf of San Blas.
3 Gulf of Santa Fé.
1624 Gulf of St. Lawrence

1625 Gulf of Triste.
6 Gulf of Uraba.
7 Gulf Stream.
8 Gulliver's Hole.
9 Gull Islands.
1630 Gull Rock.
1 Gun Boat Shoal.
2 Gun Key.
3 Gurnet Head.
4 Gustavia Town.
5 Gut of Canso.
6 Guyacanes.
7 Guyana.
8 Gysborough Harbor.
9 Gwinn's Island, Va.

H.

1640 Habitant's Bay.
1 Hack Cove.
2 Haddock Harbor.
3 Hadlock's Harbor.
4 Hagget's Cove.
5 Ha Ha Bay.
6 Ha Ha.
7 Ha Ha Harbor.
8 Hain's Point.
9 Haldimand Cape.
1650 Haldimand Port.
1 Haley's Cove.
2 Half Island Cove.
3 Half Moon Bay.
4 Half Moon Key.
5 Half Moon Reef, Texas.
6 Half Way Rock.
7 Halibut Point, Mass.
8 Halifax.
9 Halifax Bay.
1660 Hamilton.
1 Hampton, Va.
2 Hampton Bar.
3 Hampton Harbor.
4 Hampton Roads, Va.
5 Handkerchief Shoal.
6 Hanover County, Va.
7 Hanover Island.
8 Hant's Harbor.
9 Harbor Briton.
1670 Harbor Buffet.
1 Harbor Delute, Me.
2 Harbor Femme.
3 Harbor Grace.
4 Harbor Island.
5 Harbor La Conte.
6 Harbor Main.
1677 Harbor Millè.
1678 Harbor Parish, Mass.
9 Harding's Rock, Mass.
1680 Hardy Peninsula.
1 Hardy's Rock, Mass.
2 Hare Bay.
3 Hare Harbor.
4 Hare's Ears Point.
5 Harpswell Sound, Me.
6 Hart Island.
7 Harvey Reef.
8 Hatchett's Reef.
9 Hat Island.
1690 Hat Key.
1 Hatteras, Cape.
2 Hatteras Cove.
3 Hatteras Inlet.
4 Haute Island.
5 Haut Fond.
6 Haut Fond Shoals.
7 Havana.
8 Havre de Grace, Md.
9 Hawke Bay.
1700 Hawke Channel, Fla.
1 Hawke Inlet.
2 Hawk's Harbor.
3 Hayti.
4 Hazard's Point.
5 Head Harbor, Me.
6 Head Harbor.
7 Head of the Passes, Mississippi River.
8 Health Islands.
9 Heart's Content Harbor.
1710 Heath Point.
1 Hedge Fence, Mass.
2 Helena, St.
3 Helena Sound.
4 Hell Gate.
5 Hemos Island.
6 Hen and Chickens.
7 Hen and Chickens, Del. Bay.
8 Hen and Chickens, N. S.
9 Hen and Chickens, Fla.
1720 Hender's Island.
1 Henderson Island, Me.
2 Hendrick's Head, Me.
3 Heneagua Island.
4 Henley Island.
5 Henley Ledges.
6 Henlopen, Cape.
7 Henne Bay.
8 Henry, Cape.
9 Hereford, N. J.
1730 Herins Bay.
1 Hermanos Island.
1732 Hermitage Bay.

1733 Hermite Island.
4 Herring Cove, Mass.
5 Herring Cove, N. S.
6 Herring Gut Harbor, Me.
7 Herring Island.
8 Herring Neck Harbor.
9 Hickman's Harbor.
1740 Hidden Harbor.
1 Highlands of Navesink, N. J.
2 Higney.
3 Higgin's Point.
4 Hilliard's Harbor.
5 Hillsborough.
6 Hillsborough Bay.
7 Hillsborough Inlet, Fla.
8 Hind Island.
9 Hill's Point.
1750 Hilton Head.
1 Hinchinbroke Rocks.
2 Hispaniola.
3 Hodgkin's Cove, Mass.
4 Hog Bay.
5 Hog Channel.
6 Hog Fish Cut.
7 Hog Inlet.
8 Hog Island Harbor, Mass.
9 Hog Island.
1760 Hogland, Va.
1 Hog Island Light-house.
2 Hogsties.
3 Holandes Channel.
4 Holandes Point.
5 Holderness Island.
6 Hole in the Wall.
7 Holland Cove.
8 Holland Harbor.
9 Holland Point.
1770 Holland's Island, Md.
1 Holland's Straits.
2 Hollin's Harbor, N. S.
3 Holme's Hole, Mass.
4 Holyrood Harbor.
5 Honda River.
6 Honduras.
7 Hood Port.
8 Hooper's Strait, Md.
9 Hooping Harbor.
1780 Hope Harbor.
1 Horne's Neck.
2 Horn, Cape.
3 Hornos Island.
4 Horse Hammock.
5 Horse Island.
6 Horse Shoe, N. S.
7 Horse Shoe, Va.
788 Horse Shoe Point.
1789 Horsehead Shoals.
1790 Horton, N. S.
1 Hospital Key.
2 Hospital Rock.
3 How Harbor.
4 Howell's Point.
5 House Harbor.
6 Hubert's Cove.
7 Hudson's Bay.
8 Hudson's River.
9 Huevo Island.
1800 Hughlett's Point.
1 Hull's Cove, Me.
2 Humber River.
3 Hunger's Creek.
4 Hunting Creek.
5 Hunting Island, S. C.
6 Huntington Harbor.
7 Huntington Bay.
8 Huron, Lake.
9 Hurricane Bay.
1810 Hussey's Sound.
1 Hutchinson's Island.
2 Hyannis, Mass.
3 Hydra Rock.
4 Hypocrite Passage, Mass.

## I.

5 Iaquarine Bay.
6 Icacos Point.
7 Icague.
8 Idaparatuba.
9 Iguane River.
1820 Ildefonso Island.
1 Ilha Grande Bay.
2 Illinois River.
3 Incurrucu River.
4 Independent Harbor.
5 Indian Arm.
6 Indian Bay.
7 Indian Cove.
8 Indian Harbor.
9 Indian Head.
1830 Indian Keys.
1 Indian Key, Fla.
2 Indian Harbor, Fla.
3 Indian Point Shoal.
4 Indian River Shoal, Fla.
5 Indian River, Fla.
6 Indian Rocks.
7 Indian River Inlet.
8 Indies, East.
9 Indies, West.
1840 Indios River.
1841 Ingram River.

1842 Ingram Cove.
3 Ingormachoix Bay.
4 Inland Harbor.
5 Inman Rock.
6 Ipswich Island.
7 Ipswich, Mass.
8 Ireland.
9 Irish Point.
1850 Ironbound Island.
1 Iron Island.
2 Isaac's Harbor.
3 Isabella Island.
4 Isabella Point.
5 Isabella Reefs.
6 Isla de Congrejo.
7 Isla de Pajaros.
8 Isla de Pinos.
9 Isla de Vernados.
1860 Isla Fuerto.
1 Islas de Aves.
2 Island of Columbier.
3 Island of St. Paul.
4 Isle au Haute, Me.
5 Isle do Mel.
6 Isle of Beata.
7 Isle of Ramea.
8 Isle of Sable, N. S.
9 Isle of Wight Shoal, Del. Bay.
1870 Isle Ramieres.
1 Isle of Pines.
2 Isles of Shoals.
3 Isthmus Bay.
4 Itacolomi Mount.
5 Itapacoraya Point.
6 Italy.

J.

7 Jackson's Arm.
8 Jack Taylor's Reef.
9 Jacmel.
1880 Jacob's Harborhead.
1 Jacquemel.
2 Jagenos Island.
3 Jageson's Island.
4 Jago, St.
5 Jagua Harbor.
6 Jaguaripe River.
7 Jamaica.
8 James River.
9 Janeiro, Rio de.
1890 Janes Island.
1 Janvrin Harbor.
2 Janvrin Shoal.
3 Japan.
1894 Jacquemel Bay.
1895 Jaquet Bank.
6 Jaragua River.
7 Jardinellos.
8 Jardines.
9 Jatibonica River.
1900 Javinal Point.
1 Jayua Island.
2 Jean Ravel Road.
3 Jedore Harbor.
4 Jeffrey's Bank.
5 Jegogan Harbor.
6 Jekyl Island.
7 Jeremie.
8 Jericoacoara.
9 Jerseyman's Harbor.
1910 Jestico Harbor.
1 Jesus Maria Point.
2 Joano.
3 Joatinga Point.
4 Jobano.
5 Joe Flogger Shoal.
6 Joe's Hole.
7 John's Bay.
8 John le Bay Bay.
9 John's, St., Fla.
1920 John's, St., Island.
1 Johnson Harbor.
2 Jolie, Port.
3 Jolly Island.
4 Jolvos Island.
5 Jones's Harbor.
6 Jones's Island.
7 Jones's Point, Potomac.
8 Jordan's Point, Va.
9 Jordan River.
1930 Josef Pobre Point.
1 Joujou River.
2 Jourimin Islands.
3 Juan, St.
4 Juan del Pozo.
5 Juan d'Olio.
6 Juan Louis Key.
7 Judge and Apostle Rocks.
8 Judith Point, R. I.
9 Juliana Bay.
1940 Jupiter Inlet, Fla.
1 Jupiter Inlet Light-house.
2 Jururu Port.

K.

3 Kate Harbor.
4 Keel's Harbor.
5 Keeper's Rocks.
6 Kennebeck, Me.
1947 Kennebunk, Me.

|  |  |
|---|---|
| 1948 | Kensington. |
| 9 | Kent County, Md. |
| 1950 | Kent Harbor. |
| 1 | Kent Island, Md. |
| 2 | Kentucky. |
| 3 | Kepple Harbor. |
| 4 | Kettle Bottoms, Potomac. |
| 5 | Key Anclote, Fla. |
| 6 | Key Arenas. |
| 7 | Key Baril. |
| 8 | Key Biscayno, Fla. |
| 9 | Key Bivoras, Fla. |
| 1960 | Key Bokel. |
| 1 | Key Confites. |
| 2 | Key de Cruz. |
| 3 | Key Francis. |
| 4 | Key Largo, Fla. |
| 5 | Key Largo. |
| 6 | Key Melchoir Rodrigues, Fla. |
| 7 | Key Roman, Fla. |
| 8 | Key Romano. |
| 9 | Key Sal. |
| 1970 | Key Sanibel, Fla. |
| 1 | Key Vacas, Fla. |
| 2 | Key Verde. |
| 3 | Key West, Fla. |
| 4 | Key Tavernier, Fla. |
| 5 | Kiawa Island. |
| 6 | Kiawa River. |
| 7 | Kimberly's Reef. |
| 8 | King's Bay. |
| 9 | King's Creek. |
| 1980 | King's Harbor. |
| 1 | Kingsley's Cut. |
| 2 | Kingston Bay. |
| 3 | Kingston. |
| 4 | Kingston, Canada. |
| 5 | Kirby Rocks. |
| 6 | Kitty Vitty. |
| 7 | Knowles Harbor. |
| 8 | Knoll Shoal. |
| | **L.** |
| 9 | La Baie du Parc. |
| 1990 | Labrador. |
| 1 | Labrador Harbor. |
| 2 | La Bras d'Or. |
| 3 | La Caldera. |
| 4 | La Caleta. |
| 5 | La Coronas. |
| 6 | La Conte Harbor. |
| 7 | La Cone Harbor. |
| 1998 | Lago de St. Rita. |
| 1999 | Laguayra. |
| 2000 | Laguna City. |
| 1 | Laguna. |
| 2 | La Folle. |
| 3 | La Hache City. |
| 4 | La Hune Bay. |
| 5 | Laja Shoal. |
| 6 | Lake George, Fla. |
| 7 | Lake of Terminos. |
| 8 | Lake Pontchartrain, La. |
| 9 | La Laja Shoal. |
| 2010 | Las Manchas. |
| 1 | La Mar. |
| 2 | Lambert's Cove. |
| 3 | Lamentin Point. |
| 4 | La Moine Harbor. |
| 5 | La Naybe. |
| 6 | Lance de Loup. |
| 7 | Lance Union Cove. |
| 8 | Landfall Islands. |
| 9 | L'Anguille Isle. |
| 2020 | Langley Island. |
| 1 | L'Anse-a-Veau. |
| 2 | L'Anse-a-L'eau. |
| 3 | La Pamillos. |
| 4 | La Piragua. |
| 5 | La Perche. |
| 6 | La Poile Bay. |
| 7 | La Punta. |
| 8 | Largo Key. |
| 9 | Lark Harbor. |
| 2030 | La Riviere Salee. |
| 1 | La Romana. |
| 2 | La Satina. |
| 3 | Las Minas. |
| 4 | La Scie Harbor. |
| 5 | Latitude Bay. |
| 6 | Laun Bay and Island. |
| 7 | Laura Harbor. |
| 8 | Laurent Shoal. |
| 9 | La Vache. |
| 2040 | La Vache Harbor. |
| 1 | Lavandera Shoal. |
| 2 | Lavanderas. |
| 3 | Lavantados. |
| 4 | La Vela de Coro. |
| 5 | Lawford Channel, S. C. |
| 6 | Lawrence, St., River. |
| 7 | La Tete Harbor. |
| 8 | Lazaretto Point. |
| 9 | Leander Shoal. |
| 2050 | Leblanc Harbor. |
| 1 | L'Ebert Port. |
| 2 | Ledges. |
| 3 | Le Diamant Isle. |
| 2054 | Leeward Islands. |

2055 Leeward Stocking Island.
6 Le Have River.
7 Leighton Rock.
8 Leith Harbor.
9 Lee Laage.
2060 Le Mouton.
1 Le Maire Strait.
2 Lennox Island.
3 Lennox Passage.
4 Leon Harbor.
5 Lepreau Point.
6 Lerma.
7 Les Alcatraces.
8 Les Baleines.
9 Les Chardoniers.
2070 Lewes, Del.
1 Lewis Reef.
2 Liberty.
3 Light-house Island, S. C.
4 Lima.
5 Limbe Channel.
6 Lime Key.
7 Lime River.
8 Lingan.
9 Linkhorn Bay.
2C80 Linnyard Bay.
1 Lion's Den.
2 Liscomb Harbor.
3 Little Adventure Cove.
4 Little Annemessix.
5 Little Arachat Harbor.
6 Little Bahama Bank.
7 Little Bay.
8 Little Brewster Island.
9 Little Bruen Harbor.
2090 Little Cape Morgan.
1 Little Catalina Bay.
2 Little Cat Arms.
3 Little Catt Island.
4 Little Choptank.
5 Little Coney Arms.
6 Little Corn Island.
7 Little Courtland Bay.
8 Little Cumberland Island, Ga.
9 Little Curazao Island.
2100 Little Egg Harbor.
1 Little Exuma Island.
2 Little Fish Harbor.
3 Little Fogo Islands.
4 Little Gallows Harbor.
5 Little George Bank.
6 Little Gonave Isle.
7 Little Gulf of Baru.
8 Little Gull Bank.
9 Little Gull Island.
2110 Little Harbor Deep.
2111 Little Harbor.
2 Little Harbor of Jeboque.
3 Little Heneagua.
4 Little Hope.
5 Little Isaacs.
6 Little Island.
7 Little Matchipongo.
8 Little Mark Island.
9 Little Matacumbe, Fla.
2120 Little Martinique.
1 Little Miquelon Island.
2 Little Mortier Bay.
3 Little Paradise Harbor.
4 Little Placentia Harbor.
5 Little Portuguese.
6 Little Quirpon Harbor.
7 Little River.
8 Little Round Harbor.
9 Little Round Shoal.
2130 Little Saba.
1 Little Sandy Harbor.
2 Little South Harbor.
3 Little St. Julien's Harbor.
4 Little St. Lawrence.
5 Little Tobago.
6 Little Talbot Island.
7 Little Turk.
8 Little Watts Island.
9 Little Warsaw Island.
2140 Liverpool Bay.
1 Liverpool Point.
2 Livisa Harbor.
3 Lloyd's Neck and Harbor.
4 Lobos Island.
5 Lobster Harbor.
6 Lobster Rocks.
7 Lodazar.
8 Loggerhead Key.
9 Lombard Cove.
2150 London.
1 London, New.
2 Londonderry Island.
3 Londonderry.
4 Londoner's Island.
5 Londoner's Rock.
6 London Isle.
7 Long Beach.
8 Long Branch.
9 Long Harbor.
2160 Long Island Bay.
1 Long Island Harbor.
2 Long Island.
3 Long Island Sound, N. Y.
4 Long Key.
5 Long Spit.
2166 Long's Wharf.

2167 Long Ledge.
8 Long Island, Mass.
9 Long Reef.
2170 Lookout, Cape.
1 Lort Bay.
2 Los Algodones.
3 Los Randitos.
4 Louisbury Harbor.
5 Louisburg.
6 Louis Port.
7 Louis, Saint.
8 Louisiana.
9 Lounging Island.
2180 Loup Ministre.
1 Loup St. Mary.
2 Low's Point.
3 Lower Cedar Point.
4 Lower Sound Point.
5 Lua River.
6 Lucea Harbor.
7 Lucia Island.
8 Lucia, St.
9 Lunenburg Bay.
2190 Lurcher Rock.
1 Lynch's Bay.
2 Lynhaven Bay.
3 Lynn Haven Inlet.

M.

4 Macao Town.
5 Macaripe Cove.
6 Macao Village.
7 Machbridge Head.
8 Macoris Port.
9 Mace's Bay.
2200 Machipungo Shoals.
1 Machias.
2 Machipongo.
3 Machodac Creek.
4 Machos Key.
5 Mackerel Rock.
6 Macdonald Shoal.
7 Mackensie Shoal.
8 Mac Nab's Island.
9 Macouria River.
2210 Madagascar Rock.
1 Madagascar Shoal.
2 Madeira Island.
3 Magalhaen Straits.
4 Magdalena.
5 Magdalen Island.
6 Magdalen Islands.
2217 Magdalen River.
2218 Magothy River.
9 Mahon's Ditch Light.
2220 Mahone Bay.
1 Majana Point.
2 Mala Pasa.
3 Malaquash.
4 Malagueta Bay.
5 Mal Bay.
6 Maldonado.
7 Malignant Cove.
8 Malpeque Bay.
9 Manan Island.
2230 Manan Ledge.
1 Manare.
2 Manassas Gap.
3 Manassas Junction.
4 Manati Harbor.
5 Manchas.
6 Manchester.
7 Manchac Pass.
8 Manheigan Island.
9 Manchester, Mass.
2240 Manchioneal Point.
1 Manduba Point.
2 Manduga.
3 Mangrove Island, Fla.
4 Manoken River.
5 Manoel Luiz Shoal.
6 Man-of-War Bay.
7 Man-of-War Bay, Tobago.
8 Man-of-War Keys.
9 Man-of-War Rocks.
2250 Man-of-War Rock.
1 Manzanilla Bay.
2 Manzanilla.
3 Manzanilla Harbor.
4 Manzanilla Point.
5 Maquerau Point.
6 Marabona Bay.
7 Maraccas Bay.
8 Maracaibo.
9 Marache.
2260 Marajo Islands.
1 Maracuno Inlet.
2 Maranbaya.
3 Maranham.
4 Maravi Port.
5 Marblehead.
6 March Harbor.
7 Marcus Hook.
8 Margaret's Bay.
9 Margaretta Island.
2270 Marguerite Island.
1 Maria Gorda Bay.
2 Maria's Ledge.
2273 Marie Galante.

2274 Marie and Joseph.
5 Marice Islands.
6 Marigot Bay.
7 Mariguana.
8 Mariel.
9 Mark Island.
2280 Marlborough, Md.
1 Marlborough Point.
2 Marle Head.
3 Marion Island.
4 Marion, Fort.
5 Maroni River.
6 Marowyne River.
7 Marquese Key, Fla.
8 Marseilles.
9 Marshall Point.
2290 Marsh Isle, La.
1 Martha Brae Harbor.
2 Martha's Vineyard.
3 Martinique.
4 Martin Shoal.
5 Martin Vas Rocks.
6 Martin Bay.
7 Martin's Industry, S. C.
8 Mary's, St.
9 Maryland.
2300 Maryland Point.
1 Masio Harbor.
2 Mason's Bay.
3 Matagorda.
4 Matahambre Bay.
5 Mata Harbor.
6 Matanzas.
7 Matanzas, Fla.
8 Matanzas Point.
9 Maternillos Point.
2310 Mattawoman.
1 Mason's Creek.
2 Mathias Point, Potomac.
3 Matinicus Island.
4 Matinilla Reef.
5 Matompkin Harbor.
6 Matoon Port.
7 Mattapoisett Harbor.
8 Maud's Bank.
9 Mauger Key.
2320 Mauritius.
1 Mayabeque Point.
2 Mayaguana.
3 Mayaguer.
4 Mayero Bay.
5 May, Cape.
6 May Island.
7 Mayport Mills.
8 May River.
2329 Mayo, Island of.

2330 McCobb's Island.
1 McCree's Shoal.
2 Mecatina Harbor.
3 Mecklenburg Harbor.
4 Media Luna.
5 Mediterranean.
6 Media casa Point.
7 Medway River.
8 Meek Island.
9 Meger's Island.
2340 Memory Rock.
1 Meogenes Island.
2 Merasheen Island.
3 Merchantman Harbor.
4 Merida.
5 Merigonish Harbor.
6 Merigonish Island.
7 Merrimac River.
8 Merrill's Light-house, La.
9 Messorgo Creek.
2350 Metomkin Inlet.
1 Metway Port.
2 Mexico.
3 Miami River.
4 Michaux Point.
5 Middle Arm.
6 Middleburg.
7 Middle Cove.
8 Middle Ground.
9 Middle Ground, L. I. Sound.
2360 Middle Island.
1 Middle Passage.
2 Middle Race Rock.
3 Middle River.
4 Middle Shoal.
5 Midway Inlet.
6 Miel Harbor.
7 Mile Creek.
8 Milford.
9 Milky Way.
2370 Millstone Narrows.
1 Mill Creek.
2 Milne Bank.
3 Mine Creek.
4 Mindrin's Cove.
5 Mink Island Bay.
6 Mink Hill.
7 Minorca.
8 Minot's Ledge.
9 Miramichi Bar.
2380 Miramichi Bay.
1 Mira por-vos Shoal.
2 Miray Bay.
3 Miscouche Shoal.
4 Misequash River.
2385 Misery Islands.

2386 Mispillion Creek.
7 Mistaken Cove.
8 Mistaken Point.
9 Mistanogue Bay.
2390 Misteriosa Bank.
1 Mississippi River.
2 Missouri.
3 Missouri River.
4 Moa.
5 Moal.
6 Mobile Bay.
7 Mob Jack Bay.
8 Mochina Harbor.
9 Moela Island.
2400 Mohawk.
1 Mona Island.
2 Mona Islands.
3 Monas Shoal.
4 Money Key.
5 Monges del Nortes.
6 Monillo Key.
7 Monito Island.
8 Monomoy Point.
9 Mono.
2410 Monos Island.
1 Montague Shoal.
2 Monte Christi Bank.
3 Montego Bay.
4 Monte de Trigo.
5 Monte Grande.
6 Monte Rey Key.
7 Montevideo.
8 Montpelier.
9 Montreal.
2420 Montauk Point.
1 Monte Vides.
2 Montgomery, Ala.
3 Montserrat.
4 Monument River.
5 Moose-a-Bek Head.
6 Moose Island.
7 Morant Point.
8 Morant Keys.
9 Morant Bay.
2430 Morgan Island.
1 Morgan River.
2 Morgan Point.
3 Morne Rouge.
4 Morocco.
5 Momables Bay.
6 Mosquito Shore.
7 Morris Island.
8 Morris Island.
9 Morris Cove.
2440 Morro Blanco.
2441 Morro Castle.
2442 Morro Point.
3 Morrosquillo Gulf.
4 Mortier Bey.
5 Mortan Island.
6 Moselle Shoal.
7 Mosqueiras.
8 Mosquito Bank.
9 Mosquito Coast.
2450 Mosquito Cove.
1 Mosquito Harbor, Me.
2 Mosquito Harbor.
3 Mosquito Inlet, Fla.
4 Mouchor Quaire Shoal.
5 Mount Desert Island.
6 Mount Low.
7 Mount Prospect.
8 Mount Sarmiento.
9 Mount Skyring.
2460 Mousselier Pass.
1 Mouton Keys.
2 Moustique Key.
3 Mouton Port.
4 Mozambique.
5 Mucacas Shoal.
6 Mud River.
7 Mulas Point.
8 Mulatas Islands.
9 Mullegash Point.
2470 Mullet Key.
1 Murgain Bay.
2 Murray Harbor.
3 Murr Islands.
4 Murrell's Inlet.
5 Muscle Harbor.
6 Muscle Ridge.
7 Mushaboon.
8 Muskeket Channel.
9 Musqueteers.
2480 Musquash Harbor.

N.

1 Nag's Head, N. C.
2 Nantasket Roads.
3 Nanticoke River.
4 Nantucket Harbor.
5 Nantucket Shoals.
6 Naos Harbor.
7 Naples.
8 Naranjo Port.
9 Narragansett Bay.
2490 Narrow Guages Harbor.
1 Narrows, N. Y.
2 Nashawina.
2493 Nash's Island.

2494 Nassau Bay.
5 Nassau.
6 Nassau River.
7 Nassau Sound.
8 Nausett Beach.
9 Nautilus Shoals.
2500 Navas Port.
1 Navasa.
2 Naval Hospital, Norfolk.
3 Navesink Lights, N. J.
4 Navy Bay.
5 Necunkey Cliff.
6 Neddock Cape.
7 Ned's Point.
8 Negril Harbor.
9 Negrillo Shoal.
2510 Negrillo.
1 Negro Cape.
2 Negro Island.
3 Negro Point.
4 Neiva Bay.
5 Netherlands.
6 Neobsco Point.
7 Neptune Rocks.
8 Net Rocks.
9 Netsbuctoke.
2520 Neuse River.
1 Neuva Island.
2 Nevis Island.
3 New Bedford.
4 Newbern, N. C.
5 New Brunswick.
6 Newburyport.
7 New Castle, Del.
8 New Castle.
9 New Castle Island.
2530 New Canal, La.
1 New England.
2 New Ferrolle Bay.
3 Newfoundland.
4 New Hampshire.
5 New Harbor Ledges.
6 New Harbor.
7 New Haven.
8 New Inlet.
9 New Islands.
2540 New Jersey.
1 New London.
2 New Matacumbe.
3 Newman's Sound.
4 New Meadows.
5 New Orleans.
6 New Perlican Harbor.
7 New Point Comfort.
8 Newport.
2549 Newport's News, James Riv.
2550 New Providence.
1 New River Inlet.
2 New Shoal.
3 New South Shoal.
4 New Smyrna.
5 New Topsail Inlet.
6 New Year Harbor.
7 New Year Sound.
8 New York.
9 Neyba Bay.
2560 Niagara.
1 Niantic Harbor.
2 Nicaragua.
3 Nicolas Shoal.
4 Nick's Mate.
5 Nipe Harbor.
6 Nipper's Harbor.
7 Nobsque Point.
8 Noddy Harbor.
9 Noir Island.
2570 Nombre de Dios Harbor.
1 Nomini Cliffs.
2 Non Such Harbor.
3 Non Such Harbor.
4 Norfolk, Va..
5 Norman Cape.
6 Norman's Island.
7 Norman's Woe.
8 North Broad Cove.
9 North Cape.
2580 North Carolina.
1 North Channel.
2 North Cove.
3 North Darien.
4 North Dumplin.
5 North-east Arm.
6 North Edisto.
7 Northern Ledges.
8 Northern Monks.
9 Northern Triangle.
2590 Northampton County, Va.
1 North Harbor.
2 North Inlet.
3 North Island.
4 North Point.
5 North Road.
6 North Sea.
7 Northport.
8 North Reef.
9 North Run.
2600 North Sidney Harbor.
1 Northumberland Strait.
2 Nottingham County, Va.
3 North-west Arm.
2604 North-west Channel, Key West.

| | |
|---|---|
| 2605 | North-west Harbor. |
| 6 | Norway. |
| 7 | Noswaddox. |
| 8 | Nueva River. |
| 9 | Nuevas Grandes Port. |
| 2610 | Nuevas River. |
| 1 | Nuevitas. |
| 2 | Nyatt Point. |
| | O. |
| 3 | Oar Bay. |
| 4 | Oak Island. |
| 5 | Observation Cape. |
| 6 | Observation River. |
| 7 | Occahannock Creek. |
| 8 | Occasional Harbor. |
| 9 | Occoquan. |
| 2620 | Occoquan Creek. |
| 1 | Ocho Rios. |
| 2 | Ocoa Point. |
| 3 | Ocoa River. |
| 4 | Ocracoke, N. C. |
| 5 | Ocracoke Creek. |
| 6 | Ocumara Island. |
| 7 | Odiorne's Point. |
| 8 | Ogeechee River. |
| 9 | Okonofrisky River. |
| 2630 | Olandas Point. |
| 1 | Old Cape Francis. |
| 2 | Old Channel. |
| 3 | Old Ferrolle Island. |
| 4 | Old Field Point. |
| 5 | Old Harbor. |
| 6 | Old Harry Head. |
| 7 | Old Harry Rock. |
| 8 | Old House Cove. |
| 9 | Old Jerusalem. |
| 2640 | Old Man. |
| 1 | Old Man's Bay. |
| 2 | Old Matecumbe. |
| 3 | Old Plantation Creek. |
| 4 | Old Point Comfort. |
| 5 | Old Port au Choix. |
| 6 | Old Road. |
| 7 | Old Rhode's Key. |
| 8 | Old Shoal. |
| 9 | Old Silas. |
| 2650 | Old Stage Harbor. |
| 1 | Old Town. |
| 2 | Olinda City. |
| 3 | Oliver Island. |
| 4 | Omoa. |
| 5 | Ontario Lake. |
| 6 | One Bush Reef. |
| 2657 | Onslow. |
| 2658 | Oporto. |
| 9 | Ora Cabeca. |
| 2660 | Orange Bay. |
| 1 | Orange Keys. |
| 2 | Orange Isles. |
| 3 | Oregon Inlet, N. C. |
| 4 | Orchila Island. |
| 5 | Orinoco River. |
| 6 | Oro Islands. |
| 7 | Oropouche River. |
| 8 | Orosco Mount. |
| 9 | Orphan Island. |
| 2670 | Orpheus Island. |
| 1 | Orton's Point. |
| 2 | Ortiz Bank. |
| 3 | Oruba Island. |
| 4 | Orwell Bay. |
| 5 | Ossabau. |
| 6 | Oswald Keys. |
| 7 | Oswego. |
| 8 | Otter Bay. |
| 9 | Otter Island. |
| 2680 | Otway Bay. |
| 1 | Ouetique Island. |
| 2 | Outer Bank. |
| 3 | Outer Harbor. |
| 4 | Outer Shoals. |
| 5 | Overall Channel. |
| 6 | Owl's Head Harbor. |
| 7 | Owl's Head. |
| 8 | Oxford, Md. |
| 9 | Oyapoc River. |
| 2690 | Oyster Bay. |
| 1 | Oyster Bank. |
| 2 | Oyster Beds, Ga. |
| 3 | Oyster Pond. |
| 4 | Ozuma River. |
| | P. |
| 5 | Packet Rock. |
| 6 | Pacific Reef, Fla. |
| 7 | Packsaddle Bay. |
| 8 | Pacific Ocean. |
| 9 | Padre Harbor. |
| 2700 | Padre Island, Texas. |
| 1 | Padre Point. |
| 2 | Palomas Key. |
| 3 | Palanta Key. |
| 4 | Palenque. |
| 5 | Palermo. |
| 6 | Palestine. |
| 7 | Palmas Coast. |
| 8 | Palmer's Island. |
| 9 | Pajaro Shoal. |
| 2710 | Palmas Bay. |

2711 Palmas Cape.
2 Palma Bay, Majorca.
3 Pamlico Point.
4 Pamlico Sound.
5 Palm Island.
6 Pampatar.
7 Pamartar.
8 Panoma.
9 Panella Rocks.
2720 Paquet Harbor.
1 Para.
2 Paramaribo River.
3 Paramore Bank.
4 Paramore Island.
5 Paranagua Bay.
6 Paradise Sound.
7 Paradise Creek.
8 Paraguay.
9 Parana River.
2730 Parham.
1 Paris.
2 Parma.
3 Park Bay.
4 Parkham.
5 Pascagoula.
6 Pasqua Cape.
7 Passa del Cabello.
8 Passamaquoddy Bay.
9 Passe a l'Outre.
2740 Pass Christian.
1 Passage Isles.
2 Passages.
3 Pass Cavallo.
4 Pass Manchac.
5 Pass Island.
6 Patagonia.
7 Panmure Island.
8 Patapsco River.
9 Partridge Bay.
2750 Patridge Island.
1 Pasbebiac Roadstead.
2 Pasquotank River.
3 Pasquehannock Creek.
4 Patch Rock.
5 Patuxent River.
6 Pauroma River.
7 Paya.
8 Paz, La.
9 Peaked Bay.
2760 Peak of Orizaba.
1 Peak of Tarquino.
2 Pea Patch.
3 Pealetuvier's Bay.
4 Pearl Lagoon.
5 Pearl Reef.
2766 Pedro Bay.
2767 Pedro Key.
8 Pedro Shoals.
9 Pelican Keys.
2770 Pelican Point.
1 Pelican Shoal.
2 Penguin Islands.
3 Penguin Island.
4 Penikese Island.
5 Penmequid Harbor.
6 Pennsylvania.
7 Peninsula Point.
8 Penobscot Bay.
9 Penobscot River.
2780 Pensacola.
1 Peraya Key.
2 Perce Town.
3 Percival River.
4 Perlas Bay.
5 Perdigo Bay.
6 Perkins' Island.
7 Pernambuco.
8 Perrysville, Md.
9 Persia.
2790 Persian Gulf.
1 Peru.
2 Pertigalette Bay.
3 Persimmon Point.
4 Pescador Isles.
5 Petcudia River.
6 Petersburg, Va.
7 Peter's Island.
8 Petit Bois Island.
9 Petit Passage.
2800 Petite Trou.
1 Petite Terre Island.
2 Petit Fort Harbor.
3 Petit Passage.
4 Petite Pene.
5 Petit Degrat Inlet.
6 Petty Harbor.
7 Philadelphia.
8 Phillipsburg.
9 Phillips' Cove.
2810 Phillips' Rocks.
1 Piankctank.
2 Picayo Port.
3 Picarre Harbor.
4 Pickle Bank.
5 Pickle Reef.
6 Pictou Island.
7 Pictou Island Bank.
8 Pictou Road.
9 Pictou.
2820 Piedras Islet.
1 Piedras Keys.
2822 Piendas Islands.

2823 Pierre Joseph's Islet.
4 Pierre de Gros Cape.
5 Pigeon Cove.
6 Pigeon Hill Harbor.
7 Pigeon Island.
8 Pigeon Key.
9 Pigeon Keys.
2830 Pilot Rock.
1 Pindar's Reef.
2 Pine Islands.
3 Pinette Harbor.
4 Piney Point.
5 Pine's Key.
6 Pink Rock.
7 Piper's Hole.
8 Pirasonungo.
9 Pirate Island.
2840 Pirates' Bay.
1 Piscataway, Md.
2 Pistolet Bay.
3 Pitre's Cove.
4 Pitts' Harbor.
5 Pitts' Town.
6 Placentia Bay.
7 Placer de la Paz.
8 Plana Keys.
9 Plaster Cove.
2850 Plate Cove.
1 Plata River.
2 Platform.
3 Plattsburg, N. Y.
4 Playa de Miel.
5 Playa Larga.
6 Playa de Huidres.
7 Pleasant Bay.
8 Pleasant River.
9 Pleasant House Creek.
2860 Pleasonton's Island.
1 Plumb Gut.
2 Plum Island.
3 Plum Point.
4 Plymouth, Mass.
5 Plymouth, N. C.
6 Pochick Rip.
7 Pocillos.
8 Pocklington Island.
9 Poco Harbor.
2870 Pocomoke Bay.
1 Pocomoke River.
2 Pocosin.
3 Poge Cape.
4 Pogwash Harbor.
5 Pohick.
6 Polard.
7 Polrick Run.
2878 Pollock Rip.
2879 Point Agugas.
2880 Point Alderton.
1 Point Charles.
2 Point a Petre.
3 Point au Fer.
4 Point au Gaul.
5 Point Balona.
6 Point Barracos.
7 Point Barnes.
8 Point Isabel, Texas.
9 Point Judith.
2890 Point Lance.
1 Point Lepreau.
2 Point Llana.
3 Point Lookout, Md.
4 Point Lucretia.
5 Point la Hayne.
6 Point Los Morillos.
7 Point Martel.
8 Point Macoube.
9 Point Macoripre.
2900 Point Manabique.
1 Point of Shoals.
2 Point No Point.
3 Point Manare.
4 Point Manduri.
5 Point Manzanilla.
6 Point Maternillos.
7 Point May.
8 Point Morros.
9 Point Mulas.
2910 Point Negra.
1 Point Negro.
2 Point Pascal.
3 Point Padre.
4 Point Pedernales.
5 Point Petre.
6 Point Peter.
7 Point Pevis.
8 Point Piedras.
9 Point Rich.
2920 Point Rasa del Laore.
1 Point St. Francis.
2 Point St. Juan.
3 Point Ubero.
4 Point Bernal.
5 Point Brava, Brazil.
6 Point Brava, Cuba.
7 Point Canas.
8 Point Canvas.
9 Point Chateau.
2930 Point Colrado.
1 Point Chupara.
2 Point Covarrulias.
3 Point Concord.
2934 Point del Tunar.

2935 Point Desconocida.
6 Point des Trois.
7 Point Escondido.
8 Point Escribanos.
9 Point Espada.
2940 Point Espinello.
1 Point Ferrolle.
2 Point Galeota.
3 Point Gammon.
4 Point Gorda.
5 Point Gravois.
6 Point Guigero.
7 Point Guarico.
8 Point Holandes.
9 Point Indio.
2950 Point Icacos.
1 Point Jaragua.
2 Point Javinal.
3 Point Jesus Maria.
4 Point Jicaco.
5 Point Joro.
6 Point Jucacas.
7 Point Valiente.
8 Point Willie.
9 Point Xicalango.
2960 Policarpo Cove.
1 Pollock Shoal.
2 Pomquet Harbor.
3 Ponce.
4 Pomket Harbor.
5 Poole Island.
6 Pope's Creek.
7 Pope's Harbor.
8 Pope's Rock.
9 Poplar Island.
2970 Poplar Point.
1 Potomac River.
2 Poquosin.
3 Porcos Island.
4 Porcupine Cape.
5 Porcupine Island.
6 Porpoise Cape.
7 Port Antonio.
8 Port a Port.
9 Port au Basque.
2980 Port au Choix.
1 Port au Prince.
2 Port Bonaventura.
3 Port Basil Hall.
4 Port Cavallo.
5 Port Caballos.
6 Port Casilda.
7 Port Castries.
8 Port Cavanas.
9 Port Cayaguaneque.
2990 Port Charlotte.
2991 Port Clerke.
2 Port Cook.
3 Port Dauphin.
4 Port Desire.
5 Port Durham.
6 Port Espagne.
7 Port El Roque.
8 Port Escondido.
9 Port Francois.
3000 Port Grave Bay.
1 Port Haldimand.
2 Port Hariet.
3 Port Hoppner.
4 Port Hora.
5 Port Ioaque.
6 Port Jolie.
7 Port Jackson.
8 Port Jururu.
9 Port Louis.
3010 Port Laguna.
1 Port Lamentin.
2 Portland Harbor.
3 Portland, Me.
4 Portland, Jamaica.
5 Port L'Ebert.
6 Port Louis.
7 Port Latour.
8 Port Maravi.
9 Port Marnham.
3020 Port Maria.
1 Port Mariel.
2 Port Matoon.
3 Port Maxwell.
4 Port Metway.
5 Port Morant.
6 Port Moustique.
7 Port Mouton.
8 Port Maranyo.
9 Port Naras.
3030 Porto Bello, Colombia.
1 Porto Bello.
2 Port Cabello.
3 Port Cavannas.
4 Port of Macoris.
5 Port of Sama.
6 Port Orange.
7 Port Penn, Del.
8 Porto Praya.
9 Porto Rico.
3040 Porto Santo.
1 Porto Seguro.
2 Porto Veto.
3 Port Paix.
4 Port Parry.
5 Port Piment.
3046 Port Plata.

3047 Port Roseway.
8 Port Royal, Jamaica.
9 Port Royal, S. C.
3050 Port Royal, Martinique.
1 Port Royal, Mosquito Coast.
2 Port Saunders.
3 Port Salut.
4 Port Scarborough.
5 Port Tobacco.
6 Portsmouth, N. H.
7 Portsmouth, Va.
8 Port St. Elena.
9 Portuguese Guyana.
3060 Portugal.
1 Port Vancouver.
2 Port Vita.
3 Port William.
4 Posey's Bluff.
5 Potomac Creek.
6 Potomac River.
7 Poulament Bay.
8 Poule Reef.
9 Pownell Bay.
3070 Pownell's Run.
1 Pozuelos Bay.
2 Prado City.
3 Prentice Creek.
4 Premier Shoals.
5 Presque Harbor.
6 Prickly Pear Islands.
7 Prim Island Point.
8 Prince Apulca River.
9 Prince Edward's Island.
3080 Prince Rupert's Bay.
1 Prince's Bay, N. J.
2 Prince's Bay, W. I.
3 Prickly Point.
4 Proctorsville.
5 Prospect Harbor.
6 Prospect Cape.
7 Providence, Caicos.
8 Providence, W. I.
9 Providence Channel.
3090 Providence, R. I.
1 Provincetown.
2 Provision Islands.
3 Provision Ports.
4 Pubnico Harbor.
5 Puerto Casilda.
6 Puerto de Cavannas.
7 Puerto de Cispata.
8 Puerto del Mariel.
9 Puerto del Padre.
3100 Puerto de Manati.
1 Puerto de Plata.
3102 Puerto de Santa Barbara.
3103 Puerto Escondido, Cuba.
4 Puerto Escondido, Col.
5 Puerto Francis.
6 Puerto Viejo.
7 Puerto Viejo de Azua.
8 Pugwash Reef.
9 Pulaski Fort.
3110 Punta Broqueles.
1 Punta Cana.
2 Punta Castilla.
3 Punta Catalina.
4 Punta Caucedo.
5 Punta del Agorroba.
6 Punta de Guaniguilla.
7 Punta del Bergentin.
8 Punta de Carlos.
9 Punta del Escarpado Roxo.
3120 Punta de Piedras.
1 Punta Escoces.
2 Punta Espada.
3 Punta Frayle.
4 Punto Foreillo.
5 Punta Macao.
6 Punta Martel.
7 Punta Real de Cabo Roxo.
8 Punta Sal.
9 Puntanal.
3130 Puntilla Reef.
1 Purwick Cove.

Q.

2 Quaco.
3 Quantico.
4 Quebec.
5 Queen's Bay.
6 Quiabon River.
7 Quick's Hole.
8 Queimada Island.
9 Quilmes Town.
3140 Quirpon Harbor.
1 Quisset Harbor.
2 Quita Sueno Bank.
3 Quito.

R.

4 Race Cape.
5 Race Point.
6 Raccoon Point.
7 Ragged Harbor.
8 Ragged Head.
9 Ragged Islands, W. I.
3150 Ragged Island.
1 Ragged Point.
3152 Ram Islands.

3153 Ramea Harbor.
4 Ramdom Sound.
5 Rancho de Cura.
6 Rappahannock River.
7 Rasa Island.
8 Raspberry Harbor.
9 Rastico Harbor.
3160 Rat Island.
1 Rattan Island.
2 Rattones River.
3 Rattlesnake Shoals.
4 Rebecca Shoal.
5 Rebellion Road.
6 Receife Port.
7 Red Bay.
8 Red Cape.
9 Redfish Bar.
3170 Red Harbor.
1 Red Head.
2 Red Island.
3 Red Island Harbors.
4 Red River.
5 Red Sea.
6 Redondo Island.
7 Redondo, Cuba.
8 Redondo Rock.
9 Reedy Island.
3180 Reef Point.
1 Rehoboth Bay.
2 Reid's Rock.
3 Remire Islets.
4 Rendezvous Bay.
5 Rendezvous, No. 1.
6 Rendezvous, No. 2.
7 Rendezvous, No. 3.
8 Rendezvous, No. 4.
9 Rendezvous, No. 5.
3190 Rendezvous, No. 6.
1 Renowes Rocks.
2 Repulse Bay.
3 Rhode Island.
4 Richard's Harbor.
5 Richibucto Bar.
6 Richmond.
7 Richmond, Va.
8 Richmonds Island.
9 Rich Inlet.
3200 Rich Point.
1 Rickard's Channel.
2 Riding Rocks.
3 Rifleman Reef.
4 Rigolets.
5 Riker's Island.
6 Rio Bueno Harbor.
7 Rio de la Plata.
3208 Rio del Norte.
3209 Rio de Miel.
3210 Rio de Pedernales.
1 Rio de San Fernando.
2 Rio Doce.
3 Rio Dulce.
4 Rio Grande.
5 Rio Grande de San Pedro.
6 Rio Grande, Texas.
7 Rio Janeiro.
8 Rio Lagartos.
9 Rio Negro.
3220 Rio Para.
1 Rio Salado.
2 Rio San Francisco.
3 Riocito.
4 Ristigouche Harbor.
5 River John.
6 River of Tupilco.
7 River Philip.
8 River Plate.
9 River St. Ander.
3230 Road of Naso.
1 Road Harbor.
2 Roanoke Island.
3 Roanoke River.
4 Roaring Bull.
5 Robbin's Point.
6 Robbin's Reef.
7 Robeirao Town.
8 Robinhood's Bay.
9 Roca Partida.
3240 Roccas.
1 Rochalois Reef.
2 Rochelle, New.
3 Rochester.
4 Rockaway Inlet.
5 Rock Harbor.
6 Rocky Bay.
7 Rocky Point.
8 Rodriguez Key.
9 Rodriguez Reef.
3250 Roger's Island.
1 Rogue's Bay.
2 Rogue's Island Harbor.
3 Rollo Bay.
4 Romana River.
5 Roman Cape.
6 Romer.
7 Roques.
8 Roque, St.
9 Rosario Island.
3260 Rosario Key.
1 Rosas Bay.
2 Roseau Town.
3 Roseau, Dominica.
3264 Rose Blanche Harbor.

3265 Rose and Crown.
6 Roseway Port.
7 Rogue's Bay.
8 Rosier's Bluff.
9 Rotterdam.
3270 Round Harbor.
1 Round Island.
2 Roy Ledge.
3 Royal Shoal.
4 Rozier Cape.
5 Ruatan Island.
6 Rum Key.
7 Rupert's Bay.
8 Rugged Island Harbor.
9 Ryder's Harbor.

S.

3280 Saba.
1 Sabanilla.
2 Sabine Pass Light-house.
3 Sabine River.
4 Sable Cape.
5 Sable Cove.
6 Sable Island Bank.
7 Sable Island.
8 Sable River.
9 Saco.
3290 Saco Grande.
1 Saco Island.
2 Sackett's Harbor.
3 Sacrificios Island.
4 Saddle Back Islet.
5 Saddle Back Ledge.
6 Saddle Island.
7 Sagona Island.
8 Sagua la Grande.
9 Sail Harbor.
3300 Saintes.
1 Salado Chico River.
2 Salado River.
3 Salamanquilla.
4 Salem.
5 Salem Cove.
6 Sale Trou.
7 Salibia River.
8 Salinas Point.
9 Salinas.
3310 Salina.
1 Salisbury.
2 Salmedina.
3 Salmedina Shoal.
4 Salmon Cove.
5 Salmon River.
6 Salt Key.
3317 Salt Key Bank.
3318 Salt Lake Bay.
9 Salt River Cove.
3320 Salt River.
1 Salvador, St.
2 Salvage Bay.
3 Salvages.
4 Saluria.
5 Sama Port.
6 Samana Bay.
7 Sambro Harbor.
8 Sambro Light-house.
9 Sambro Key.
3330 Samson Rocks.
1 Sand Cove Reef.
2 Sand Hill Cove.
3 Sand Island, Ala.
4 Sand Key, Fla.
5 Sand Key, W. I.
6 Sand Island.
7 Sand Point.
8 Sand Shoal Inlet.
9 Sand's Point.
3340 Sandbury Cove.
1 Sandwich Bay.
2 Sandwich Islands.
3 Sandwich.
4 Sandy Bay.
5 Sandy Cove.
6 Sandy Hook, N. J.
7 Sandy Hook Channel.
8 Sandy Island Bay.
9 Sandy Island.
3350 Sandy Key.
1 Sandy Point, Md.
2 Sandy Point Bay.
3 Sandy Point.
4 Sandy Spit.
5 Sandbury Cove.
6 San Agustin.
7 San Blas.
8 San Bernardo.
9 San Christoval Bay.
3360 San Fulgentia.
1 Sanibel Island.
2 San Juan de Nicaragua.
3 San Juan de Ulua.
4 Sankaty Head.
5 Sans Fond Harbor.
6 Santa Anna Island.
7 Santa Catalina Island, M. C.
8 Santa Catalina Island, W. I.
9 Santa Cruz Bay.
3370 Santa Cruz, Brazil.
1 Santa Cruz, W. I.
2 Santa Cruz River.
3373 Santa Martha.

3374 Santarem Channel.
5 Santee River.
6 Santero Town.
7 Santiago de Tolu.
8 Saint Marcello.
9 Santa Fé.
3380 Santos.
1 Saone Island.
2 Sapatabar.
3 Sapelo Island.
4 Sapelo entrance.
5 Sapelo Sound.
6 Sapin Ledge.
7 Sagua le Grande.
8 Sarramacca River.
9 Sardinero River.
3390 Sardinia.
1 Sarmiento River.
2 Sarrana Bank.
3 Sasarai Channel.
4 Sassafras River.
5 Satan's Rock.
6 Satilla River.
7 Saunder's Harbor.
8 Sausett.
9 Savage Cove.
3400 Savage Harbor.
1 Savanna de le Mar.
2 Savannah.
3 Savanna Key.
4 Savanna la Mar.
5 Savannah River.
6 Savoy.
7 Sawyer's Bluff.
8 Saxony.
9 Saybrook.
3410 Scarborough.
1 Scatara Island.
2 Schaperham Bay.
3 Schoolmaster Reef.
4 Schooner's Cove.
5 Scituate.
6 Scoodie River.
7 Scotland.
8 Sea Bear Bay.
9 Sea Cow.
3420 Seal Island.
1 Seal Islands.
2 Sealing Bight.
3 Seal Rocks.
4 Seal Rocks.
5 Seahorse Reef.
6 Sea Lion Rock.
7 Seara.
8 Sear's Island.
3429 Searl's Rocks.

3430 Sebastian Harbor.
1 S. E. Cape.
2 Segovia River.
3 Seguin Light-house.
4 Senee Bay.
5 Seranilla Bank.
6 Sergipe River.
7 Serpent's Island.
8 Severn River, Va.
9 Severn River, Md.
3440 Sewell's Point, Va.
1 Seville.
2 Shagawannock Reef.
3 Shag Harbor.
4 Shag Rock.
5 Shag Island.
6 Shag Bay.
7 Shallow Bay.
8 Shalloway Island.
9 Sharp's Creek.
3450 Sharp's Island.
1 Shaw's Point.
2 Sheratica Bay.
3 Sheep Keys.
4 Sheep's Cove.
5 Sheep's Head.
6 Sheepscut River.
7 Sheet Harbor.
8 Shelburne Harbor.
9 Shell Keys Light-house.
3460 Shelter Island.
1 Shendor's Point.
2 Ship Cove.
3 Ship Harbor.
4 Shipman Point.
5 Ship Island.
6 Ship Passage.
7 Shipping Point.
8 Ship Shoal Inlet.
9 Ship Shoal Light-house.
3470 Shoal Bay.
1 Shoe Cove.
2 Shoreham.
3 Shovelful Shoal.
4 Shrewsbury Inlet.
5 Shut in Harbor.
6 Sicily.
7 Sierra Leone.
8 Siguanca Bay.
9 Silan, Gulf of.
3480 Silver Key Bank.
1 Silver Key Passage.
2 Silver Spring Harbor.
3 Simon's Bay.
4 Sinamara River.
3485 Sinu River.

| | | | |
|---|---|---|---|
| 3486 | Sinepuxent Shoals. | 3542 | Sow and Pigs. |
| 7 | Sippican Harbor. | 3 | Spain. |
| 8 | Sisal. | 4 | Spaniard's Bay. |
| 9 | Sisibou River. | 5 | Spanish Guyana. |
| 3490 | Slew Channel. | 6 | Spanish Room Harbor. |
| 1 | Smith Island. | 7 | Spanish Rock. |
| 2 | Smith's Island. | 8 | Spanish Town Island. |
| 3 | Smithson's Shoal. | 9 | Sparrow Cove. |
| 4 | Smith's Sound. | 3550 | Spear Cape. |
| 5 | Smith's Point, Va. | 1 | Spear Harbor. |
| 6 | Smithville, N. C. | 2 | Spear Island. |
| 7 | Smutty Nose Island. | 3 | Spear Shoal. |
| 8 | Smyrna. | 4 | Specutia Island, Md. |
| 9 | Smyrna, Del. | 5 | Spencer's Inlet. |
| 3500 | Snake Island. | 6 | Spiring's Bay. |
| 1 | Snake Key. | 7 | Spiritu Santo. |
| 2 | Snag Rock. | 8 | Spit and Red Buoy. |
| 3 | Sneed's Point. | 9 | Spotted Island. |
| 4 | Snug Cove. | 3560 | Sprague's Point. |
| 5 | Snug Harbor. | 1 | Spreightstown. |
| 6 | Soco River. | 2 | Spruce Creek Harbor. |
| 7 | Sod Channel. | 3 | Spry Harbor. |
| 8 | Soldier Key. | 4 | Squam Inlet. |
| 9 | Sombrero Island. | 5 | Squam. |
| 3510 | Sombrero Key. | 6 | Square Handkerchief. |
| 1 | Sombrero Reef. | 7 | Square Island Harbor. |
| 2 | Somers Islands. | 8 | Squibnocket. |
| 3 | Sola Islet. | 9 | S. S. W. Key. |
| 4 | Sophia Harbor. | 3570 | Stafford County, Va. |
| 5 | Sound, L. I. | 1 | Stag Road. |
| 6 | Sound Point. | 2 | Stanley Shoals. |
| 7 | South America. | 3 | Stanley Harbor. |
| 8 | Southampton County, Va. | 4 | Stanhope Points. |
| 9 | South Bar. | 5 | Star Island. |
| 3520 | South Broad Cove. | 6 | Starting Rock. |
| 1 | South Carolina. | 7 | Staten Island. |
| 2 | South Edisto River. | 8 | Staten Island. |
| 3 | South Harbor. | 9 | Statira Shoal. |
| 4 | South Newport River. | 3580 | Stewart's Bay. |
| 5 | South Sea. | 1 | Stingray Point, Va. |
| 6 | South Shoal. | 2 | Stinking Islands. |
| 7 | South Pass. | 3 | Stirrup Keys. |
| 8 | South Point. | 4 | Stokes Bay. |
| 9 | South River. | 5 | Stone Key. |
| 3530 | South Saddle Hills. | 6 | Stone Horse. |
| 1 | Southward. | 7 | Stonington. |
| 2 | Soathward Bay. | 8 | Stono Inlet, S. C. |
| 3 | Southwest Breaker. | 9 | Stony Patches. |
| 4 | Southwest Harbor. | 3590 | Stony Point. |
| 5 | Southwest Island. | 1 | Strait le Maire. |
| 6 | Southwest Point, Anticosti. | 2 | Stratford. |
| 7 | Southwest Arm. | 3 | Sturgeon Creek. |
| 8 | Southwest Reef, La. | 4 | Stump Inlet. |
| 9 | South Point. | 5 | St. Anastasia Island. |
| 3540 | Southern Point. | 6 | St. Ander. |
| 3541 | Southerland Island. | 3597 | St. Andrew's Bay. |

| | |
|---|---|
| 3598 | St. Andrew's Harbor. |
| 9 | St. Andrew's Channel. |
| 3600 | St. Andrew's Sound. |
| 1 | St. Andrew's Island. |
| 2 | St. Anne Harbor. |
| 3 | St. Anne's Bay. |
| 4 | St. Anne's Harbor. |
| 5 | St. Anthony Cape. |
| 6 | St. Anthony's Harbor. |
| 7 | St. Antonio Cape. |
| 8 | St. Aubin Island. |
| 9 | St. Augustine, Fla. |
| 3610 | St. Augustine, Brazil. |
| 1 | St. Augustin. |
| 2 | St. Barbe Bay. |
| 3 | St. Bartholomews. |
| 4 | St. Bernard. |
| 5 | St. Catherine's Sound. |
| 6 | St. Catherine's River. |
| 7 | St. Catherines. |
| 8 | St. Croix River. |
| 9 | St. Croix. |
| 3620 | St. David's Head. |
| 1 | St. Domingo City. |
| 2 | St. Domingo Key. |
| 3 | St. Domingo. |
| 4 | St. Elena. |
| 5 | St. Esprit Harbor. |
| 6 | St. Esprit Reef. |
| 7 | St. Eustatius Island. |
| 8 | St. Francis' Cape. |
| 9 | St. Francisco River. |
| 3630 | St. George's Bay. |
| 1 | St. George's Bay. |
| 2 | St. George's Harbor. |
| 3 | St. George's Sound. |
| 4 | St. Genevieve Bay. |
| 5 | St. Helena Sound. |
| 6 | St. Jago de Cuba. |
| 7 | St. Jago. |
| 8 | St. Jago de Tolu. |
| 9 | St. Jaques Harbor. |
| 3640 | St. Joao Island. |
| 1 | St. John's Bay. |
| 2 | St. John's Cape. |
| 3 | St. John's Harbor, N. B. |
| 4 | St. John's. |
| 5 | St. John's Harbor, N. F. |
| 6 | St. John's Harbor, Nic. |
| 7 | St. John's Island. |
| 8 | St. John's Town. |
| 9 | St. Joseph's Bay. |
| 3650 | St. Juan Cape. |
| 1 | St. Kitt's Island. |
| 2 | St. Lawrence River. |
| 3653 | St. Lewis' River. |
| 3654 | St. Lorenzo Bay. |
| 5 | St. Louis, Mo. |
| 6 | St. Louis Harbor. |
| 7 | St. Louis, Bay of. |
| 8 | St. Lucia. |
| 9 | St. Lucia Inlet. |
| 3660 | St. Lunaire Bay. |
| 1 | St. Marco Bay. |
| 2 | St. Marc. |
| 3 | St. Maria Cape. |
| 4 | St. Margaret's Bay. |
| 5 | St. Mary's Cape. |
| 6 | St. Mark's, Fla. |
| 7 | St. Mark's, Brazil. |
| 8 | St. Martin's Cove. |
| 9 | St. Martin's Town. |
| 3670 | St. Martin's. |
| 1 | St. Martha Cape. |
| 2 | St. Martha Grande. |
| 3 | St. Mary's Cape. |
| 4 | St. Mary's Bay. |
| 5 | St. Mary's. |
| 6 | St. Mary's Harbor. |
| 7 | St. Mary's Bay and River. |
| 8 | St. Michael's Bay and Cape. |
| 9 | St. Nicholas Channel. |
| 3680 | St. Nicholas Mole. |
| 1 | St. Patrick's Channel. |
| 2 | St. Paul Island. |
| 3 | St. Peter's Bay. |
| 4 | St. Peter's Island. |
| 5 | St. Peter's Harbor. |
| 6 | St. Peter's. |
| 7 | St. Philip's Reef. |
| 8 | St. Roque Cape. |
| 9 | St. Roman Cape. |
| 3690 | St. Rosas Bay. |
| 1 | St. Salvador. |
| 2 | St. Salvador, or Cat Island, |
| 3 | W. I. |
| | St. Sebastian Island. |
| 4 | St. Shot's Bay. |
| 5 | St. Simon's. |
| 6 | St. Thomas's Island. |
| 7 | St. Vincent's. |
| 8 | Sugar Loaf. |
| 9 | Sullivan Island. |
| 3700 | Sunbury. |
| 1 | Sunken Rock, Trinidad. |
| 2 | Surinam. |
| 3 | Susquehannah River. |
| 4 | Suwanee River. |
| 5 | Swan Islands, Col. |
| 6 | Swan Islands, W. C. |
| 7 | Swan Point. |
| 3708 | Swash Channel. |

| | |
|---|---|
| 3709 | Sweden. |
| 3710 | Sweet Bay. |
| 1 | S. W. Bay. |
| 2 | S. W. Passage. |
| 3 | S. W. Harbor. |
| 4 | S. W. Reef. |
| 5 | S. W. Rock. |
| 6 | Swimmer Bank. |
| 7 | Sydney Harbor. |
| 8 | Syracuse. |
| 9 | Swordfish Point. |

T.

| | |
|---|---|
| 3720 | Tabano. |
| 1 | Tabasco. |
| 2 | Tabb's Inlet. |
| 3 | Table Bay. |
| 4 | Taco Harbor. |
| 5 | Tacurucu Island. |
| 6 | Talbot County, Md. |
| 7 | Talbot Island. |
| 8 | Talley's Point. |
| 9 | Tamandare Harbor. |
| 3730 | Tambor Island. |
| 1 | Tampa Bay. |
| 2 | Tampico. |
| 3 | Tanamo Harbor. |
| 4 | Tangier Harbor. |
| 5 | Tangier Island. |
| 6 | Tanguijo. |
| 7 | Tanner's Creek. |
| 8 | Tappahannock. |
| 9 | Tar Bay. |
| 3740 | Tarena Keys. |
| 1 | Tarpaulin Cove. |
| 2 | Tarrant Harbor. |
| 3 | Tartan Bay. |
| 4 | Tatamagouche Bay. |
| 5 | Tate Cape. |
| 6 | Tutuock Island. |
| 7 | Tavernier's Bay, Fla. |
| 8 | Tavernier's Key, Fla. |
| 9 | Taylor's Bay. |
| 3750 | Taypu Point. |
| 1 | Tchefuncti River, La. |
| 2 | Teatable Key, Fla. |
| 3 | Temple Cape. |
| 4 | Tennallytown, Md. |
| 5 | Ten Pound Island. |
| 6 | Terrin Point. |
| 7 | Terre de Bass. |
| 8 | Testigos Island. |
| 9 | Texas. |
| 3760 | Thames River. |
| 3761 | Thatcher's Island. |
| 2 | The Isaacs. |
| 3 | Thetis Bay. |
| 4 | Thimble. |
| 5 | Thomas Bay. |
| 6 | Thomas Head. |
| 7 | Thomas Cape. |
| 8 | Thomas Point, Md. |
| 9 | Thoroughfare. |
| 3770 | Three Islands. |
| 1 | Three Fathom Bank. |
| 2 | Through Channel. |
| 3 | Thrumcap Shoal. |
| 4 | Thrumcap Island. |
| 5 | Thurin's Bay. |
| 6 | Tiburon Bay. |
| 7 | Tiburon Cape. |
| 8 | Tickle Channel. |
| 9 | Tierra del Fuego. |
| 3780 | Tiger Island. |
| 1 | Tiger Keys. |
| 2 | Tigioca. |
| 3 | Tignish River. |
| 4 | Tigrillo Bay. |
| 5 | Timbalier Island. |
| 6 | Timballier Bay, La. |
| 7 | Tinnicum Island. |
| 8 | Tobago. |
| 9 | Toco Bay. |
| 3790 | Tod Port. |
| 1 | Tolu. |
| 2 | Tom's Harbor. |
| 3 | Tonala River. |
| 4 | Tongula River. |
| 5 | Torbay. |
| 6 | Tormentine Reef. |
| 7 | Torres. |
| 8 | Toro Point. |
| 9 | Torquetoque Islet. |
| 3800 | Tortola. |
| 1 | Tortue Island. |
| 2 | Tortuga. |
| 3 | Tortuga Island. |
| 4 | Tortugas. |
| 5 | Tortugas Fort. |
| 6 | Tortuguero. |
| 7 | Toulinquet Harbor. |
| 8 | Toulinquet Island. |
| 9 | Tower Rocks. |
| 3810 | Townsend Harbor. |
| 1 | Tracadie Harbor. |
| 2 | Tracadigash Point. |
| 3 | Treble Island. |
| 4 | Trebuppy. |
| 3815 | Trepassey Harbor. |

| | |
|---|---|
| 3816 | Triangles. |
| 7 | Triangle Shoals. |
| 8 | Tributaria de Minerva. |
| 9 | Trinidad, Cuba. |
| 3820 | Trinidad Island. |
| 1 | Trinity Bay, |
| 2 | Trinity Harbor. |
| 3 | Trinity. |
| 4 | Trinity Ledge. |
| 5 | Triton Harbor. |
| 6 | Triunfo de la Cruz. |
| 7 | Tripoli. |
| 8 | Triumph Reef. |
| 9 | Trois Maries Point. |
| 3830 | Tropezou. |
| 1 | Trout Rock. |
| 2 | Troy Island. |
| 3 | Truro. |
| 4 | Truxillo River. |
| 5 | Tryon River. |
| 6 | Tucacos Bay. |
| 7 | Tuckanuck Island. |
| 8 | Tucker's Island. |
| 9 | Tuma Island. |
| 3840 | Turbalton Bay. |
| 1 | Tunis. |
| 2 | Turiamo Harbor. |
| 3 | Turivazo Point. |
| 4 | Turin. |
| 5 | Turkey. |
| 6 | Turkey Point, Md. |
| 7 | Turk's Island Passage. |
| 8 | Turtle Harbor. |
| 9 | Turtle Heads. |
| 3850 | Turtle Island. |
| 1 | Turtle Reef. |
| 2 | Turtle Rocks. |
| 3 | Tusket River. |
| 4 | Tuspan River. |
| 5 | Tutoia, Brazil. |
| 6 | Tutumates Island. |
| 7 | Tweeds or Great Harbor. |
| 8 | Tybee. |
| 9 | Tybee Island. |
| 3860 | Tyler's Creek. |
| 1 | Tyrell's Bay. |
| 2 | Tyrell's Bay, Tobago. |

## U.

| | |
|---|---|
| 3 | Ubes, St. |
| 4 | Umbrella Key. |
| 5 | Umbrella Passage. |
| 6 | Una de Gato. |
| 7 | Unare Bay. |
| 3868 | Union Mills. |
| 3869 | United States. |
| 3870 | Union River. |
| 1 | Upper Cedar Point. |
| 2 | Upper Jetty. |
| 3 | Upshur's Point. |
| 4 | Uralia. |
| 5 | Uraine Bay. |
| 6 | Urbanna. |
| 7 | Uruguay River. |
| 8 | Utila Island. |

## V.

| | |
|---|---|
| 9 | Valetta, La. |
| 3880 | Valiente Point. |
| 1 | Valentine Harbor. |
| 2 | Valient Channel. |
| 3 | Vasasousa Bay. |
| 4 | Valasco. |
| 5 | Valparaiso. |
| 6 | Venados. |
| 7 | Venezuela. |
| 8 | Venice. |
| 9 | Venus Cove. |
| 3890 | Vera Cruz. |
| 1 | Verde Cape. |
| 2 | Verde Island. |
| 3 | Vermeille Point. |
| 4 | Vermillion Bay. |
| 5 | Vermont. |
| 6 | Vernon River. |
| 7 | Verte Bay. |
| 8 | Vestal Rock. |
| 9 | Victoria Island. |
| 3900 | Vicque Island. |
| 1 | Vigia. |
| 2 | Villa Grande. |
| 3 | Villa Nova do Prinzeza. |
| 4 | Vinas Point. |
| 5 | Vincent, St. |
| 6 | Vincent, Cape St. |
| 7 | Vine Island. |
| 8 | Vineyard Sound. |
| 9 | Vinhas Island. |
| 3910 | Viper Key. |
| 1 | Virgin Gorda. |
| 2 | Virgin Cape. |
| 3 | Virgin Islands. |
| 4 | Virginia. |
| 5 | Virgin Rocks. |
| 6 | Virgin's Passage. |
| 7 | Visarinkum. |
| 8 | Vita Port. |
| 3919 | Volage Bank. |

## W.

|  |  |
|---|---|
| 3920 | Wadham Island. |
| 1 | Wachepreague, Va. |
| 2 | Wade's Point. |
| 3 | Waldoborough. |
| 4 | Wales. |
| 5 | Wales, New South. |
| 6 | Wallace Harbor. |
| 7 | Wank's River. |
| 8 | Warcaller River. |
| 9 | Wareham. |
| 3930 | Warnari River. |
| 1 | Warsaw. |
| 2 | Warsaw Island. |
| 3 | Warrington Shoal. |
| 4 | Warwick. |
| 5 | Washball Shoal. |
| 6 | Washington City. |
| 7 | Washington, N. C. |
| 8 | Wasting Islet. |
| 9 | Watchman, Cape. |
| 3940 | Water Cove. |
| 1 | Waterford. |
| 2 | Waterloo. |
| 3 | Water Key. |
| 4 | Watering Bay. |
| 5 | Wateman Island. |
| 6 | Watling's Island. |
| 7 | Watts' Island. |
| 8 | Waugh Shoal. |
| 9 | Wedge Island. |
| 3950 | Week Island. |
| 1 | Wellfleet Bay. |
| 2 | West Bay Harbor. |
| 3 | West Chop, Holmes' Hole. |
| 4 | West Harbor. |
| 5 | West Indies. |
| 6 | Western Entrance. |
| 7 | Western Islands. |
| 8 | Western Passage. |
| 9 | Westminster, Md. |
| 3960 | Westmoreland, Va. |
| 1 | West Point. |
| 2 | Westward Arm. |
| 3 | Weymouth. |
| 4 | Whale Bank. |
| 5 | Whale Key. |
| 6 | Whale Rock. |
| 7 | Whale Back. |
| 8 | White Bay. |
| 9 | White Bear Bay. |
| 3970 | White Cliff. |
| 1 | White Haven. |
| 2 | White Head. |
| 3973 | White Hills. |
| 3974 | White Horse Reef. |
| 5 | White Horses. |
| 6 | White Horse Point. |
| 7 | White Islands. |
| 8 | White Rock. |
| 9 | White Sands. |
| 3980 | White Shoals. |
| 1 | White Sand Bay. |
| 2 | Whiteman Rock. |
| 3 | Whittle Bay. |
| 4 | Whittle, Cape. |
| 5 | Whittle Bay. |
| 6 | Whookamagh. |
| 7 | Wicomico. |
| 8 | Willoughby. |
| 9 | Willoughby's Spit. |
| 3990 | Wilmington, N. C. |
| 1 | Wilmington, Del. |
| 2 | Wimble Shoals. |
| 3 | Winchester, Va. |
| 4 | Windmill Point. |
| 5 | Windsor. |
| 6 | Windsor River. |
| 7 | Windham River. |
| 8 | Windward Islands. |
| 9 | Windward Channel. |
| 4000 | Windward Passage. |
| 1 | Wine Harbor. |
| 2 | Winter Harbor. |
| 3 | Winter Island. |
| 4 | Winter Quarter Shoal. |
| 5 | Winyah Bay, S. C. |
| 6 | Withy Wood Bay. |
| 7 | Wolf Bay. |
| 8 | Wolf Key. |
| 9 | Wolf Island. |
| 4010 | Wolf's Cove. |
| 1 | Wolf Trap. |
| 2 | Wood End. |
| 3 | Woodbridge Bay |
| 4 | Wooding Island. |
| 5 | Wood Island. |
| 6 | Woodland. |
| 7 | Wood's Harbor. |
| 8 | Wood's Hole. |
| 9 | Woolwich. |
| 4020 | Wreck Hill. |
| 1 | Wreck Reef. |
| 2 | Wrecked Ship Shoal. |

## X.

|  |  |
|---|---|
| 3 | Xaqua Harbor. |
| 4 | Xibari Harbor, Cuba |
| 5 | Xicalango Point. |
| 4026 | Xingui River. |

# HOMOGRAPHIC SYMBOLS

FOR

# DAY SIGNALS,

BASED UPON

THE PLAN OF CAPTAIN WILMOT, R. N., C. B.

## PLAN OF HOMOGRAPH.

*To be made with a Sword, Tiller, Stick, Stretcher, and a Handkerchief, or Flag.*

| Position. | No. | Figure. | Position. | No. | Figure. |
|---|---|---|---|---|---|
| *Sword in right hand perpendicular over the Body.* | 1 |  | *Sword in right hand perpendicular over the Body, left arm extended.* | 6 |  |
| *Sword elevated 45° arm always extended.* | 2 |  | *Sword elevated in right hand 45°, left arm extended.* | 7 |  |
| *Sword horizontal in right hand.* | 3 |  | *Sword in right hand horizontal, left arm extended.* | 8 |  |
| *Sword depressed 45° in right hand.* | 4 |  | *Sword in right hand depressed 45°, left arm extended.* | 9 |  |
| *Sword in left hand extended horizontally* | 5 |  | *Sword held horizontally over the head with both hands.* | 0 |  |

## PLAN OF HOMOGRAPH.

*To be made with a Sword, Tiller, Stick, Stretcher, and a Handkerchief, or Flag.*

| Nos. | Figure. | Position. |
|---|---|---|
| 1*st Repeater and Affirmative.* |  | *Sword in each hand extended perpendicular over the head.* |
| 2*d Repeater and Negative.* |  | *Sword in each hand extended horizontally.* |
| 3*d Repeater.* |  | *Hat off, left arm extended.* |
| *Preparatory.* |  | *Handkerchief or Flag spread.* |
| *Answering.* | *Sword waved over the head with right arm.* | |
| *Numeral.* |  | *Sword in rigth hand extended horizontally, left arm held perpendicular over the head.* |
| *Interrogatory.* | *Sword in each hand waved over the head.* | |
| *At the end of each complete signal.* |  | *Hands against the hips, elbows extended.* |

# NIGHT SIGNALS.

## BY COSTON LIGHTS.

Any of the day signals in this Code may be made at night with Coston lights.

---

# OTHER NIGHT SIGNALS,

## FOR BOATS, AND BOAT-SQUADRONS.

---

When Boat-Squadrons or Boats are not provided with COSTON LIGHTS, night signals may be made with Blue Lights, Rockets, Flashes made in a flash pan, and guns and small arms.

---

|  |  |
|---|---|
| No. 1. Two Rockets, (all lights having been previously extinguished or masked.) | Action, prepare for. (To be repeated by Commanders of Divisions.) |
| No. 2. Two Rockets, (all lights having been previously extinguished or masked,) followed by a gun or volley of musketry. | Action commence. (These rockets may be sent up when the Commanding Officer is ready to commence the action, and the first gun, or volley, will be the commencement of the action, as well as the signal for general action.) |
| No. 3. One Blue Light followed by Two Rockets in succession. (Repeat if necessary at the expiration of ten minutes.) | Action discontinue. (To be repeated by Commanders of Divisions.) |
| No. 4. A Gun, guns, or a volley of musketry, followed by one Blue Light. | Aground I am, in distress, or in want of assistance. |
| No. 5. One Blue Light followed by One Rocket. | Ahead, go and reconnoiter the enemy, squadron, vessels, batteries, or proposed landing, and report to the Commanding Officer. (The division, column, vessel, or boats' distinguishing signal, must follow this signal immediately.) |
| No. 6. One Lantern held steadily, with three flashes at intervals of one minute. | Anchor, having due regard to safety and previous orders. |

| | |
|---|---|
| No 7. One Lantern, swung by hand, or, in the absence of a lantern, One Flash. | Assent, answer, or yes, in reply to a signal. |
| No. 8. One Blue Light, followed by One Rocket and Two Flashes. | Assist the vessel or boat whose situation requires it. |
| No. 9. One Lantern and Three Rockets in quick succession. | Attack, a general, with all arms. |
| No. 10. One Lantern and One Rocket, followed by One Flash. | Attack the enemy's starboard wing, division, column, or quarter. |
| No. 11. One Lantern and One Rocket, followed by Two Flashes. | Attack the enemy's port wing, division, column, or quarter. |
| No. 12. Two Lanterns horizontal, and One Flash. | Attack and carry the enemy by boarding. |
| No. 13. One Lantern, One Blue Light, followed by One Rocket. | Attack the enemy with howitzers and rifle muskets or carbines at the most effective range. |
| No. 14. Two or more Flashes with Flash Pan. | Attention, give to my movements. |
| No. 15. One Rocket, (all lights being lowered or masked out of sight.) | Board the enemy on bow and quarter. |
| No. 16. Two Blue Lights burnt in succession. | Boats, all will return to their respective vessels, stations, or rendezvous. |
| No. 17. Two Blue Lights, followed by One Rocket. | Boats, recall, all detached. |
| No. 18. One Rocket, followed by Two Blue Lights. | Chase the enemy. |
| No. 19. Two Blue Lights, followed by Two Rockets. | Chase discontinue. |
| No. 20. Two Lanterns perpendicular. | Chase has tacked, or gone on the other tack. |
| No. 21. Two Lanterns horizontal, (all other lights being masked.) | Close order take and preserve. |
| No. 22. One Lantern, where best seen, and One Blue Light. | Communicate, I wish to, with the senior officer. |
| No. 23. One Gun, or volley of musketry, followed by One Blue Light and Rocket. | Danger is discovered. It is dangerous to proceed. We are in danger. Surrounded by dangerous shoals. |
| No. 24. Two Lanterns horizontal, and Three Rockets. | Enemy, the, is in sight, is approaching; is near us. |

|  |  |
|---|---|
| No. 25. One Lantern where best seen, and Two Rockets in succession. | Enemy, the stranger is. |
| No. 26. Two Lanterns horizontal, and One Blue Light. | Follow the motions of the Commanding Officer. |
| No. 27. Two Lanterns horizontal, and Two Blue Lights. | Form, or preserve, the "Order of Columns." (See Ordnance Instructions, page 96, 1860.) |
| No. 28. Two Lanterns horizontal, and One Rocket. | Form, or preserve, the "Order of Attack, three deep." (See Ordnance Instructions, page 96, 1860.) |
| No. 29. Two Lanterns horizontal, and Two Rockets. | Form, or preserve, the "Order of Attack, two deep." (See Ordnance Instructions, page 97, 1860.) |
| No. 30. Two Lanterns perpendicular, and one Blue Light. | Form "line ahead." (See Ordnance Instructions, page 98, 1860.) |
| No. 31. Two Lanterns perpendicular, and Two Blue Lights. | "Change direction of the front." (See Ordnance Instructions, page 98, 1860.) |
| No. 32. Two Lanterns perpendicular, and One Rocket. | Form the "Order of Retreat." (See Ordnance Instructions, page 98, 1860.) |
| No. 33. Two Lanterns perpendicular, and Two Rockets. | Form, or preserve, the "First order of Steaming." (Steamers or Row-boats.) See Diagram No. 1. |

## No. 1.

FIRST ORDER OF STEAMING.

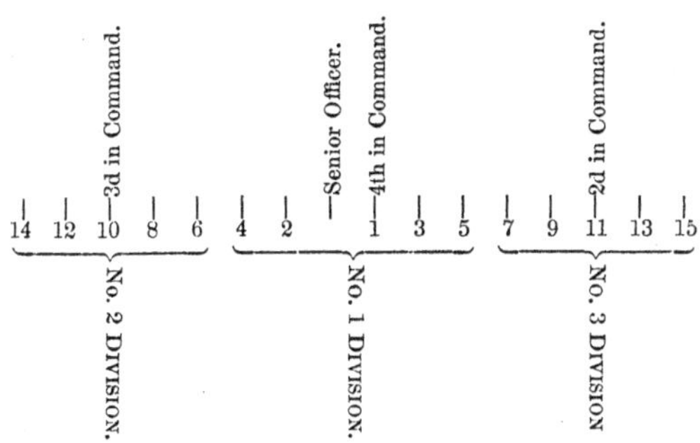

No. 34. Two Rockets in succession, followed by two Blue Lights in succession. } Form, or preserve, the "Second Order of Steaming." (Steamers or Row-boats.) See Diagram No. 2.

## No. 2.

SECOND ORDER OF STEAMING.

Third in Command.
Senior Officer.
Fourth in Command.
Second in Command.

10 | | | 11 |

12 | | 8 2 | | 1 9 | | 13

14 | | 6 4 | | 3 7 | | 15

| 5

No. 3 Division.
No. 1 Division.
No. 2 Division.

| | |
|---|---|
| No. 35. One Lantern and two Blue Lights. | Form, or preserve, the "Third Order of Steaming." (Steamers and Row-boats.) See Diagram No. 3. |

## No. 3.

### THIRD ORDER OF STEAMING.

| | |
|---|---|
| | Senior Officer. |
| 2 | 1....Fourth in Command. |
| 4 | 3 |
| 6 | 5 |
| 8 | 7 |
| Third in Command....10 | 9 |
| 12 | 11....Second in Command. |
| 14 | 13 |
| | 15 |

| | |
|---|---|
| No. 36. Two Lanterns horizontal, and One Flash. | Haul by the wind on the starboard tack. |
| No. 37. Two Lanterns horizontal, and Two Flashes. | Haul by the wind on the port tack. |
| No. 38. One Lantern, One Musket, and Flashes. | Intelligence I have of the enemy; is near, or approaching. |
| No. 39. Three Lanterns perpendicular. | Land, prepare to, in the face of the enemy. |
| No. 40. Three Lanterns perpendicular, and One Rocket. | Land immediately, and form for attack, according to prescribed plan. |
| No. 41. Three Lanterns horizontal, and One Rocket. | Landing is, or will be opposed by force. |
| No. 42. Three Lanterns horizontal. | Landing is not, or will not be opposed by force. |
| No. 43. Three Lanterns horizontal, and Two Rockets. | Landing will be attended with danger. |
| No. 44. Three Lanterns perpendicular, and One Blue Light. | Land, approach no nearer. |
| No. 45. Three Lanterns perpendicular, and Two Rockets. | Lights, all, lower, extinguish, or mask |

| | |
|---|---|
| No. 46. Three Lanterns perpendicular, and Two Blue Lights. | Make the best of your way to your rendezvous, station, ship or ships, in accordance with previous orders. |
| No. 47. One Blue Light............ | Position or positions show. (The answer to this signal will be a Blue Light.) |
| No. 48. Three Lanterns perpendicular, One Blue Light, followed by Three Rockets. | Recalls the vessel or boat, vessels or boats. (If to recall a division or column, the distinguishing signal will be made immediately after.) |
| No. 49. Three Lanterns perpendicular, One Blue, and Two Rockets in succession. | Relief, go to the, of the division, column, or boat, whose distinguishing signal will be shown. |
| No. 50. Three Lanterns perpendicular, One Blue Light, followed by One Rocket in succession. | Resume your positions in the squadron, and preserve the present order. |
| No. 51. Two Lanterns horizontal, One Blue Light, followed by One Rocket. | 1st Division or Squadron. |
| No. 52. Two Lanterns horizontal, Two Blue Lights, followed by Two Rockets. | 2d Division or Squadron. |
| No. 53. Three Lanterns horizontal, One Blue Light. | 3d Division or Squadron. |
| No. 54. Three Lanterns horizontal, Two Blue Lights. | Van Division or Squadron. |
| No. 55. Three Lanterns horizontal, One Blue Light, followed by One Rocket. | Centre Division or Squadron. |
| No. 56. Three Lanterns horizontal, One Blue Light, followed by Two Rockets. | Rear Division or Squadron. |

*Note.*—When one or more Lanterns are employed in making the foregoing signals, they are to be kept up or visible until the whole of the signal is made. When the signal is completed, the lantern or lanterns will be hauled down or masked.

Signals made with Lanterns, Blue Lights, Rockets, and Flashes, should, as a general rule, be answered by waving a lantern by hand in front of the person holding it. When no Lantern is available, the Flash Pan and a flask of powder should be in readiness to make a flash as an answer to each signal.

Special distinguishing night signals or distinctions may be given to other Vessels or Boats than those at the head of Divisions or Squadrons in using the signals made with Blue Lights, Rockets, and Lanterns; but they must be determined upon and arranged for each special occasion.

Red, Green, and White Lanterns will serve to give a number of distinctions, such as:

No. 1. One Red Lantern Light.
2. One Green Lantern Light.
3. One Red and one White perpendicular.
4. One Red and one Green perpendicular.
5. One White and one Red perpendicular.
6. One White and one Green perpendicular.
7. One Green and one White perpendicular.
8. One Green and one Red perpendicular.
9. Two Red Lanterns horizontal.
10. Two Green Lanterns horizontal.
11. One Red and one White Lantern horizontal.
12. One Red and one Green Lantern horizontal.

As all vessels of the Navy, whether propelled by steam or sails, are required by the General Order of the Navy Department to carry Red and Green lights, and to have White lights on board for exhibition according to the directions embraced in that General Order, there will necessarily be spare Colored Lanterns, or spare Colored Glass, to replace any that may be broken, which may be used on occasions when Colored Lantern lights are required in making signals.

In case there should be neither spare Colored Lanterns nor spare Colored Glass for shades to ordinary lanterns, thin Red and Green bunting stretched tightly around the horn or glass of the lanterns will give, for short distances, a sufficiently brilliant light and marked color to answer the purpose.

## PRIVATE NIGHT SIGNALS.

A private signal may be devised and made by these lights. Private signals for exhibition at night should be simple in combination, and, unlike all other signals, made with the same materials.

# BOAT SIGNALS IN FOGS.

---

| | |
|---|---|
| The sounding of Fog Horns, the long roll of drums, beating on an empty barrel, a watchman's rattle, or a boatswain's whistle. | Will denote being on the starboard tack. (To be answered by the same if on that tack.) |
| Small arms, fired singly, and at short intervals, or the ringing of a bell. | Will denote being on the port tack. (Answer according to the tack you are on.) |
| Guns, or volleys of musketry at short intervals. | Will indicate action with the enemy, or in want of assistance. The answer will be one gun, or two muskets fired in quick succession. |

The movements of BOATS SAILING OR PULLING IN CLOSE ORDER, in fogs or at night when it is not advisable to show lights, may be regulated somewhat, by the Boatswain's call.

| | |
|---|---|
| Pipe, veer, (repeat) | May indicate tack. |
| Pipe, belay, (repeat) | Down sail and out oars. (When this signal is made, if near or approaching the enemy, it is to be understood that the oars are to be muffled, and that perfect silence is to be preserved.) |
| Pipe, haul in, heave in, or walk away, (repeat.) | Make sail. |
| Pipe, sweepers, (repeat) | Close up for attack. |
| Pipe, haul and hold, (repeated in quick succession.) | Give way with a will together, for a dash at the enemy. |
| Pipe to dinner | Prepare and proceed to anchor (or land as the case may be) near the senior officer in proper order. |

STEAMERS

Having boats in tow, or not, will use their whistles to point out their positions and give information during Fogs, unless otherwise ordered by the Commanding Officer of the Squadron or Expedition.

| | |
|---|---|
| A gun, or volley of musketry, followed by a long blast of the steam-whistle, say ½ minute duration. | May indicate I am aground, or in distress, and require assistance. Disabled or damaged. |
| A long blast with the whistle, (½ minute duration,) followed by two short sharp blasts, with an interval of 5 seconds between each blast. | May indicate notice of the enemy, either approaching or stationary, but near by. |
| Two guns or volleys of musketry, followed by one long and three short blasts of the whistle, (intervals 5 seconds.) | May indicate anchor, or stop and await the orders or approach of the senior officer. |
| One long blast, (½ minute,) followed by two sharp short blasts at intervals of 5 seconds, and repeated at the expiration of 5 minutes. | May indicate danger discovered near. |
| A short blast, repeated at intervals of 10 minutes. | May indicate the positions of the different steamers. |

Other combinations may be made, or different significations may be given to those named to suit occasions and circumstances.

For the regular fog signal symbols, by steam whistle or fog horn, see introduction to Naval Signal Code, page 16.

# DISTRESS, OR ASSISTANCE SIGNALS.

TO BE MADE WITHOUT FLAGS OR SIGNAL BOOKS.

(*Boats' crews should be taught these Signals.*)

---

| | |
|---|---|
| 1. Want a Boat. | Hat, cap, flag, garment, handkerchief, bundle of sea-weed, or branch of tree or shrub, *waved by right hand from head to foot.* |
| 2. Want a boat for sick or wounded.  | Hat, cap, bundle, or branch of a tree or shrub *held perpendicularly over the head.* |
| 3. Wrecked, or in a sinking condition.  | Hat, cap, bundle, or any object which may be readily held in each hand at *arms length, perpendicular to the body.* |
| 4. In distress for food and water.  | Hat, cap, or bundle *held out in each hand at arms length over the head.* |
| 5. The enemy is approaching, or close upon me. | Hat, cap, bundle, garment, or other object *waved quickly over the head.* |

| | |
|---|---|
| 6. Cannot make any headway, or losing ground; send a line astern by a float or assistance. | Hat, cap, flag, handkerchief or garment in the *right hand, with the arm extended at full length and straight from the body.* |
| 7. Return to the shore, ship, or place of departure. | A small open flag *waved horizontally or held with both hands by the corners so as to be blown out by the wind.* |

These Signals should be continued by the person in distress, or asking for assistance, until repeated by the ship or boat addressed.

The person answering the Signals should take a prominent position, and show as much of his person as possible while repeating the signal.

The army plan of signaling may be employed instead of these arbitrary "distress signals" by those who have been taught it. A flag or a handkerchief tied to a tiller or boat hook may be used.

NUMBERS OF VESSELS AND BOATS

OF

# FLOTILLA AND BOAT SQUADRONS.

---

No. 1. Flag-ship or Boat of Boat Squadron.
2. Commander of 1st Division's Boat.
3. Commander of 2d Division's Boat.
4. Commander of 3d Division's Boat.
5.
6.
7.
8.
9.
10.
11.
12.
13.
14.
15.
16.
17.
18.
19. Commander of Steam Flotilla or Reserve.
20.
21.
22.
23.
24.
25.
26.
27.
28.
29.
30.
31.
32.
33.
34.
35.
36.
37.
38.
39.
40.

www.ingramcontent.com/pod-product-compliance
Lightning Source LLC
LaVergne TN
LVHW021400110826
845150LV00007B/1732

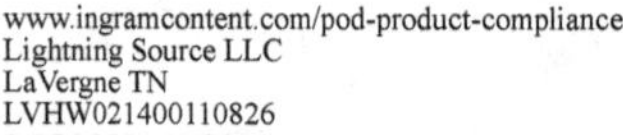

* 9 7 8 1 4 2 5 5 1 4 4 0 2 *